World employment 1995

World employment 1995

An ILO Report

International Labour Organization   Geneva

ISBN 92-2-109448-0

ISSN 1020-3079

First published 1995

Printed in Switzerland   IRL

Preface

Anxiety over employment problems, and pessimism over the prospects for resolving them, reigns in many parts of the world today. Indeed the task of creating sufficient new jobs to overcome unemployment, underemployment and problems of low pay ranks as the primary challenge for economic and social policy in countries at all levels of development across the globe. The reason why this is so is easy enough to understand. High levels of unemployment spawn a host of problems: growing inequality and social exclusion, the waste of foregone output and unutilized human resources, increasing economic insecurity, and the human suffering inflicted on the unemployed. In contrast, a high and stable rate of productive job creation is the mainspring of equitable economic and social development.

The launching of this Report on current employment problems in the world signals the intention of the International Labour Office to step up its efforts to promote national and international action to solve these problems. This is based on the firm conviction that feasible solutions *do* exist and that there is no call for defeatist attitudes; these usually become self-fulfilling prophecies. Employment problems are not predetermined outcomes of the workings of uncontrollable forces such as globalization, intensified competition, and technical change. They are the result of social choice: commissions or omissions in economic and social policies and shortcomings in institutional arrangements. The proof of this lies in the fact that countries at similar levels of development and subject to the same economic forces have achieved widely different employment outcomes. Policies and institutional arrangements at both the national and international levels can and should be improved to reverse the drift towards a global employment crisis.

This cannot, of course, be achieved easily or instantaneously. But there are firm initial steps that can be usefully taken. Foremost among these is the adoption of a common vision to inspire action. A universal commitment to the goal of full employment played this role in the shaping of the successful post-war institutions for governing the global economy. That commitment has since been eroded but, as shall be argued in the Report, it is important and timely to revive that commitment. Its weakening has led to worsening employment conditions and has foreclosed national and international actions that could have made a difference. Its revival will provide the basis for the renewed international cooperation that is so essential for solving the employment crisis.

A second basic step is to place the employment issue at the centre of the international agenda. Developments in the world economy such as the liberalization of trade and investment flows and the globalization of production have created vast new opportunities for higher rates of growth and job creation. But these have also given rise to a new generation of social tensions and reduced the effectiveness of current instruments of national and international economic and social policies. Cooperative international action is the best way of resolving this dilemma. The maintenance of an open and efficient global economic system should be a basic objective of such action but the social dimension is no less important.

Measures to promote a more equitable sharing of the costs and benefits of globalization among and within countries and to maintain and improve basic international labour standards are major social challenges. Institutional reforms to bring about a better coordination of economic and social policies would be an important means of ensuring that economic and social progress are mutually reinforcing rather than antagonistic. This is true at both the national and international levels and the ILO is prepared to play a role in helping to bring this about.

This Report appears on the eve of the World Summit for Social Development. The Summit will be a unique and timely opportunity for the international community to reaffirm its commitment to full employment and to signal the importance of launching new initiatives to deal with the mounting global employment problem and attendant social ills. As such, in undertaking its review of global employment problems, the Report has also been conscious of the need to offer ideas on national and international policies that could usefully feed into any such initiatives. But this was not the only purpose in issuing the present Report; it is also the inaugural issue of a series that will be produced regularly in the future.

15 February 1995   Michel HANSENNE
                                                          Director-General

Acknowledgements

This Report was prepared by a team headed by Eddy Lee and comprising Priya Basu, Duncan Campbell, Hélène Harasty, Alfred Pankert and Peter Peek. Support was provided by Jane Barrett, Nadejda Ebel, Chris Fry, John Jimenez, Asma Lateef, Monica Mitchell and Hilary Wyatt.

Particular thanks are due to Jack Martin, Teresa Prada de Mesa, Samir Radwan, Ali Taqi and Adrian Wood who provided helpful advice from the planning stage onwards.

Parts of the report incorporated excerpts from papers prepared by V. N. Balasubramanyam, Fred Block, Andrea Boltho, Paul Collier, Chris Freeman, Andrew Glyn, Martin Godfrey, David Greenaway, Keith Griffin, Tony Killick, Sanjaya Lall, Michael Piore, David Sapsford, Ajit Singh, Dennis Snower, Luc Soete and Guy Standing.

A number of specialists from outside the ILO prepared background papers. These included Eileen Appelbaum, David Bloom, Sam Bowles, Martin Carnoy, Kam Wing Chan, Christopher Edmonds, Herb Gintis, Paul Gregg, John Grieve-Smith, Raymond Harbridge, Alain de Janvry, Russell Lansbury, Duncan Macdonald, Roger McElrath, David Metcalf, François Michon, Chris Milner, Rinku Murgai, Waseem Noor, Bob Rowthorn, Elizabeth Sadoulet, Ronald Schettkat, Keith Sisson, Frances Stewart, Franz Traxler, Tiziano Treu, Mario Velasquez, Matthew Warning and Paul Winters.

ILO staff members who contributed background studies and data included Véronique Arthaud, Arturo Bronstein, Fred Fluitman, Rolph van der Hoeven, Frank Lisk, Roger Plant, Peter Richards and Viktor Tokman.

The team also benefited from discussions with Rebecca Blank, Jacques Gaude, John Philpott and David Soskice during various stages of its work.

Editorial assistance was provided by Inez Holmes.

Contents

Introduction

The present Report is a response to the growing worldwide concern over the problem of unemployment. In most industrialized countries unemployment has risen steadily since 1973. Its average level in the OECD countries is now around 10 per cent. In addition there is concern over the persistence of high unemployment, especially in countries of the European Community, as well as over the reduced employment prospects for unskilled workers and the related problem of rising wage inequality between skilled and unskilled workers. In the transition economies of Eastern and Central Europe there has been a dramatic emergence of mass unemployment since 1990. Unemployment rates of over 10 per cent are now common and threaten to rise further with continued economic restructuring towards a market economy. Real wages have fallen sharply and poverty has increased in many countries. In the developing world there has been a collapse of modern-sector employment in most of sub-Saharan Africa, with rising urban unemployment and substantial falls in real wages. In Latin America there was also a general deterioration in employment conditions during most of the 1980s when the bulk of job creation was in low-productivity informal-sector activities in the context of rising urban unemployment and falling real wages. It is only in Asia, especially in the rapidly growing countries of East and South-East Asia, that there has been a sustained improvement in employment conditions.

A number of recent reports and studies have addressed particular aspects of this worldwide employment problem. The European Commission White Paper on growth, competitiveness and employment and the OECD Jobs Study addressed the problem of high and persistent unemployment in the developed countries. There have also been studies of the employment crises in the transition economies and in parts of the developing world. At the same time there has been growing interest, both in academic literature and in the financial press, in the employment implications of the increasing globalization of the world economy. Most of this literature has been focused on the threat to jobs in the industrialized countries from increasing economic competition from newly industrializing countries. To date, however, there has been no comprehensive review linking together these separate strands of concern over different aspects of the employment problem. This report attempts to fill that gap.

The rationale for embarking on such a comprehensive review of the issue of employment in the global economy is basically twofold. First, the problems of unemployment in the industrialized, transition, and developing economies are, to a significant extent, interrelated, primarily by linkages through trade, foreign direct investment, and financial flows. The force of these linkages can be seen, for example,

in the strong positive impact that high growth and full employment in the industrialized countries between 1950 and 1973 had on output and employment growth in
the developing countries. Similarly, the sharp increase in interest rates in the United
States in the early 1980s precipitated the international debt crisis that led to sharp
decreases in output and employment in many developing countries in sub-Saharan
Africa and Latin America. These interrelationships are likely to become stronger
with the growing globalization of the world economy. This in turn increases the
importance of undertaking the type of global analysis of employment issues that is
being attempted in this Report.

Second, the interrelationship is not only at the level of causation but also
in terms of possible solutions to the problem. The underlying idea here is that a
coordinated and cooperative approach to tackling the unemployment problem at the
global level will yield benefits to all participating countries and result in superior
overall outcomes. The truth of this proposition can be seen most clearly in the realm
of international trade, where a coordinated expansion of world trade will lead to
greater overall employment gains than a recourse to protectionist policies. Similarly,
policies to attain higher rates of non-inflationary growth are more likely to be
successful when there is coordination of such policies across countries.

Given this perspective, the structure of the Report is as follows:

–   Part I surveys key aspects of the current globalization of the world economy.
     The focus is on the growth of world trade and of flows of foreign direct
     investment and the implications of these developments for employment. It
     includes a critical examination of fears that globalization will have negative
     effects on employment in the industrialized countries and that parts of the
     developing world are in danger of being marginalized.

–   Part II of the Report examines the employment problem in developing
     countries. It reviews salient employment trends in each of the major regions of
     the developing world, highlighting significant contrasts in performance, and
     discusses the policies that need to be followed in order to reap benefits from
     the ongoing process of globalization and to minimize the costs of adjustment.
     It also discusses additional policies that are necessary for the reduction of
     underemployment and poverty in many developing countries and concludes
     with a discussion of the causes of, and possible solutions to, the margin-
     alization of many sub-Saharan economies from the global economy.

–   Part III of the Report addresses the employment problem in the transition
     economies in Eastern and Central Europe. It reviews output and employment
     trends since the initiation of the process of transition to a market economy and

examines the scope for alleviating the unemployment problem through both overall economic policies and labour market programmes.

—   Part IV of the Report examines the employment problem in the industrialized countries. It surveys the contrasting employment performance in major groups of countries in the face of a common problem of significantly slower economic growth since 1973. It then reviews the major explanations that have been advanced for the generally poorer employment performance since 1973 as well as for differences in employment outcomes across countries. The role of macroeconomic policies is examined first. This is then followed by a detailed and critical review of the highly influential view within policy circles that labour market rigidity has been the main explanation of poor employment performance. Following upon this assessment of causes, the discussion then shifts to a consideration of policies that could be pursued to reduce unemployment.

—   The Report is rounded off in Part V with a discussion of the potential contribution of international policies to the reduction of global unemployment. Priority areas for international action are also identified.

While the Report has sought to be comprehensive in scope it has nevertheless had to concentrate on a few key themes. As a result, issues such as international migration, gender inequalities, the position of vulnerable groups, training policies and external debt and structural adjustment have either not been addressed or have been touched upon only briefly. These are all important issues in their own right which future issues of the Report might address.

Summary

1.   The present report is a response to worldwide concern over the problem of unemployment. A number of recent reports and studies have addressed the issue from the standpoint of particular groups of countries but there has, to date, been no comprehensive review of employment problems from a global perspective.

Globalization and employment

2.   Anxieties over the issue of job creation have surfaced against a backdrop of profound change in the global economy. At one level this appears ironic since the past few decades have seen steady growth in world output, in international trade, and in flows of foreign direct investment. World output has grown by at least 3 per cent per annum since 1950, although it has fallen from previously higher rates in the past two decades. World trade has grown faster than output throughout this period while flows of foreign direct investment have grown massively in recent years.

3.   The structure of output and employment has also changed radically. In terms of output there has been a significant shift out of agriculture towards industry and services, with agriculture now accounting for only 4 per cent of world output. There has been significant industrialization in developing countries, where the share of manufacturing has risen to over 20 per cent of total output, a share now similar to that in industrialized countries. In the industrialized countries there has been a marked shift towards services, which now account for nearly 65 per cent of total output. The structure of employment has changed accordingly. Similarly, there has been a major shift in the structure of world trade, where the share of manufacturing has increased rapidly and now constitutes 71 per cent of the total value of world exports. The growth of manufacturing exports from developing countries has been particularly rapid.

4.   Viewed as a whole, therefore, the world economy would appear to be creating the basis for rising prosperity and employment growth. The expansion of trade and investment flows against a background of a worldwide shift towards more open economic policies and a greater reliance on market forces should also be contributing to improved resource allocation and efficiency worldwide. Nevertheless, while essentially correct from an overall standpoint, this view of the global economy neglects differences in the position of different countries and of different social groups within these which raise serious adjustment and distributional issues.

5.   Foremost among the intercountry differences is the sharp contrast in the performance of different groups of developing countries. The rapidly industrializing

economies of East and South-East Asia have grown far faster than those of the rest of the developing world and have accounted for the major part of the gains from rising exports and manufacturing output attributed to the developing world. In contrast, Latin America is only beginning to recover from the economic setbacks of the debt crisis of the 1980s, while sub-Saharan Africa is still mired in economic stagnation. The gains from expanding world trade and output have thus been unevenly distributed so far.

6. The globalization of the world economy also poses serious distributional problems within countries. The social costs of implementing major economic reforms in order to increase international competitiveness and hence reap the gains from globalization are often high. Many developing countries experiencing poor economic performance also have economic structures and policies that are still seriously distorted; these countries therefore still face a major challenge of economic reform. In the industrialized countries a major social problem is the labour market prospects of unskilled workers. This group of workers has experienced the highest incidence of unemployment, declining relative (and in some cases, absolute) wages, and reduced job prospects. This has been linked by some observers to growing import competition from low-wage economies and the relocation of low-skilled jobs to the latter. While the extent to which these factors have really been responsible has often been exaggerated, it nevertheless remains true that they have played some role. The existence of this problem fuels protectionist sentiments which could stall progress towards freer trade and investment flows, with negative effects for growth and efficiency in the global economy.

7. A basic conclusion of this report is that, while globalization generates problems such as these, the potential benefits far outweigh the costs. The optimal strategy, both from a global as well as individual-country perspective, would be to reap the considerable gains in terms of higher output and efficiency from continued globalization while dealing with the social problems that are engendered through appropriate national and international policies. Through such an approach, all parties can be better off as compared to the alternative of a move towards protectionism.

The Uruguay Round

8. The full implementation of the Uruguay Round of GATT is critical for continued progress towards a more open and productive global economy. The Uruguay Round is correctly regarded as the most ambitious and comprehensive of GATT rounds. It covered a larger number of contracting parties and a larger number of negotiating issues than any previous round. In addition to standard issues of tariff liberalization, it addressed new ones relating to foreign investment, intellectual property, and services. If all the commitments in the agreement are translated into reality then there should be significant gains in terms of trade expansion which will in turn lead to higher growth of output and employment. Some estimates show that

the agreed tariff cuts are likely to result in a 20 per cent increase in world trade and to boost world output by 5 per cent initially, and significantly more when subsequent multiplier effects are taken into account. Equally important is the fact that security of access to the markets of trading partners will be greatly increased. Ninety-nine and 59 per cent of tariffs in the industrialized and developing countries respectively will be bound. Once bound, tariffs cannot subsequently be changed unilaterally. This, together with the provisions relating to foreign investment and trade in services, constitutes an important foundation for an open and stable international economic system.

9.   While the overall impact of the Uruguay Round on employment will be favourable, there will nevertheless be problems of adjustment. The best option would be to adopt positive or proactive adjustment policies. This involves policies to smooth the transfer of resources from declining to new activities in line with a country's comparative advantage. The measures to be adopted include the retraining of workers and geographical mobility grants. Such an approach would be superior to either non-intervention or a recourse to defensive adjustment measures. Non-intervention is likely to result in slower adjustment at higher social costs. Transitional unemployment can become persistent through hysteresis effects while slower adjustment will also tend to strengthen political forces opposed to trade liberalization. Similarly, recourse to defensive adjustment through measures such as voluntary export restrictions and anti-dumping legislation has been shown to involve high deadweight costs and consequent welfare losses.

Foreign direct investment (FDI)

10.   An important new development is the increasingly important role of multinational enterprises (MNEs) in world trade and production. Foreign direct invest-ment by such enterprises has grown significantly faster than world output and trade, and faster than domestic investment. Flows to developing countries have increased particularly rapidly and there has been a marked change in attitudes and policies towards foreign investment in these countries. Instead of previous suspicions and controls there is now a generally welcoming attitude. This derives from a growing appreciation of the benefits to be derived from such investment in terms of job creation and the learning and spillover effects from the introduction of new techno-logy. By 1992 about 73 million jobs had been directly created by MNEs worldwide; of these 12 million were in developing countries. Including jobs that were created indirectly would lead to a doubling of these numbers. While the number of jobs created in developing countries is still only 2 per cent of total employment in these countries, the proportion is significantly higher in some countries which have received large amounts of foreign investment. Employment attributable to MNEs is as high as 20 per cent of non-agricultural employment in some of these. Moreover,

employment creation by MNEs is likely to expand significantly with the growing globalization of their activities. In particular, technological developments have created new scope for increased out-sourcing of service activities, thereby creating new employment opportunities for developing countries with the required supplies of trained workers.

11.   While the opportunities for employment creation through MNEs are likely to continue to expand rapidly, these benefits have not been widely diffused so far. Foreign direct investment in developing countries has remained concentrated in only a few of them. In 1992, ten countries accounted for 76 per cent of the total stock of foreign direct investment in developing countries, while the 47 least developed countries accounted for only 0.6 per cent of total flows. Moreover, the prospects for the least developed countries are likely to remain bleak, with intensified competition among countries to attract FDI. The entry into the FDI scene of currently "under-invested" countries such as India is likely to attract a substantial share of future flows. The spectacular inflow of FDI into China in recent years has illustrated how significant this effect can be.

Concerns over globalization

12.   The problem of the marginalization of the least developed countries, and growing international inequality as a result of globalization is an emerging area of concern. Another area of concern over globalization is apprehension in the industrialized countries over job losses. Alarmist views on the job-destroying effects of imports from, and the relocation of production to, developing countries are often heard. It is argued that imports from low-wage economies destroy jobs both directly through the displacement of production as well as indirectly through the labour-saving technical change that is induced. Extreme versions of these arguments fear that wages in the industrialized countries will be pulled down through the working of the factor-price equalization theorem and that the diffusion of western technology to low-wage producers will give them an unbeatable competitive advantage. Arguments such as these have fuelled protectionist sentiments in the industrialized countries.

13.   Such alarm is in fact unwarranted. It is based on the flawed assumption that trade and investment flows are essentially a zero-sum game. The evidence that there are considerable mutual benefits for both industrialized and developing countries is typically overlooked. For example, trade between the industrialized countries and the newly industrializing countries (NICs) (the main source of import penetration) has been in balance; exports from industrialized countries to the NICs have grown as fast as imports from these countries. This is to be expected since faster growth and rising incomes in developing countries will lead to increasing demand for imports of capital goods, technology, and other products from the industrialized countries. Moreover, there will be the benefits from increased competition in the world

economy in the form of lower prices, the economies of scale made possible by larger markets, and expanded investment opportunities.

14.   A similar virtuous circle of mutual benefits operates in the case of investment flows. Far from being a one-way process of exporting jobs to low-wage countries, foreign direct investment in fact generates significant benefits to the capital-exporting country. Such investments often generate increased exports of, for example, technology, components, and other productive inputs. There are also benefits in terms of the return flow of profits which could boost investment and from the generalized gains through the "lifting-all-boats" effect of greater efficiency of resource allocation in the world economy. It is also important to note that an outflow of investment is often not a simple subtraction from funds that would otherwise have been available for domestic investment. Foreign investment often provides the only available outlet for expansion in industries which face saturated domestic markets. Given that production "know-how" and intangibles such as market reputation are typically industry-specific, it does not follow that domestic investment would have occurred in the absence of foreign investment. Similarly, product-cycle considerations often make it rational to invest abroad in the mature phase of an industry when production technology becomes standardized and allows production to be broken down into a number of relatively unskilled tasks. Comparative advantage therefore shifts to low-wage economies at this stage of the product cycle. So long as product innovation continues in the industrialized countries such relocation of production yields mutual benefits to both capital-exporting and capital-receiving countries.

15.   To stress mutual benefits from trade and investment flows is not, however, to deny that there are real costs of adjustment, especially in the short run. But, as argued earlier, it is best to deal with these problems directly through domestic policy rather than through forgoing the clear net benefits of participating in the global economy.

16.   Another apprehension connected to globalization is that the rapid spread of new technologies is destroying a significant number of jobs. But technical change both destroys old jobs and creates new ones and there are also important indirect benefits from the pervasive spread of a major new technology such as Information and Communication Technology (ICT). The spread of ICT can create the basis for a virtuous circle of growth in which investment is high, labour productivity grows fast but output grows even faster, so that there is net growth of employment.

Developing countries

17.   The economic performance of developing countries in different regions of the world has diverged significantly since the early 1980s and employment performance has varied accordingly. In East and South-East Asia high and sustained rates of economic growth have led to rapid growth of modern-sector jobs, rising real wages

and, in some cases, even labour shortages. By contrast, in sub-Saharan Africa economic stagnation or retrogression has led to a collapse of modern-sector employment, falling labour earnings, rising urban unemployment and a bloating of low-productivity informal-sector employment. In Latin America, there was also a similar deterioration of employment conditions during the 1980s though the situation has begun to improve in recent years.

18.   The main mechanism through which high growth was transmitted into favourable employment performance in Asia was the rapid growth of manufacturing exports. This was the main impulse for the rapid growth of labour demand in the modern sector that provided expanding opportunities for the labour force to shift into more productive and better paid jobs. The growth of manufacturing exports and jobs has in turn been boosted by significant inflows of foreign direct investment in several of these countries. In this sense, therefore, successful response to the opportunities created by globalization was a key explanation of their superior economic performance.

Responding to globalization

19.   The problem of employment creation in developing countries now has to be viewed within the new context of an increasingly globalized economy. Globalization sets limits on the effectiveness of traditional instruments for influencing the level and quality of employment but, on the whole, the impact on job creation is likely to be favourable provided the right policies are adopted. The increased importance of trading success and the attraction of foreign investment as policy objectives is likely to lead to improved economic management. This will be reflected in greater macroeconomic stability, more liberal trade regimes, the avoidance of currency overvaluation, and less distorted relative prices. All this will have favourable effects on the demand for labour. There is, however, the danger that globalization will have negative effects on labour standards. The increased footlooseness of MNEs, combined with pressures to attract and retain foreign investment, could lead to a debasement of labour standards. This makes it important to give fresh impetus to cooperative international action to protect them.

20.   Within this new context, a fundamental objective of economic policy in developing countries should be to capture as much as possible of the potential gains from expanding trade and investment flows. In general this will involve the adoption of more open economic policies that will guide production and trade towards activities in line with a country's comparative advantage. For a significant number of countries, but by no means all, this will imply the adoption of export-oriented industrialization policies. For countries with abundant land and natural resources, as is true for many countries in sub-Saharan Africa and Latin America, comparative advantage will continue to lie in primary production. In these cases the benefits of globalization can be captured through increasing and diversifying agricultural and

other primary commodity exports and increased processing of these products. Nevertheless, regardless of where comparative advantage lies it still makes sense to adopt open economic policies and to avoid the artificial promotion or protection of activities which have no hope of becoming internationally competitive.

21. In general, the adoption of export-oriented policies will be desirable. However, the adoption of export-oriented policies is not synonymous with the adoption of pure laissez-faire policies. While failed policies of "classical" import substitution should be avoided, there will often be a need for government intervention. For example, intervention to correct failures in both product and factor markets will improve efficiency. Similarly, the protection of infant industries will be economically sound, provided it is strictly limited to industries with genuine comparative advantage and includes strong incentives for these industries to upgrade their capabilities.

22. The successful attraction of FDI can be a powerful spur to rapid industrialization and employment creation, and adopting policies to this end is an important means of gaining access to the benefits of globalization. Apart from factors that policy cannot directly affect (such as geographical location and the resource base), important variables affecting the flow of FDI are economic and political stability, a favourable attitude towards private enterprise in general, good infrastructure and macroeconomic management, clear and transparent policies towards investors, and a trade and industrial regime that allows MNEs to operate in internationally competitive conditions. Within this general framework it may be desirable to target the entry of foreign investment into sectors or activities that particularly benefit employment creation.

23. The adoption of these trade liberalization and investment promotion policies will, for many countries, amount to a far-reaching programme of economic reform. Countries which still suffer from macroeconomic instability and a heavy burden of external debt, which still have high levels of protection, and which are still heavily regulated face particularly difficult adjustment problems. While adjustment is unavoidable, precipitate and ill-designed programmes are unlikely to be successful and will inflict unnecessarily high social costs in the process. Adjustment programmes should therefore be carefully designed so as to allow sufficient time to introduce supportive measures to increase the capacity of economic agents to respond to new economic incentives. Care should also be taken to ensure that effective redeployment and safety net measures are in place before implementing reforms which involve significant redundancies and reduce the living standards of the poor. Involving labour ministries and the social partners in the design and implementation of adjustment programmes is an important means of ensuring that social costs are minimized and that there is essential social support of the programmes. The capacity of labour ministries to design and implement redeployment and safety net measures should also be strengthened.

24.   Economic liberalization which has characterized adaptation to globalization has, in some developing countries, also exposed weaknesses in national
patterns of labour market regulation. This is to be expected, since, as in Latin
America, labour market institutions which may have been appropriate to earlier
development models and more closed economies have been slow to adapt to new
economic regimes. Reform of inappropriate regulations is therefore called for,
particularly where these have sheltered a protected formal sector at the expense of
widening the gulf between these workers and those in the unprotected informal
economy. Yet it would be wrong to assume that labour market regulation is the major
impediment to change when it is in fact the wholesale transformation of an uncompetitive industrial structure and inward-oriented development model that is the far
greater challenge. Neither is it true that it is the absence of labour market regulation
that explains the economic success of the dynamic Asian economies. The pursuit of
effective export-oriented industrialization strategies was a far more important factor
behind the economic success of that region. Moreover, labour market institutions have
not been uniform across these countries and rapid growth has continued in spite of the
growing maturity of labour market institutions in some of them.

Reducing underemployment and poverty

25.   While a successful response to globalization is of strategic importance
for generating a higher number of productive modern-sector jobs, this will not by itself
be sufficient. In many developing countries the majority of the labour force are still
employed in the low-productivity rural and urban informal sectors of the economy.
Underemployment is endemic and most of the poverty in these countries is in fact
concentrated in these sectors. It is thus important that development policies should not
be biased against them and that measures to reduce underemployment and poverty be
given priority in government programmes.

26.   This need for a balanced strategy can be illustrated with respect to
policies to raise the rate of investment. Such policies are critical for raising the rate of
growth of output and employment in an economy. The most successful developing
countries have all had high rates of investment in both physical and human capital. But
it is not enough merely to have high rates of investment; it is equally important to raise
the productivity of capital and to ensure that it is efficiently allocated across sectors.
In developing countries capital markets are often distorted, with producers in the rural
and informal sectors having very limited access to formal credit markets. They thus
face a high cost of capital and this depresses productivity. Reform of capital markets
to ensure more equal access would thus be important for improving productivity in the
rural and urban informal sectors. The implementation of innovative credit schemes
targeted at small producers has shown impressive results in a number of countries.
Capital market reforms would also promote higher rates of employment growth, since

a characteristic of distorted capital markets is that capital is artificially cheapened, hence promoting an unwarranted degree of capital-intensity in production.

27. The urban informal sector in developing countries comprises a wide variety of activities ranging from petty services to small-scale production with the potential for being upgraded and absorbed into the modern sector. Since this sector as a whole serves a safety net function of absorbing surplus labour, the general policy towards it should be to remove administrative and other obstacles to its growth. In addition, the modernizing segment of the sector should be promoted through facilitating access to credit, productive inputs and knowledge of improved techniques of production, and through promoting linkages with the modern sector.

28. It is important to provide continued state support to the small farm sector on both efficiency and equity grounds. Investments in rural infrastructure and in credit and agricultural extension programmes have high economic returns in terms of improved productivity. This in turn makes an important contribution to alleviating poverty since there is typically a very high incidence of poverty among small farmers. Economic liberalization often improves economic opportunities for the agricultural sector through higher producer prices, reduced taxes, and the enhancement of export potential. However, the response of producers to these new opportunities has often been poor because of the reduction or withdrawal of state support to the small farm sector. Such policy errors should be rectified in order to enable small farmers to benefit fully from the new opportunities created by economic liberalization.

29. In addition to supportive policies towards the urban informal and rural sectors, direct measures to alleviate poverty are necessary. Employment creation programmes are an important instrument for alleviating the considerable underemployment that exists in many developing countries. For example, rural public works provide valuable income supplements to the underemployed poor while creating productive assets that enhance productivity and future employment prospects. Special employment programmes can also provide basic income support to the unemployed during economic crises. It is also important to provide a modicum of economic security to the poor since they have no other means of providing this for themselves. Such expenditures, apart from being justified on equity grounds, also yield net economic benefits since they involve, at most, only a minor trade-off with efficiency. Expenditures that are effectively targeted to improving the access of the poor to basic social services such as health care and education are particularly important and can often be funded through a reallocation of government spending away from unproductive and inequitable uses.

The marginalization of Africa

30. There is growing concern over the marginalization of many countries in sub-Saharan Africa from the benefits of globalization. The shares of this region in

world trade and investment have declined to negligible proportions and its economies have become more inward-oriented during a period in which all others have become more integrated into the global economy. It is highly likely that this has been an important cause of the dismal economic performance of African countries.

31.   Until the late 1980s it was straightforward to explain this marginalization of Africa in terms of domestic policies which were hostile both to the private sector in general and to the export sector and foreign capital in particular. During the 1980s, usually under the auspices of structural adjustment programmes, these policies were to an extent reversed. While it could be argued that these policy reforms have not gone far enough, it is more likely that more basic factors than just a gap in policy reforms are at work in explaining Africa's marginalization. The higher degree of risk in African economies, arising from both external shocks and frequent abrupt shifts in policy, deters investment. In addition severe deficiencies in the institutional structure, such as insecure property rights and weak judicial and accountancy systems, make investment highly illiquid and thus unattractive. As a result of this inhospitable investment climate neither domestic nor foreign investment has been able to contribute to overcoming Africa's marginalization.

32.   Reversing Africa's marginalization from the world economy will ultimately require comprehensive efforts by governments to reduce policy risks and other deterrents to both domestic and foreign investment. In the meantime reforms to current aid programmes and policy conditionality can help to improve the situation. Aid transfers as currently conceived are essentially transfers of foreign exchange to the public sector which appreciate the exchange rate and raise public expenditure, both absolutely and relatively to GDP. This has negative effects in terms of reduced exports and the crowding out of the private sector in general. These negative effects could be mitigated by transferring most aid to the private sector in general and the export sector in particular. In addition, policy conditionality could be redesigned to be retrospective rather than prospective, that is, rewarding actual past performance rather than mere promises for policy reform which are often not honoured. This will provide stronger incentives for governments to actually implement policy reforms.

Transition economies

33.   The initial years of the transition process in the former centrally planned economies in East and Central Europe have been characterized by sharp falls in output, the rapid emergence of mass unemployment, and rising inequality and poverty. Although there was a relative improvement in some countries by 1994, the outlook remains bleak, especially in the former USSR. On the whole, the transition process has turned out to be more difficult than foreseen. The restructuring of heavily distorted economies insulated for decades from both domestic and international market forces and the building of new market institutions from scratch has proved to

be a truly daunting and time-consuming task. The social cost has been high even in connection with only the partial transformation that has been achieved so far.

34.   A disturbing aspect of developments so far is that the share of the transition economies in world trade has fallen sharply and inflows of foreign direct investment have been negligible. Yet this cannot really be rectified until the transition to a market economy is complete since this is an essential precondition for these economies to become internationally competitive. The transition therefore needs to be completed as rapidly as possible. But there are two constraints on how fast this can proceed. One is the fact that some aspects of the transition, particularly the building of new institutions, are inherently slow. The other is the risk of aggravating the already very high social costs of transition.

35.   A major challenge is therefore to manage the pace of trade liberalization, enterprise restructuring and privatization so that the best balance is found between the imperative of efficiency and the need to contain social costs within tolerable limits. Proponents of rapid change argue that anything less would thwart the whole transition, that is, the choice is an all-or-nothing one between instant restructuring or no progress at all towards a market economy. This does not appear to be true since there exist policy instruments which make it feasible to manage a more gradual process of change that nevertheless still heads in the right direction. The gradual approach should not, of course, rely on a continuation of indiscriminate and unconditional protection through soft credits to state-owned enterprises or the imposition of import quotas. Such measures would indeed freeze necessary progress in restructuring. Instead time-bound assistance that is conditional upon progress in restructuring should be offered to targeted enterprises that show promise of future viability.

36.   The problem of mass unemployment in the transition economies will ultimately be solved only by the expansion of output and the creation of jobs in new activities in line with comparative advantage in these economies. With further progress towards market-determined price signals and the removal of production subsidies, a clearer picture will emerge of competitive production opportunities in both the domestic and world markets. A key determinant of the capacity to respond to these new opportunities is the rate of investment. A high rate of investment is necessary in order to upgrade physical infrastructure and to create productive capacity in new activities. Achieving this will require the completion of reforms to create a reliable system of property rights and well functioning capital markets. These are essential for improving the climate for both domestic and foreign investment. In addition to raising the rate of investment a major effort in training and retraining will also be required in order to adjust the mix of skills to the requirements of the new structure of production.

37.   It is also important to strengthen labour market policies, since these have achieved only modest results so far. The capacity to implement active labour market policies is particularly weak and employment services need to be greatly reinforced.

This will allow for more effective redeployment and retraining measures that are of critical importance given the magnitude of the economic restructuring that is under way. In particular, there is a need to boost enterprise-based training which has been severely cut back in the wake of enterprise restructuring. A new government-supported institutional framework for providing such training needs to be created to replace the previous system where the entire responsibility rested with enterprises. There is also scope for increased effort with respect to the implementation of measures such as public works and the promotion of self-employment, which have only been used to a limited extent so far. The decline in social protection as a result of progressive disentitlement to benefits with increased targeting and the application of means tests also needs to be arrested. Social protection should be increasingly combined with training and other active labour market measures. In addition, mechanisms for tripartite consultations and negotiations need to be strengthened through supporting the development of strong, representative, and effective social partners.

Industrialized countries

38.   Unemployment began to rise in the industrialized countries after the first oil shock in 1973, when the rate of economic growth dropped by half. Although the rate of economic growth has been, on the whole, similar in these countries between 1974 and 1994, employment performance has varied from one to another. While unemployment has fluctuated at around 6 per cent in the United States since the early 1960s and has remained virtually unchanged at around 2 per cent in Japan, it has risen significantly in Europe. In the European Community it has risen steadily since 1974 apart from the marked drop between 1986 and 1990 due to the economic recovery which followed the oil counter-shock. By 1994 unemployment stood at the unprecedentedly high level of 12 per cent. Even in the EFTA countries (Austria, Finland, Norway, Switzerland and Sweden), where unemployment was significantly lower than most other OECD countries throughout the 1980s, it has risen sharply since 1990.

39.   These differences in employment performance reflect varying rates at which labour productivity declined in response to slower economic growth after 1974. In the United States, the EFTA countries, and to a lesser extent Japan, the slackening in labour productivity has completely offset the slow-down in growth so that employment creation continued at the same rate as in the 1960s. In contrast, in the countries of the European Union, except the Netherlands and Ireland, labour productivity has declined by smaller margins and employment growth has consequently been slight.

40.   These contrasting patterns in the rate of growth of labour productivity in turn implied different rates of increase in real wages. There was thus a trade-off between employment creation and increases in real wages. Countries such as the United States which had higher rates of employment growth also had lower rates of growth of labour productivity and hence wages. In the European Community, on the other hand, higher

productivity growth has allowed higher wage increases but this has been at the cost of higher unemployment. Put more starkly, the contrast is between persistent unemployment in Europe and stagnant or even declining wages for the working poor in the United States. Some countries, such as Sweden, have managed to avoid both these extremes through having narrower wage differentials and creating jobs in the public sector. This has, however, been at the risk of building up inflationary pressures and depleting public finances.

Causes of rising unemployment

41. Two basic sets of causes of the rise in unemployment in many industrialized countries have been identified. The first focuses on economic policies and their impact on growth and hence on employment, while the second attributes differences in employment performance to differences in labour market regulation. These two sets of causes are not mutually exclusive although much recent analysis has tended to focus exclusively on one or the other within a monocausal framework.

42. Between the first and second oil shocks (1974-79), differences in economic policy across countries were not an important explanation of varying employment performance. Most governments reacted to the first oil shock with expansionary budgetary policies and easy money policies. The result was a rapid return to sustained growth (although at only half of previous levels) but with persistent inflation. The purchasing power of wage earners was maintained through wage indexation and most of the adjustment had to be borne by enterprises, whose profits diminished considerably. In this context of growing disequilibria, economic policy reactions were very different following the second oil shock: the struggle against inflation and the reestablishment of profit margins of enterprises became of prime importance. But within this general reorientation, policies began to diverge, leading to differences in growth rates and employment performance. In the first half of the 1980s a wide divergence between budgetary policies in the United States and Europe emerged. Whereas increased public expenditure and reduced taxes combined to support activity in the United States, budgetary policies remained neutral or highly restrictive in Europe. The result was a return to high growth in the United States in a context of growing public and foreign trade deficits, whereas growth remained slow in Europe. It was not until the latter half of the 1980s, as a result of the oil counter-shock and the relaxation of monetary policies following the stock exchange crash of 1987, that growth picked up again in Europe. By the early 1990s, however, the German recession in the aftermath of reunification and highly restrictive monetary policies gradually pushed Europe into recession. In contrast, the American economy, under the impetus of a broad relaxation of monetary policy, experienced its strongest recovery in ten years in 1992-93.

43. Apart from these differences in macroeconomic policies, differences in the mechanisms through which disinflation was achieved also partly explained

differences in employment outcomes. Disinflation was paid for directly by wage earners in the United States, who saw a sharp drop in their real wages in the first half of the 1980s. In Europe it was achieved through the maintenance of a high level of unemployment. Since 1980 the operation of the European Monetary System has also contributed to high unemployment through the deflationary bias it imparted to monetary policy. Monetary policy has been dictated by German objectives of low inflation and has been tight. High interest rates in turn also constrained budgetary expansion by raising the cost of government borrowing. Moreover the absence of an institutional mechanism for coordinating budgetary policies in Europe reinforced this deflationary bias. Without policy coordination, isolated attempts at reflation would soon be halted by balance of payments constraints.

44.   An influential body of opinion considers differences in labour market regulation to be the central explanation of contrasting employment performance across countries. Specifically, labour market rigidity in Europe – strong unions, stringent employment protection, generous welfare provisions – in contrast to the relatively unregulated labour market in the United States is held to be the main explanation of poor employment performance in Europe.

45.   A basic argument within this framework has been that wages in Europe have been too high, thereby reducing the demand for labour. Excessive wages reduce profits and thus investment, thereby reducing employment through a shrinking of productive capacity. The employment intensity of investment is also reduced through the labour-saving induced by excessive wages. The empirical evidence suggests that from the first oil shock to the mid-1980s excessive wage increases did indeed contribute to rising unemployment in Europe. However, from the mid-1980s onwards this no longer appears to be true. Real wage gaps had disappeared as countries abandoned automatic wage indexation and wage increases became lower than productivity increases. By the end of the 1980s the share of wages in value added had declined to its early 1970s level while profit margins were also restored. Nevertheless, European unemployment has remained high in spite of this elimination of excessive wage levels since the mid-1980s. This suggests that, contrary to the "excessive wage" argument, other factors were causing the persistence of high unemployment.

46.   A strand of argument that is closely related to the "excessive wage" explanation of high unemployment focuses on the labour market rigidities caused by inappropriate industrial relations systems. A major claim here is that very decentralized bargaining structures yield the best employment outcomes because they ensure the greatest degree of wage flexibility. This greater flexibility is argued to apply both to aggregate adjustments of real wages to overall macroeconomic conditions as well as to adjustments in relative wages. The evidence in support of this view is, however, at best unclear. The literature on the relationship between the degree of centralization in wage bargaining and macroeconomic performance has not yielded clear conclusions, at least over time. Nor does the experience of some countries with reforms to

institute decentralized systems unambiguously demonstrate the alleged superiority of such systems. In the United Kingdom real wages have risen faster than productivity growth and aggregate employment has not increased, in spite of the decline in union density and decentralization of wage bargaining. Moreover, the fact that three of the world's most successful economies, the United States, Japan and Germany, all have vastly different levels and coverage of bargaining and union density undermines the case for the superiority of decentralized systems. This is reinforced by the fact that flexible adjustments in wages can occur under widely differing industrial relations systems. Austria, with a highly corporatist system, has the highest inter-industry wage spread in Europe, while Japan has been able to control wage inflation in spite of having a decentralized industrial relations system. All this suggests the overall conclusion that a variety of industrial relations systems can ensure wage flexibility and the coordination of wage policy with macroeconomic objectives.

47.   The existence of minimum wages has also been identified as a cause of poor employment performance. However, the bulk of empirical evidence largely finds the impact of minimum wages on employment to be insignificant. In any case, in the majority of industrialized countries statutory minimum wages declined relative to average wages in the 1980s. In practice wage floors can be established not only by statutory minima but also through the administrative extension to all workers of minimum wages resulting from collective agreements. This practice has also been criticized as having negative employment effects but such criticisms are not wholly convincing. Minimum wages resulting from collective bargaining are not impervious to market forces. Besides, they yield benefits in terms of promoting the coordination of wage bargaining.

48.   Another concern over the price of labour relates to high levels of payroll taxes. It is argued that these high non-wage labour costs reduce labour hiring and encourage the adoption of labour-saving technology. However, the available evidence suggests that in spite of differences in the share of non-wage labour costs in total labour costs, the share of wages in value added is similar across countries. This is consistent with the theoretical expectation that in the long run the incidence of payroll taxes is ultimately shifted back to wage earners. Nevertheless, in the short to medium term reductions in non-wage labour costs can increase employment. In particular, the reduction or elimination of payroll taxes on low wages would increase the employment of low-skilled workers.

49.   High levels and long durations of unemployment benefits have also been widely blamed for aggravating unemployment through undermining the incentive to work. The evidence indicates that the level of benefits does indeed affect the duration of unemployment spells but the effects are small. The general order of magnitude is that a 10 per cent increase in benefits leads to a 3 per cent increase in the average duration of unemployment spells. The level of benefits thus cannot by itself account for high levels of European unemployment, since observed levels of unemployment

are higher than what such estimates would predict. The evidence also suggests that the duration of benefits also affects the duration of unemployment. Long-lasting and generous unemployment benefits may reduce the incentive to work most strongly among low-paid workers, thus causing them to be disproportionately represented among the long-term unemployed. The economic advantages of a well-functioning unemployment benefits system are thus clear and targeted reforms warrant discussion.

50.   Employment security rules have often been cited as a deterrent to job creation. The case against these rules is that by raising "firing costs" they reduce the incentive to hire and also impede labour market adjustments. There is some empirical support for this view but also much evidence that employment security rules have not been a major factor in explaining high unemployment. A number of European countries relaxed these rules in the 1980s with the objective of increasing employment but instead of giving a significant boost to overall employment the main effect was to shift the structure of employment towards temporary or fixed-term jobs. This illustrates the general point that employment security rules do not block labour market adjustments but only alter the path of adjustment. Adjustment to changing labour market conditions can occur not only through changes in the numbers employed but also through changes in hours worked. Similarly, the impact of employment protection may be to reduce employment fluctuations over the economic cycle, hoarding labour in a downturn and hiring less in an upturn, while leaving overall employment relatively unchanged. Such considerations probably explain the fact that in spite of higher levels of employment protection in Europe than in the United States, patterns of labour reallocation across sectors are similar. This observation is also consistent with the view that the creation of long-term jobs is primarily determined by firms' expectations of the stability of labour demand with "firing costs" having at best only a minor influence.

51.   The foregoing review of evidence suggests that labour market rigidities have not been an underlying cause of past labour market performance. Labour market performance has deteriorated since the first oil shock irrespective of differences in labour market regulation, suggesting that a more fundamental common factor (or factors) has been at work. International shifts in trade, employment and technology could be among these fundamental causes of deteriorating labour market performance. The manifestations of this deterioration have, however, differed, taking the form of rising inequality and falling wages in the less regulated United States labour market and high unemployment in the more regulated European setting. In any case, even if the issue of ultimate causation is left aside it remains debatable whether it is regulation of the labour market that has been the main impediment to job creation. For example, anti-competitive regulations in European product markets – ranging from zoning laws to a variety of regulatory barriers to entry – have been found to be a more serious impediment to job creation than labour market regulation.

52. This debate over labour market regulation is, however, not simply an academic one but has implications for the reform of existing labour market regulation. Some concrete proposals for reform are in fact on the current policy agenda in several countries. It is important that the social partners be involved not only in the general debate on these proposals but also in the actual formulation of new regulations. Social concertation in this area will be essential for arriving at a harmonious balance between the competing demands of economic efficiency and social protection.

Reducing unemployment

53. Most projections of long-term employment scenarios indicate that rates of growth higher than the trend since 1974 are required in order to restore full employment, particularly in Europe. Yet most countries face severe constraints in pursuing policies to achieve higher growth. These include current macroeconomic imbalances, high long-term real interest rates determined on global financial markets independently of national policy, and the limits placed on expansionary policies in a single country by an increasingly globalized world economy. Attempts by a single country to reflate carry the risk of engendering an unsustainable external deficit and speculative pressures on the exchange rate. Coordinated recovery is a way of breaking these constraints. The balance of payments constraint will be loosened both by higher demand among trading partners who are also reflating and by the fact that the loss of competitiveness will be limited since all trading partners will be subject to similar inflationary pressures. Moreover the initial expansionary effect will be reinforced since each country stimulates the growth of its trading partners.

54. Such a coordinated recovery will not, however, be easy to achieve. Certain countries may consider that they have already done much in the way of budgetary stimulation while some others still face inflationary pressures. On the whole, however, it appears that a basis for policy coordination exists in the present conjuncture. The level of capacity utilization is generally low, making it unlikely that growth will be checked by supply constraints in the short run. Moreover, most countries have current unemployment rates that are markedly above the NAIRU (non-accelerating inflation rate of unemployment), indicating that there is scope for expansion without generating serious inflationary pressures. Indeed inflation remains generally under control. This, together with high prevailing interest rates in Europe, indicates that there is room for manoeuvre with respect to monetary policy. However, many observers are of the view that there is little scope for expansionary fiscal policy given the high current levels of public debt in most countries. This pessimistic view is not entirely warranted. The problem of sustainability of the public debt is to a large extent linked to the high level of real interest rates in a context of slow growth. A reduction of interest rates in the context of a coordinated recovery will reduce the debt-servicing burden and hence increase the sustainability of public debt.

This will be reinforced by the favourable impact of a higher level of activity on revenues.

55.   While all avenues for raising growth rates through changes in macro-economic policy should be explored, attention also needs to be paid to the growth-augmenting benefits of successful adjustment to opportunities in the global economy. The industrialized countries stand to benefit significantly from a generalized increase in international trade and demand. Growth in the developing and transition economies will provide expanding markets for the high-technology, high value-added and capital-intensive products in which the industrialized countries have a comparative advantage. The expansion of such activities should have a net positive effect on employment, even when the losses due to the abandonment of low-skilled and labour-intensive activities are taken into account. The focus should thus be on positive adjustment policies to deal with the problem of labour redeployment out of un-competitive industries rather than on protectionist policies. Policies to improve competitiveness through investments in human capital, research and development, and infrastructure will be of particular importance.

56.   It will, of course, also be important to deal with issues of labour market policy. But it must at the same time be recognized that there are strong limits to the extent to which a reliance on such policies alone can solve the unemployment problem. In particular, a purely (or mainly) deregulatory route to greater labour market flexibility will not be a panacea. Far from being a simple solution that confers only benefits it is likely to involve a trade-off in terms of greater inequality and poverty. It will also involve the sacrifice of the considerable benefits that flow from an appropriately regulated labour market.

57.   The benefits of appropriate labour market regulation are often over-looked. A major economic benefit from regulation derives from the fact that it often responds to market failures and thus improves market functioning. For example, employment security increases both the propensity of firms to train and the will-ingness of workers to invest in upgrading their skills. Similarly rules that protect the income and employment security of workers can increase productive efficiency by creating incentives for competition to occur more through product market innovation and product market strategy.

58.   The limits to what can be achieved through labour market deregulation alone are best illustrated by the issue of wage cuts. Proponents argue that a major benefit of deregulation will be to lower currently excessive wage levels and that this in turn will raise employment significantly. There are several reasons for doubting the validity of this proposition. First, it is debatable whether wages are still too high after the wage moderation of the 1980s. Second, the impact of changes in relative factor prices on capital-labour substitution is slow since it operates only at the margin through new investment. Moreover, empirical findings on the impact of labour costs on employ-ment show that large wage cuts are required in order to achieve only small increases

in employment. Third, a reduction of wage costs will increase competitiveness (and hence employment) only if it is applied in a single country.

59.   These doubts over the effects of labour market deregulation do not, of course, imply that all labour market regulations should be retained in their current form. A case in point are the rigidities imposed by regulations on the length and organization of working time. These can frustrate voluntary labour supply decisions, new working time and work organization patterns, and thus job growth. Changes in this area have been a widespread source of greater labour market flexibility since the 1980s and have often linked the expansion of operating time, innovation in shiftwork patterns, and job creation or preservation with a reduction in individual working hours. The continued removal of regulatory impediments to voluntary labour supply choices should be encouraged. Selective reforms to existing labour market regulations are indeed also necessary to tackle serious problems such as low pay, the worsening employment prospects of unskilled workers and the need to improve training and workplace performance in order to meet the challenges posed by new technology and production systems.

60.   There is general agreement that training should develop flexibility in workers since they are now likely to change jobs several times in their working life. This is difficult to ensure in a deregulated labour market since labour turnover would increase and erode incentives to train. An important distinction is between decentralized settings, such as the United States, where labour market adjustment occurs primarily through the external labour market, and countries such as Japan or Germany, where the existence of long-term trust relationships between management and labour and of well-developed systems of employment security directs adjustment mainly through the internal labour market. In the former settings, it is important to create or adapt training infrastructures external to the firm so that training shortfalls do not occur. In the latter settings, strong training systems, whether at firm or economy-wide levels, already exist. These may require additional strengthening if the frequency of job changes increases considerably.

61.   New production systems require extensive cooperation between labour and management and the participation of workers in business decisions from which they were previously excluded. Here again the "decollectivization" of labour-management relations that is implied by deregulation will be dysfunctional. In contrast, strong organs of workplace employee participation will yield significant benefits in terms of greater productivity and the more rapid and efficient diffusion of new technology.

62.   Labour market reforms are also required to deal with the problem of declining job prospects for low-skilled workers. Two broad policy routes for encouraging the required creation of jobs for the low-skilled can be envisaged; pressing wages down through labour market deregulation or employment subsidies. The fundamental difference between the two options is distributional. The question is whether low-

skilled workers as a whole should pay for increased employment by cuts in relative pay, or whether the costs should be borne generally out of taxation. The choice is ultimately a political one and cannot be seriously settled on the grounds of the allocative inefficiencies of subsidies.

63.   Tax-financed expenditures to create jobs can be used either for employment subsidies or for direct job creation in the provision of social services and improving infrastructure. It is an important, though often under-appreciated, feature of the contemporary Welfare State that the net cost of the additional public spending to the taxpayer is far less than the gross cost if the workers concerned would otherwise have remained unemployed. In most OECD countries the net cost of job creation by the public sector would be no more than 20 per cent of the gross cost. Nevertheless, it remains an open question whether the electorate will accept the additional taxation that will still be involved. In addition, wage restraint will be necessary in order to prevent the higher consumption resulting from increased employment from pushing up inflation.

64.   There is some agreement among policy-makers that unemployment benefit systems in most industrialized countries are in need of reform. Current systems of financing employment benefits through payroll taxes raise labour costs, at least in the short run. Therefore, financing unemployment benefits through expenditure taxes may generally be expected to have a favourable effect on employment: expenditure taxes lead to lower labour costs and higher take-home pay than do payroll taxes. This raises firms' incentives to employ and workers' incentives to seek work. Other options for reform have also been suggested. One is to lower the cost of unskilled labour through introducing progressivity in the financing of unemployment benefits. Another is to convert unemployment benefits into employment vouchers; since this would give the unemployed – particularly the long-term unemployed – a new option: to use a portion of their unemployment benefits, if they so wish, as vouchers for employers to hire them. In the context of persistent unemployment such innovative ideas warrant discussion; specific policy proposals will, of course, depend on the characteristics of individual settings.

65.   While the reform of unemployment benefits along such lines can yield gains to the long-term unemployed, it will not deal with the wider problem of the working poor. Employment subsidies to low-paid workers could provide a solution. Providing a subsidy to employers to hire low-wage workers would increase both job opportunities and earnings for the low-paid. Such subsidies can be justified on moral grounds and on the basis of the social benefits of lower unemployment. There will also be economic benefits through the strengthening of the motivation of the low-paid to retain a job and work diligently. There is, however, the drawback of the efficiency cost of the higher taxes that may be necessary to fund the subsidies. Although the benefits are likely to outweigh this, there does still remain the question of the political acceptability of higher taxes.

The challenge of global full employment

66.   The challenge of restoring full employment is formidable in most parts of the world. No simple and painless solutions are readily available and defeatist attitudes are common. But complex and difficult as it is, restoring full employment is feasible with sufficient political will and the right combination of international and national policies. There will be vast benefits from a renewed commitment by all nations to the objective of full employment. Such a common commitment will facilitate co-operative international action to achieve higher growth in the world economy and expanding trade and investment flows, all of which will have a favourable impact on job creation worldwide. In contrast, the alternative of seeking individual solutions will lower world welfare and lead to a more divided, unequal, and politically turbulent world.

67.   The current employment situation stands in striking contrast to the situation that prevailed between 1950 and 1973 when the industrialized countries enjoyed full employment and when most developing countries experienced steady growth in output and modern-sector employment. Three key factors made this possible: the high priority given to the objective of full employment in the international economic system; the social consensus in the industrialized countries over the distribution of national income that made non-inflationary growth feasible; and stable monetary and trading arrangements in the global economic system. The breakdown of all these features of the international economy has made it more difficult to maintain full employment. In particular the breakdown of the Bretton Woods system and huge increases in speculative international financial flows have imposed severe constraints on national macroeconomic policies and created a bias towards restrictive monetary policies in the world economy. This has been aggravated by the breakdown of the domestic mechanisms for securing non-inflationary growth in industrialized countries.

68.   This background underscores the importance of cooperative international action in order to restore full employment. Reform of the international monetary system to dampen the destabilizing effects of speculative financial flows on exchange and interest rates and greater coordination of macroeconomic policies will permit higher growth in the world economy. Similarly, a stable institutional framework for promoting freer international trade and flows of direct investment will improve resource allocation and efficiency in the world economy and boost economic growth and employment creation. In this connection a new impetus to international co-operation to enforce basic labour standards will help to defuse protectionist sentiments based on perceptions that the non-observance of such standards is a major source of unfair competition in international trade. Such international action on labour standards will also be essential for counteracting pressures towards a debasement of labour standards generated by increasing competition for export markets and foreign

investment. International action to assist the least developed countries in overcoming their marginalization from the global economy and to provide adjustment assistance to countries facing severe adjustment difficulties will also help to reduce international inequality and sustain the process of globalization.

69.   An important step towards initiating the desired international action is to give higher priority to employment and social objectives in the formulation of international economic policies. The forthcoming World Summit for Social Development provides a timely opportunity for the international community to commit itself towards achieving this. This would be highly appropriate since the fundamental solution to the social problems to be addressed by the Summit lies in the creation of the conditions for generating higher rates of growth of output and employment in the world economy. Beyond this, a specific mechanism for ensuring higher priority to employment issues would be to include ministers of labour in deliberations on economic policy at both the national and international levels. This could be reinforced by bringing about better coordination and closer collaboration between international institutions responsible for economic and social policies and those responsible for employment and social issues.

1 PART ONE

Globalization and employment

Salient trends

Changes in the world economy in the past few decades have affected both the level and the structure of employment across the globe. Total world output has grown by more than 3 per cent per annum since 1960. Between 1966 and 1973 growth rates were close to 5 per cent per annum before slowing down to 3.5 per cent between 1974 and 1980 and 3.3 per cent in the 1980s. The present decade has seen a further deceleration to 1.1 per cent, but this is largely due to the recession of the early 1990s in major industrialized countries (table 1). With the current recovery, global output is projected to return to the 3 per cent range that has prevailed since 1974.[1] These growth rates have exceeded population growth, yielding a steady increase in per capita global output (table 2). In 1990 total world output in real terms was almost double what it had been in 1970 and real per capita output was around 26 per cent higher. From this viewpoint, that is, if we abstract from problems of distribution between and within countries, it is apparent that there has been considerable global economic progress. Yet the world today is still afflicted by serious problems of unemployment, underemployment, inequality and poverty.

The structure of world production has also changed radically. In 1960 10.4 per cent of total output was in agriculture, 28.4 per cent in manufacturing and 50.4 per cent in services. By 1990 these proportions had become 4.4, 21.4, and 62.4 per cent respectively. In the industrialized countries the biggest shift was from manufacturing to services, with the latter now accounting for nearly 65 per cent of total output compared to 21 per cent for manufacturing. In the developing countries the main shift was from agriculture to manufacturing with the former now accounting for less than 15 per cent of output. The share of manufacturing in total output in both industrialized and developing countries is now about the same, although the trends are moving in opposite directions (table 3 and figure 1).

The structure of employment has changed accordingly. By 1989-91, in the industrialized countries only 7 per cent were employed in agriculture while employment in industry had dropped to 26 per cent. In the developing countries the share of agricultural employment had dropped to 61 per cent while that of industrial employment had risen to 14 per cent. Again abstracting from intercountry differences, we can say that the world's working population roughly divides into 48 per cent in agriculture, 17 per cent in industry and 35 per cent in services (table 4).

Table 1.   **World output summary,[1] 1966-93**

	1966-73	1974-80	1981-90	1991-93
World total	**4.9**	**3.5**	**3.3**	**1.1**
Developed countries	**4.7**	**3.2**	**3.2**	**1.2**
Eastern Europe & Central Asia	**7.0**	**4.5**	**2.3**	**–9.8**
Developing countries	**6.4**	**4.8**	**3.6**	**4.6**
East Asia	8.0	7.0	7.9	8.3
China	8.9	6.3	9.9	11.2
South Asia	3.6	3.9	5.6	3.5
Sub-Saharan Africa	5.0	3.0	1.9	1.7
Latin America & Caribbean	6.8	4.8	2.0	3.2
Middle East & North Africa	7.0	4.6	0.4	3.0

[1] Average annual percentage growth rates of GDP, measured in market prices and expressed in 1987 prices and exchange rates.

Source: World Bank: *Global economic prospects and developing countries*, p. 7, table 1.1 (Washington, 1994).

The gaps between the shifts in the structure of output and of employment give a rough indication of differences in productivity. Agricultural employment is now predominantly in low-income countries, where productivity levels are very low. World poverty is consequently concentrated in the rural areas of these countries.

Looking at the world economy in this abstract way is a useful device for drawing attention to some salient features of change in the past three decades. But the world is not a single unified economy and it is in intercountry differences and relationships that the most interesting issues lie.

The growth in world output has been unevenly distributed. Not surprisingly, since they accounted for 69 per cent of world output in 1965, the industrialized countries have had growth rates only slightly below the world average in all three subsequent decades. Many developing countries grew significantly faster in the 1960s and 1970s but have grown only slightly faster in the 1980s. In the early 1990s their growth rates have picked up again. This coincided with the recession in the industrialized countries so the growth gap between the developing and industrial world (as measured by subtracting the industrialized countries' annual average GDP growth from the developing countries' growth) has been larger during the 1991-93 period than in

Table 2.   **Growth of real per capita output,[1] 1960-90**

	1960-70	1970-80	1980-90
Developed countries	**4.0**	**2.2**	**2.2**
Eastern Europe	**5.7**	**4.5**	**1.6**
Developing countries	**3.3**	**3.1**	**1.2**
Sub-Saharan Africa	0.6	0.9	–0.9
East Asia	3.6	4.6	6.3
China	3.6	3.6	8.2
South Asia	1.4	1.1	3.1
Latin America	2.5	3.1	–0.5

[1] Average annual percentage rate of growth of real per capita GDP, constant prices.

Source: United Nations: *Statistical Database* (New York, 1993).

Table 3. **Structure of world output (percentage of GDP)**[1]

	Agriculture				Manufacturing[2]				Services			
	1960	1970	1980	1990	1960	1970	1980	1990	1960	1970	1980	1990
World	**10.4**	**6.9**	**5.6**	**4.4**	**28.4**	**26.1**	**22.4**	**21.4**	**50.6**	**56.4**	**57.0**	**62.4**
Industrial countries	**6.3**	**3.9**	**3.4**	**2.5**	**31.0**	**27.7**	**23.6**	**21.5**	**51.6**	**58.3**	**60.2**	**64.7**
USA	4.0	2.8	2.6	1.7	29.0	25.2	21.8	18.5	57.2	62.7	63.8	70.3
Japan	13.1	6.1	3.7	2.4	35.1	36.0	29.2	28.9	40.9	47.2	54.4	55.8
Europe	8.8	4.8	3.6	3.0	34.7	30.5	24.0	21.5	43.8	54.3	59.2	63.8
Developing countries	**31.6**	**22.4**	**14.7**	**14.6**	**15.6**	**17.8**	**17.6**	**20.7**	**42.8**	**48.1**	**44.2**	**49.8**
Latin America & Caribbean	16.5	11.9	9.5	8.5	21.1	22.8	23.5	22.3	50.6	55.3	54.5	57.5
Africa[3]	45.8	33.1	25.1	30.2	5.8	8.6	7.7	10.9	37.5	44.0	39.9	41.6
Asia[4]	38.0	23.9	17.8	17.4	14.4	15.1	15.4	20.9	37.1	42.5	37.9	45.9
South & South-East Asia	44.0	35.6	24.7	18.9	13.7	15.6	19.8	22.9	36.2	41.9	43.5	46.6

[1] Figures in the columns do not add up to 100 since the construction sector is left out, as is non-manufacturing industrial output. [2] Figures for manufacturing do not represent total industrial activity. [3] Excluding North Africa. [4] Includes all developing countries in the region; the figure for 1965 is used instead of the 1960 figure.

Source: United Nations, op. cit.

any other period since 1966 (table 1). However, given the significantly higher rates of population growth in developing countries, the gap in growth rates between these countries and the industrialized nations was much smaller in terms of per capita real GDP, with the gap being negative during the 1960s and 1980s (table 2). Indeed during the 1980s per capita growth rates in the developing countries were only half those in the industrialized countries. The net outcome of this pattern of growth rates was that the relative shares of the industrialized and developing countries did not change much over the last two decades. The share of Eastern European and Central Asian transition economies in world output declined dramatically, by almost one-half, between 1970 and 1992.[2] Growth rates in these countries have slowed down steadily since 1966, with the region facing a negative annual average GDP growth rate of nearly 10 per cent per annum in the early 1990s, as compared to a positive 7 per cent per annum growth during 1966-73 (table 1).

A striking aspect of change has been the growing divergence in growth rates among different regions of the developing world. Growth rates in sub-Saharan Africa and Latin America have decelerated since the 1960s while those in Asia have accelerated. The differences became very pronounced during the debt-troubled

Table 4. **Structure of world employment, 1965 and 1989-91**

	Agriculture		Industry		Services	
	1965	1989-91	1965	1989-91	1965	1989-91
World	**57**	**48**	**19**	**17**	**24**	**35**
Industrialized countries	22	7	37	26	41	67
Developing countries	72	61	11	14	17	25
East & South-East Asia[1]	73	50	9	18	18	32
Sub-Saharan Africa	79	67	8	9	13	24

[1] Figures for 1960 instead of 1965; industry includes only manufacturing.

Source: ILO labour statistics on diskette (Geneva, 1994).

Figure 1.
Structure of production, 1960 and 1990

Industrial countries   **Developing countries**

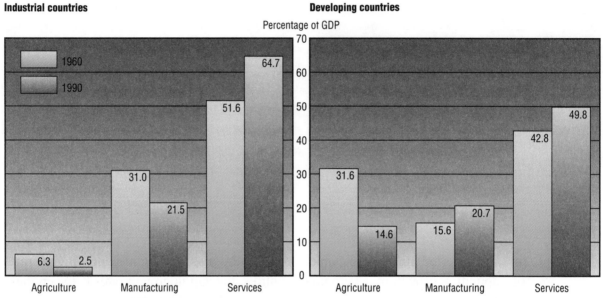

Source: United Nations: *Statistical Database* (New York, 1993).

1980s when the first two regions experienced negative per capita output growth while per capita output grew by 6.3 and 3.1 per cent respectively in East and South Asia. Since then most Latin American countries have begun to recover although growth rates are still significantly lower than in Asia. Sub-Saharan Africa on the other hand continues to decline, giving rise to concern over its marginalization from the world economy. The outcome of these divergences is that the developing world is now far more differentiated economically than it was in 1960. For most of the post-war period world trade grew significantly faster than output. Between 1950 and 1973 world trade grew at between 7 and 8 per cent per annum. It slowed down to 3.1 per cent between 1974 and 1983, when the world economy suffered from the effects of the two oil shocks and the debt crisis, but recovered to close to its previous trend level between 1984 and 1989 (table 5). It has slowed down again but is expected to increase with the recovery in the industrialized countries. This sustained and rapid growth in world trade has meant that national economies in most parts of the world have become more interrelated and open. For example, export-to-GDP ratios increased in many countries between 1970 and 1992, although the pattern was uneven. A majority of OECD countries experienced increases and there was no case where the ratio fell. Particularly large increases were recorded in the United States (from 5.8 to 10.6 per cent), Germany (21 to 33 per cent) and France (15 to 23 per cent). The export-to-GDP ratio also increased in the majority of Asian countries and in about half of Latin American countries but in only a minority of sub-Saharan countries. Thus, apart from most of sub-Saharan Africa, there is a general trend towards greater openness in international trade.

Table 5. **Growth of world trade, 1950-94 (annual average percentage rate of growth)**

	1950-73	1974-83	1984-89	1990	1991-94
World trade[1]					
Volume	7.7	3.1	6.4	4.6	3.8
Value	n.a.	8.9	3.0	8.3	-0.7
Volume of exports					
Industrial countries	n.a.	3.9	5.9	5.8	2.8
Transition economies[2]	n.a.	3.6[4]	2.4	-9.5	-15.0[3]
Developing countries	n.a.	-1.9	7.3	8.7	8.2
Four Asian NIEs	n.a.	12.2	13.6	6.2	11.4
Sub-Saharan Africa	n.a.	-0.6	2.4	7.7	-2.8
Imports					
Industrial countries	n.a.	2.8	7.9	4.8	2.9
Transition economies[2]	n.a.	2.2[4]	2.9	-5.1	-13.5[3]
Developing countries	n.a.	7.0	3.3	5.5	11.2
Four Asian NIEs	n.a.	9.0	13.2	12.5	12.0
Sub-Saharan Africa	n.a.	-0.5	0.9	1.8	-2.4

n.a. = not available.
[1] Average of annual percentage change for world exports and imports – includes trade of industrial and developing countries and transition economies, except trade among the states of the former USSR.   [2] Eastern Europe and former USSR.   [3] Average for 1991-92 only.   [4] Average for 1980-83 only.

Source: United Nations: *Statistical Database*, op. cit., and IMF: *World Economic Outlook* (Washington, various issues).

This development is partly due to trade liberalization measures that occurred especially in the 1980s. The growth of regional trading arrangements such as the European Common Market, NAFTA, MERCOSUR, and ASEAN was an important element. But apart from this there was also a wave of trade liberalization in developing countries which had previously pursued import-substitution industrialization strategies. Around 15 of the 27 developing countries, for which information on tariffs is available, reduced the levels of tariffs and equivalent import charges during the 1980s.[3] Another four countries had already achieved low average tariff levels by the beginning of the 1980s.[4] Thus, by the late 1980s, the majority of developing countries for which data are available had significantly reduced tariff levels compared to previous decades. These countries were concentrated mainly in Latin America and Asia.

As regards non-tariff measures, 18 of the 26 developing countries for which such information is available significantly relaxed such measures during the 1980s.[5] In another two countries the incidence of non-tariff measures was already very low by 1985.[6] Real effective exchange rates were also corrected for previous overvaluation in a number of developing countries, a development which favoured the growth of exports.[7]

The structure of world trade also changed significantly in several respects. The share of manufacturing in total world exports rose from 61 per cent in 1965 to 71 per cent in 1990. This was particularly striking for developing countries, where manufactured goods now constitute over half of total exports, being most dramatic in South and South-East Asia, where 78 per cent of exports now consist of manufactures (table 6). By contrast, Latin America and Africa remain predominantly exporters of

Figure 2.
Share in world trade percentage, developed and developing world

Percentage share

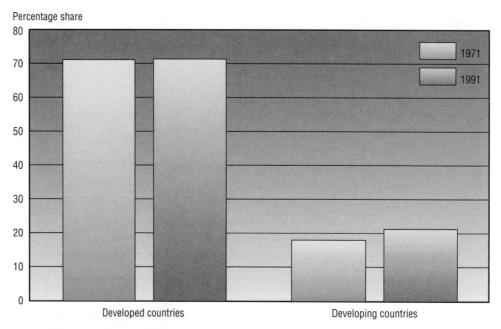

Source: UNCTAD: *Handbook of International Trade and Development Statistics* (New York, various issues).

primary products, even though the share of manufactured exports did increase. On the other hand, the share of manufactures in the total exports of the transitional Eastern European economies actually fell in 1990 as compared to previous years. Manufactured exports from high-income countries increased by 4.5 per cent per annum during the 1980s, but the corresponding growth rate for developing countries was 7.6 per cent. Within this latter group Asian growth outstripped the other regions: manufactured exports grew by 12.4 per cent per annum in East Asia and by 9.1 per cent in South Asia (table 7).

Shares in world trade changed accordingly. The share of Asian developing countries increased from 4.6 to 12.5 per cent between 1970 and 1991 but those of Latin America and sub-Saharan Africa fell. The overall developing country share increased only slightly as a result of these divergences in performance. Over the same period the share of the former socialist countries fell from 10 to 5 per cent. The upshot is that the share of the developed market economies remained unchanged at 71 per cent. Thus the major shift was a redistribution among the non-industrialized countries, with Asia gaining relative to the rest (see figures 2 and 3).

The bulk of the increase in world trade has been intra-OECD; the shares of intra-OECD exports increased throughout the last three decades, from about 70 per cent in 1958-60 to over 76 per cent in 1990-91. Parallel with this, intra-developing country trade also increased: the share of exports from these countries to other developing countries rose from about 24 to over 32 per cent over this period; much of this trading was within Asia (table 8).

Figure 3.
Share in world trade percentage, major developing regions

Percentage share

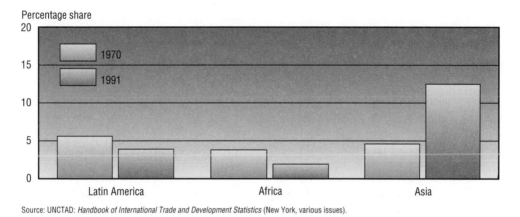

Source: UNCTAD: *Handbook of International Trade and Development Statistics* (New York, various issues).

In spite of this overall trend there is one significant aspect of North-South trade that has given rise to concern and controversy in the North.

This is the rapid growth of manufactured exports from the South, primarily from the dynamic Asian economies and China. Imports of manufactures from these latter countries grew by nearly 15 per cent per annum in Japan and the United States, and by close to 13 per cent per annum in the European Union between 1980 and 1990 (table 7). This continues a trend which began with rapid growth in the four original Asian newly industrializing economies in the 1960s. As a result of this growth, the developing countries' share of manufactured exports to the developed market economies increased from 5 to 14 per cent between 1970 and 1990.

During the last three decades, flows of portfolio and direct investment also increased rapidly: average annual FDI flows in the world economy increased substantially from US$21 billion in the 1970s to US$126 billion by 1992. Together with the rapid increase in world trade this has led to a burgeoning academic literature and policy discussion on the implications of increasing globalization of the economy. This process has affected, and will continue to affect, the structure of global produc-

Table 6.   **Manufactures as a percentage of total exports, 1970-90**

	1970	1980	1990
World	**60.9**	**64.2**	**71.1**
Developed countries	**72.0**	**70.9**	**78.0**
Eastern Europe	**59.1**	**50.2**	**43.9**
Developing countries	**18.5**	**18.5**	**53.9**
Asia	28.4	23.5	65.5
South and South-East Asia	43.4	51.0	77.7
Latin America	10.6	14.7	30.8
Africa	7.0	4.0	15.1[1]

[1] Corresponding figure for sub-Saharan African region for 1990 was 13 per cent. It may be noted that this figure is largely attributable to three countries: Cameroon, Côte d'Ivoire and Mauritius, which together account for one half of SSA's total manufacturing exports.

Source: UNCTAD: *Handbook of International Trade and Development Statistics* (New York, various issues).

Table 7. **Growth of trade in manufactures, 1980-90 (average growth rate, percentage)**

From: / To:	Developed countries[1]					Developing countries[2]							All countries
	US	EC	Japan	Other developed countries	All developed countries	East Asia	South Asia	Europe	MENA	SSA	Latin America and the Caribbean	All developing countries	
Developed countries[1]	**7.7**	**6.0**	**10.7**	**5.3**	**6.3**	**6.7**	**3.1**	**2.3**	**–9.0**	**–6.2**	**–1.5**	**–1.0**	**4.5**
US		4.9	9.0	6.1	6.0	6.9	2.3	2.3	–9.5	–7.4	0.7	0.2	4.1
EC	6.4	5.7	12.7	4.3	6.6	6.5	2.9	3.1	–8.3	–5.7	–3.4	–2.0	3.9
Japan	7.8	8.8		5.1	7.1	4.5	1.1	–3.1	–12.7	–8.0	–4.2	–1.6	4.2
Other high income	8.5	7.3	11.4	6.5	7.7	11.4	6.8	1.6	–7.7	–5.8	–3.0	1.7	6.5
Developing countries[2]	**13.0**	**8.1**	**14.5**	**10.9**	**10.6**	**13.4**	**6.1**	**2.7**	**–0.2**	**–4.6**	**1.5**	**2.3**	**7.6**
East Asia & Pacific	14.6	12.8	14.8	11.4	13.1	13.6	8.3	10.0	2.3	5.2	11.3	8.6	12.4
South Asia	15.6	11.9	19.0	9.0	12.8	11.2	4.8	4.4	–8.2	–1.9	15.9	1.6	9.1
Latin America	11.1	5.1	7.1	11.0	9.2	19.9	16.7	2.8	–1.8	–2.9	–0.3	0.9	5.6
All countries	**8.4**	**6.2**	**11.6**	**5.8**	**6.7**	**7.2**	**3.6**	**2.4**	**–7.9**	**–6.0**	**–1.2**	**–0.5**	**4.8**

[1] All high-income countries classified according to World Bank classification.   [2] All middle- and low-income countries classified according to World Bank classification.

Source: World Bank: *Global economic prospects and the developing countries* (Washington, 1992, p. 65).

tion and patterns of growth. It promises vast gains in economic efficiency and higher growth but it also imposes the need for major adjustments in countries across the globe. These adjustments will centre on changes in the structure of production and hence in that of employment. Large numbers of workers will have to shift from declining to growing activities and problems of transitional unemployment will have to be faced. How well this process is managed will be an important determinant of whether globalization is sustained and its potential benefits are reaped.

A major development that will influence the future evolution of world trade is the completion of the Uruguay Round of GATT negotiations. The next section of the report therefore examines its potential effects on world trade and employment. This will be followed by an examination of recent developments in foreign direct investment flows and their impact on employment prospects.

Table 8. **World exports by destination, selected periods, 1958-91 (percentage of total value exports by origin)**

Origin	Destination	
	Industrialized countries	Developing countries
Industrialized countries[1]		
1958-60	69.3	27.2
1978-80	71.5	24.0
1987-89	77.0	19.6
1990-91	76.5	20.2
Developing countries[2]		
1958-60	72.3	23.7
1978-80	70.7	25.1
1987-89	64.7	30.2
1990-91	62.0	32.5

[1] Represents the value of exports from industrialized countries to industrialized countries as well as to developing countries, measured as a percentage of total value of exports originating in industrialized countries.   [2] Is the value of exports from developing countries to industrialized countries and to developing countries including socialist economies in Asia, measured as a percentage of total exports originating in developing countries.

Source: UNCTAD: *Handbook of International Trade and Development Statistics*, various issues.

Trade and employment: The Uruguay Round

Background

The Uruguay Round is correctly regarded as the most ambitious and comprehensive of all of GATT's rounds. It involved a larger number of Contracting Parties (CPs) than any previous round (109) and covered a larger number of negotiating issues (15). In addition to revisiting old issues like tariff liberalization, it addressed new ones relating to foreign investment, intellectual property and services.

A major potential effect of the agreement is to reinforce the trend towards greater openness to trade and rapid increases in trade flows. This will result from the tariff reforms contained in the agreement. There are essentially three ingredients to these: a zero-for-zero component which will result in tariff-free trade in 11 sectors;[8] a liberalization component that will reduce mean tariffs on industrial goods by some 38 per cent (on a trade-weighted basis); and a harmonization component which subjects higher tariffs to deeper cuts. As a result, the trade-weighted average tariff in industrial countries will decline from 6.4 per cent to 4 per cent, and some 40 per cent of imports will enter duty free. Reductions are, however, below average (20 per cent) in respect of some of the main industrial exports of developing countries (textiles, clothing and leather products), though the reduction is from initially higher levels. Although it has not been widely commented upon, another crucial outcome is that the proportion of tariffs which are bound in industrial countries will increase from 78 per cent to 97 per cent; even more significantly, the proportion bound in developing countries will increase from 21 per cent to 65 per cent. Once tariffs are bound, they cannot be unilaterally altered.

For non-agricultural goods, the tariff-reduction commitments will be implemented over time in up to five equal stages,[9] the first being on the entry into force of the Agreement establishing the World Trade Organization (WTO).

Apart from tariff reductions, there will also be a move towards reducing non-tariff barriers. As tariffs declined as a result of earlier GATT rounds there had been some substitution of non-tariff barriers (NTBs) for tariffs. Their discriminatory application (especially against newly industrializing countries (NICs) and less developed countries (LDCs)) and their opacity have tended to erode GATT authority. The Uruguay Round therefore established major commitments to correct this, including a prohibition on the use of voluntary export restraints (VERs), orderly marketing agreements and other extra-legal instruments.

The Uruguay Round also extends trade liberalization to new sectors. For example, temperate-zone agriculture has for the first time been subject to liberalization under GATT. The market access agreement requires the tariffication of existing NTBs, the binding of the resultant tariffs and their reduction by 36 per cent over six years in industrialized countries and over ten years in LDCs, with the least developed being exempted. Domestic support measures are to be reduced by 20 per cent in industrialized countries and 13.3 per cent in LDCs. Export subsidies are to be reduced by 36 per cent in value terms and 21 per cent in volume terms (on 1986-90 bases) in industrialized countries. Lower reductions of 24 per cent and 14 per cent respectively are required of LDCs, with no further concessions for the least developed. However, there are special provisions relating to food aid and assistance to the least developed and net food-importing LDCs. Although, as in other areas, these reforms are to be phased in over a six-to-ten-year period, they represent very significant liberalization in an erstwhile completely sheltered sector.

Another sector to which trade liberalization has been extended is textiles and clothing. Hitherto trade in this sector has been subject to a legal derogation from GATT non-discrimination requirements. The Uruguay Round agreement commits CPs to a phased run-down of the Multifibres Arrangement (MFA) over the period 1995-2005 and the complete integration of textiles and clothing into the GATT system. Four phases are envisaged: 1995-98, 1998-2002, 2002-05 and post-2005. At the beginning of Phases I, II and III, CPs will be required to have integrated products accounting for not less than 16 per cent, 17 per cent and 18 per cent respectively of their total imports of textiles and clothing. Post-2005, all products will be fully integrated. Annual growth rates for quotas of products still subject to MFA provisions within each phase have been set at 16 per cent, 25 per cent and 27 per cent above the growth rates in each of the previous phases. There will be a limited safeguard provision available of a maximum three-year duration (non-renewable), in instances where serious prejudice can be established.

In addition, further tariff liberalization has been agreed for natural-resource-based and tropical products. These are of obvious interest to some LDCs.

New issues covered by the agreement are also likely to facilitate increased flows of foreign direct investment and increased trade in services. The trade-related investment measures (TRIMs) agreement maintains the existing provisions, notably, Articles III and XI of the GATT. Any TRIMs inconsistent with these are prohibited. These measures include some that are currently widely used, such as local content requirements and trade balancing requirements. Pre-existing measures have to be phased out within two years (industrialized countries), five years (developing countries) or seven years (least developed countries). Arrangements for monitoring phase-out and uncovering cases of instrument substitution will be put in place. More importantly, there is a commitment to evaluate the role of TRIMs in the wider context of competition policy in the medium term.

The General Agreement on Trade in Services (GATS) is more limited in scope than was hoped when the Round was launched but takes an important first step in regulating the services sector. The agreement specifies a range of basic obligations which include the treatment of national services sectors and the most favoured nation commitments. A schedule is established for progressive liberalization of trade and the specific institutional provisions required to accomplish this. Finally, for a number of sectors (financial services, telecommunications, air transport services), detailed implementation schedules are provided.

Implications for market access and employment

What the foregoing will add up to in terms of actual market access improvements and prospects for trade expansion is, of course, difficult to foretell. Ultimately it is the translation of commitments into reality that will trigger an increase in employment. Where many of the Uruguay Round agreements are concerned, it is difficult to comment with any precision on what will happen to trade flows. There is uncertainty about what will follow from the GATS, agreements on trade-related intellectual property rights (TRIPs) and TRIMs and the redrafting of GATT provisions on anti-dumping, subsidies and so on. Nevertheless, the balance of probabilities holds out hope of beneficial effects on trade flows.

A number of evaluations of the Round have been completed, both qualitative and quantitative.[10] The latter have generally concluded that global net benefits from the Round will be at least $200 billion per annum. Such estimates typically originate from computable general equilibrium (CGE) models. Although these models tend to focus on primarily income measures, some also evaluate employment effects, albeit in highly aggregative terms. Given the modelling techniques being used, the estimates are inevitably post-adjustment, i.e. they assume that all of the trade agreements are implemented and the system as a whole has settled into a new equilibrium. Such estimates, while useful, are limited; in particular, they ignore the transitional employment changes.

Because changes in tariff and non-tariff measures can be expressed numerically and used in models of trade flows, one can say more about the impact of reforms in this area. Basically, the relevant ingredients of the Uruguay Round Agreement are the larger number of bound tariff reductions in average tariff levels and reductions in tariff escalation. Although the importance of the first is often forgotten, it is, in fact, vital. Once tariffs are bound they cannot be unilaterally raised again. Any changes are subject to negotiation and, if implemented, to compensation. In other words, they provide security of access of imports: the percentage of imports entering developed countries under bound rates will increase from 94 per cent to 99 per cent; that in developing countries from 14 per cent to 59 per cent. The latter is a dramatic change and can be expected to affect both South-South and North-South trade.

As regards tariff cuts, developed countries, which account for some 70 per cent of total global trade, have reduced tariffs on over 40 per cent of their imports. Average tariff cuts of some 38 per cent apply to imports valued at over $900 billion. A similar percentage reduction applies to some $100 billion of agricultural trade. Even if these cuts were evenly applied across all exporting countries and all products, their biggest impact would be on trade expansion in the North, since more than 50 per cent of global trade is North-North trade, most of which, moreover, is in trade in manufactures.

Furthermore, several features of the tariff deal reinforce North-North trade. The main one is that the cuts are not evenly distributed. In particular, deeper cuts apply to products of interest to industrialized exporting countries, while tariff cuts are shallower for products where developing countries and NICs enjoy a comparative advantage (for instance, the average reductions in textiles and clothing; leather, footwear and travel goods; fish and fish products; and transport equipment, are 22 per cent, 18 per cent, 26 per cent and 23 per cent respectively). However, a second factor may counter this to some extent, namely the impact of the reforms on tariff escalation. The harmonization component of the agreement has served to increase tariff escalation in North-North trade since the reduction in tariffs on semi-manufactures is greater than that on manufactures.

For these reasons, all quantitative analyses predict that the greatest volume changes in trade will be in North-North trade in manufactures.[11]

There will nevertheless be significant impacts on North-South trade expansion. Substantial increases in global trade volumes are predicted, with total trade rising by 20 per cent.[12] Within this overall expansion, large increases in certain types of North-South trade are predicted. The liberalization of Northern agricultural markets is expected to benefit middle-income agricultural exporters such as Argentina, Brazil and Indonesia. The main source of this trade expansion will be via the lowering of non-tariff barriers: those which currently exist under the MFA, those which are due to be tariffed under the terms of the agriculture agreement and those which could be phased out as a result of the proscription of VERs and the reframing of Article XIX of the GATT. Thus the potential exists for considerable trade expansion, if access to Northern industrial and agricultural markets improves.

Overall, the Round would appear to give greatest opportunity for the expansion of Southern exports to the North, given the liberalization of textiles, clothing, agricultural and manufacturing markets in the North. If so, this will clearly augment employment in the South and deplete it in the North, in the short run at least. Moreover, some research suggests that the jobs which will be displaced in the North are low-skilled jobs.[13] It is possible that significant short-term adjustment frictions in developed countries could be associated with such trade expansion. If so, it could lead to greater reliance on defensive adjustment measures.

So far the discussion has concentrated on the effect of relative price changes (as a result of tariff adjustments) on trade flows, but it is vitally important not to ignore income effects. There is a substantial literature which suggests that the growth of real output and the growth of trade are positively correlated. It is certain that the Round will give a boost to growth. Clearly, that in turn can be expected to

Table 9. **Sectoral employment changes in the North and South**
(resulting from implementing the Uruguay Round)

	Agriculture	Intermediates (basic)	Mining	Light industries	Forestry & fishing	Capital goods	High tech. manufacturing	Intermediates (manufacturing)	Services
North									
United States	−10.1	−0.3	1.2	−36.0	−0.4	3.0	4.5	1.1	0.5
Canada	−11.6	0.7	2.4	−33.3	0.2	3.2	4.0	1.2	0.7
EC	−14.0	0.9	−0.4	−23.6	1.0	3.9	12.2	2.4	1.9
Japan	−21.5	1.9	−3.2	−13.5	−1.6	2.8	3.6	2.5	0.8
Australia and New Zealand	3.6	−1.2	3.7	−28.4	0.4	−2.8	−1.3	−1.0	0.7
Other North	−14.3	1.3	−0.4	−22.7	0.9	4.2	14.9	1.8	1.4
South									
Industrializing agricultural exporters	−2.5	−0.6	−0.6	5.6	−0.2	−2.2	−4.3	−1.0	0.4
Industrializing agricultural importers	−16.6	2.9	−5.8	82.8	−4.3	−7.0	−7.8	−5.3	−2.7
Centrally planned	0.7	−0.2	0.2	4.4	0.2	−3.5	−2.4	−1.2	−0.7
Others	0.8	−1.4	2.1	8.5	−0.2	−2.0	−2.4	−1.0	−0.3

Source: T.T. Nguyen, C. Perroni and R. Wigle: "An evaluation of the Draft Final Act of the Uruguay Round", in *Economic Journal* (Oxford, Blackwell), Nov. 1993.

boost employment prospects in general. Several modelling exercises estimate net income gains in excess of $200 billion, i.e. about 5 per cent of the value of world trade. If they are realized, they will result in re-spending and further increases in trade and employment.

With or without income effects on employment, however, adjustments will need to take place in labour markets. A study by Nguyen, Perroni and Wigle takes a long-term perspective, in which total employment does not change but its structure does.[14] Table 9 sets out their predictions for the long-term, sectoral adjustments in employment in the North and South that a Uruguay-type package of trade liberalizations would produce. The notable, and not surprising, features of these results are the changes in the agricultural sector and the light industry sector dominated by textiles and clothing. Except for Australia and New Zealand, employment in agriculture is predicted to fall by between 10 and 20 per cent in the industrialized countries, while it is forecast that employment in light industry will fall by over 20 per cent in Europe and around 35 per cent in North America. Employment in the corresponding sectors of the MFA exporters is predicted to rise by as much as 80 per cent. This is the basis for the view that sectoral adjustments in the North will also involve a change in skill requirements, shifting demand away from low-skilled jobs or altering the composition (full/part-time or male/female) of employment. The employment increases in the service sectors of the North are shown in table 9 to be small in percentage terms but they are among the largest increases in absolute terms. The 1.9 per cent increase in employment in the European Community's service sector is for instance almost as large in absolute terms as the predicted employment loss in EC agriculture of 14 per cent.

The importance of positive adjustment

The previous section has shown that the Uruguay Round agreement involves, if fully implemented, major increases in market access to the industrial countries, in particular for specific imports from developing countries. The reduction of tariffs on industrial goods is likely to have its greatest impact on intra-industrial country trade. By contrast the lowering of non-tariff barriers in the agricultural and textiles sectors of the industrial North will significantly increase market access for Southern products in these sectors. The most serious adjustment and employment implications of the Round are therefore likely to be experienced in these sectors in the industrialized countries. This suggests that there will be political economy pressures within the North to resist or slow down these adjustments.

A strong case can be made that such pressures should be resisted and that there should instead be a firm commitment in all countries to implement positive adjustment measures. Improvements in market access generally lead to trade expansion, and output and employment growth in the long run, even though the process of adjustment may entail losses in real output and employment in the short run. The best policy in these circumstances is to facilitate necessary changes rather than seek to retard them.

It could be argued that no policy intervention, whether defensive or positive, is required, since markets deliver the appropriate relative price signals to direct resource reallocations. Agents, left to their own devices, will react to those price signals. Where factor mismatches occur, agents will take the appropriate action by voluntarily leaving the labour market, withdrawing physical capital from production, or investing as appropriate in retraining/retooling. This may result in some temporary loss of output which, however, should not be viewed as a cost in itself but rather as an investment and should be offset against the long-term benefits associated with higher output of the retrained labour/re-equipped capital. Thought of in this way, adjustment costs are simply the price which society pays for change.

There are, however, economic and social grounds against adopting such a laissez-faire approach. The first point to raise is one of time: how long does it actually take for factors to relocate from one sector to another? There is a large body of evidence to support the view that adjustments are unlikely to be either smooth or swift. For example, a rise in unemployment that is initially expected to be temporary can in fact turn out to be persistent. The reason is that the depreciation of labour skills over time reduces the probability of re-employment. This then results in further depreciation and so on. As a consequence the economy can get stuck in an under-employment "equilibrium" for quite a long period of time. The transitional loss of output can therefore be very high.

A second reason for intervention is that, in general, economic agents resist change, particularly if it involves a period of (even temporary) unemployment.

Typically those who benefit from tariff liberalization (primarily consumers) are not well organized and cannot articulate their case effectively. Those who perceive themselves as bearing costs (producers) are typically well organized and politically effective. The longer it takes to transfer resources from one sector to another, the more persuasive is the case that can be made to the effect that trade liberalization "causes" unemployment and therefore the stronger are the pressures against trade reforms. Since the evidence strongly suggests that liberal trade reforms confer net benefits on society, it is unfortunate if transitional costs frustrate the reform process. Adjustment policies that help to reduce such costs are therefore necessary.

Finally, it must be noted that there are social costs associated with factors of production, especially labour, being tied up in unemployment/underemployment for long periods.

Defensive adjustment measures have been extensively deployed in the past by industrialized countries in the face of competitive pressures from NICs and other LDCs. The GATT sanctions defensive adjustment under Article XIX (safeguards). When faced with a sudden upsurge in imports linked to "serious injury", a contracting party can introduce temporary protective measures. However, one of the problems with Article XIX is that it has not been widely used. If CPs have recourse to this device it should be non-discriminatory and the parties affected should have a right to negotiate compensation. As an alternative, many CPs have relied on unilateral measures such as VERs or anti-dumping action. Not only are these discriminatory; they are very difficult to remove once they are introduced. The policy of restraint which has regulated North-South trade in textiles and clothing for over 30 years is testimony to this. Through time these restraints have become more extensive in both their product and their country coverage. There is little evidence to indicate that they have promoted adjustment in textile and garment sectors in industrialized countries, but much to suggest that they have to some extent frustrated the process of specialization in LDCs.

It is, therefore, important that there should be a shift away from defensive to positive adjustment measures in order to reap the full benefits of trade liberalization. Positive adjustment policies which can broaden markets and smooth the process of resource transfers can take the form of labour retraining schemes directed at changing the skill mix of labour displaced from the import substitution sector. They can also take the form of geographical mobility grants. The actual form of the intervention depends upon the perceived nature of the obstacles to adjustment. Likewise, the institutional arrangements for managing an adjustment policy will vary from one economy to another.[15]

A number of important potential constraints on the use of defensive adjustment policies in both developed and developing countries will be introduced by the Uruguay Round agreements. The increase in tariff bindings, the prohibitions on the use of NTBs and the strengthening of safeguards, for example, are intended for this purpose. But whether the agreements really make a difference will depend almost entirely on how they are enforced. It is encouraging, however, to note that there are a number of institutional reforms aimed at the systematic strengthening of enforcement measures.

The importance of trying to make the new constraints on defensive adjustment policy work can be demonstrated by the long-run ineffectiveness and costliness of the extra-legal/grey area measures that industrialized countries have been using. One study estimates that the (deadweight) welfare cost to consumers of each person-year of employment saved by a more restrictive VER on Swedish imports of textiles and clothing was about $40,000.[16] A study of the protection of the United States footwear industry by orderly marketing agreements (OMAs) with the Republic of Korea and Taiwan, China, shows an annual welfare cost to the United States of nearly $22,000 for each job protected.[17] Of course in both of these cases a more efficient (less costly) means of protecting jobs existed. The first one showed that the average budget cost of saving a job in Swedish textiles by means of subsidies would have been about one-fifth the welfare cost of the VER.[18] Similarly, the other showed that the welfare cost of protecting each of the jobs in the United States footwear industry was nearly seven times greater with OMAs than with the equivalent tariff.[19]

The new disciplines introduced by the Uruguay Round can thus reduce the costs of defensive adjustment measures by encouraging a shift away from the more costly ones such as VERs. More importantly, they may also deter the use of defensive adjustment measures and encourage the use of positive ones. The above studies of the costs of defensive adjustment policies indicate that substantial subsidies (or subsidy equivalents of tariffs) are available to enable the countries concerned to shift into positive adjustment measures. Although the Uruguay Round Agreement introduces new provisions regarding the use of subsidies, it does not prohibit labour market policies aimed at facilitating adjustment.

Foreign direct investment

Recent trends

Together with trade expansion, the current decade is witnessing the growing significance of multinational enterprises (MNEs) in the world economy and a rapid liberalization in policies of developing countries towards trade and investment. MNEs account for ever increasing shares of world output, trade and technology. The United Nations *World Investment Report 1994* estimates that, in 1991, foreign affiliates of MNEs generated total sales of $4.8 trillion. This can be compared to total world exports in goods and services of $4.5 trillion. The stock of foreign direct investment (FDI) continues to grow faster than world GDP, domestic investment and trade and in 1993 was estimated at around $2 trillion worldwide.

Table 10. **Average annual stock of foreign direct investment, 1960-92**
(US$ billion and percentages)

	1960-70	1970-80	1981-85	1986-90	1991	1992
All countries	**104**	**313**	**618**	**1 173**	**1 854**	**1 940**
Developed countries	71	243	474	933	1 485	1 520
Developing countries	33	70	144	240	369	420
Africa (%)	19.8	21.2	16.0	11.2	11.4	11.0
Asia (%)	55.7	45.3	43.1	38.9	52.9	53.5
Latin America (%)	24.5	33.5	40.9	49.9	35.7	35.5

Source: United Nations: *World Investment Report 1994: Transnational corporations, employment and the workplace* (New York); *Transnational corporations in world development: Trends and prospects* (New York, UNCTC, 1988); and *Transnational corporations in world development: Third survey* (New York, UNCTC, 1985).

During the last three decades the world economy has witnessed a spectacular increase in the stock of FDI. The average annual stock of FDI, at current market prices, increased more than tenfold, from $104 billion during the 1960s to around $1,173 billion by the end of the 1980s. It further increased to $1,940 billion in 1992. However, it is important to note that the bulk of the (absolute) increase went to the developed rather than the developing countries; the share of developed countries in the total stock of FDI increased from around 68 per cent during the 1960s to around 80 per cent by the early 1990s (table 10).

In terms of overall trends, one of the most significant recent features of FDI is the rapid and sustained rise in flows to the developing world. After a period of relative stagnation in the wake of the debt crisis and the ensuing recession up to the mid-1980s (in 1981-85 FDI to developing countries actually declined by 4 per cent per annum), investment in the Third World revived strongly. Over the latter part of the 1980s it rose by 17 per cent per annum, with a further acceleration in the 1990s. According to the United Nations *World Investment Report 1994*, total FDI to developing countries reached a record figure of $70 billion in 1993, having increased by 125 per cent in the first three years of the decade. By contrast, there has been a sharp decline of inflows into the developed countries in the 1990s. In 1991, FDI in the OECD countries fell by 31 per cent, and in 1992 by a further 16 per cent. As a consequence, in 1992 the share of developing countries in FDI flows stood at around 32 per cent, as against an average of 24 per cent during the 1970s (table 11). It increased further to 40 per cent in 1993. If present trends continue, annual flows of FDI into the Third World could, in the medium-term, exceed those into the developed world. This would represent a major structural shift in the pattern, not just of investment, but also of the production and trade that arise from it.

As far as the composition of FDI is concerned, the trend away from the primary sector and into manufacturing and services continues. Within the latter groups, services gained at the expense of manufacturing. For instance, 51 per cent of the United States' overseas investment in 1992 was in services, compared to 41 per cent in 1985; for the United Kingdom the corresponding figures were 46 per cent and

Table 11. **Average annual flows of FDI, 1970-92**
(US$ billion and percentages)

Destination	1970-80	1981-85	1986-90	1991	1992
All countries	**21**	**50**	**155**	**149**	**126**
Developed countries	16	36	129	110	86
Developing countries	5	14	26	39	40
Africa (%)	13.0	15.3	12.0	7.9	5.1
Asia (%)	60.9	46.2	36.0	39.5	41.0
Latin America (%)	26.1	38.5	52.0	52.6	53.9

Source: United Nations: *Transnational corporations in world development: Third survey*, op. cit.; and idem: *Transnational corporations in world development: Trends and prospects*, op. cit.

35 per cent; for Japan, 66 per cent and 52 per cent; for France, 46 per cent and 47 per cent; and for Germany, 56 per cent and 53 per cent.[20] While much of the service activity is concentrated in the developed world, there are signs that liberalization has led to a substantial increase in service FDI in developing countries also. This is particularly marked in Latin America, where much of the recent revival of investment inflows has been in banking, telecommunications, hotels, retailing and similar activities. In Asia, the bulk of FDI still concentrates on manufacturing, testifying to the greater competitive capabilities built up there in industry.

The geographical distribution of FDI shows that MNE investment continues to concentrate in a few more advanced developing countries. Moreover, this concentration has grown stronger in the recent past. The ten largest recipients accounted for 76 per cent of total flows into the Third World in 1992, up from around 70 per cent in the preceding ten years (but still below the 81 per cent reached in 1981). This may be accounted for by the impressive growth in FDI into China, which attracted negligible amounts in 1981 but accounted for one quarter of all inflows to developing countries by 1992. In 1993 its dominance rose further, with inflows estimated at between $23-26 billion. This was followed by a massive 54 per cent increase in FDI in the first half of 1994 as compared to the same period in 1993.[21] These figures on concentration do not account for some new trends in FDI flows that may become significant in the near future. For instance, a number of major potential host developing countries are "underinvested" at present but are in the process of liberalizing their FDI regimes. The main one, perhaps, is India, which clearly has the potential for attracting very large amounts of investment and is starting to arouse investor interest. A recent Merrill Lynch report shows that approvals by India in 1993 came to $2.9 billion, a large jump from the $200-300 million that was the norm for the previous several years.[22]

In contrast, the 47 least developed countries have been, and continue to be, marginal to FDI flows. In 1992 such flows declined by 15 per cent to a total of $300 million, accounting for only 0.6 per cent of total flows to developing countries. Sub-Saharan Africa, in particular, received very little FDI despite widespread moves to liberalize foreign investment regimes and offer attractive incentives. Even countries undergoing strong structural adjustment programmes (like Ghana) failed to increase inward investment inflows. Clearly, there is more involved in attracting FDI than "opening up" to foreign trade and investment.

The regime governing FDI in developing countries has changed dramatically over the past decade or so. Many of the former concerns of developing country governments about the effects of MNEs seem to have evaporated. Governments now welcome FDI in a manner unprecedented in the history of economic development. The global shift of policy to market orientation and liberal economic policies has swept aside many of the apprehensions and hesitations that formerly governed inward FDI. Areas of economic activity that were formerly closed to foreign enterprises are now being opened and strong efforts are being made to woo MNEs. Utilities and infrastructure projects, where build-own-operate (BOO) and build-operate-transfer (BOT) schemes are proliferating and involving large sums of capital, are the most striking examples of these. These developments are being strongly helped by policy moves to privatize state-owned enterprises in both investing and host countries, and by pressures on governments to reduce budget deficits, increase the efficiency of infrastructure and create a climate conducive to competitive economic activity.

Participation in privatization has thus been an important mode of MNE penetration. Here, Latin America has the clear lead in the developing world. Between 1988 and 1992, $8.1 billion worth of FDI in Latin America took the form of the purchase of shares in public enterprises. This constituted 16 per cent of total FDI in Latin America, and comprised 94 per cent of total privatization-related FDI in the developing world. Eastern Europe also attracted substantial inflows of this sort: $5.2 billion in 1988-92 or 43 per cent of the total FDI in the region. Other developing regions relied much less on privatization receipts.

Effects on employment

The total number of jobs directly created by MNEs in the world as a whole is estimated at some 73 million, accounting for about 3 per cent of the total world labour force. It has been suggested that for each job created by MNEs there could be as many as a further one or two jobs generated indirectly.[23] On this basis, the total employment associated with MNEs is put at some 150 million. The 12 million jobs created by MNEs in developing countries, however, amount to a mere 2 per cent of the labour force in these countries; adding another 12 million jobs on account of possible indirect employment pushes this figure up to 4 per cent.

No doubt this overall contribution of MNEs to employment seems hardly significant at the present. There is, however, a widespread belief that FDI is a potent source of jobs and growth. The substantial growth in FDI since the mid-1980s, the pronounced change in attitudes towards it in most developing countries and the vigour with which it is advocated by international agencies suggest as much. Recent theor-

Figure 4.
Employment in transnational corporations

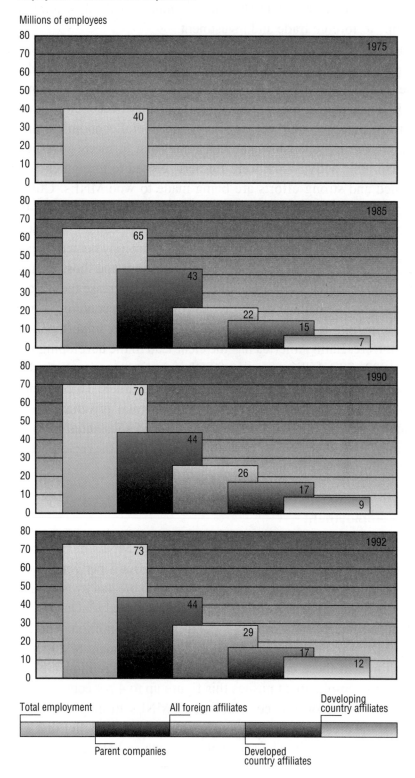

Millions of employees

Source: United Nations: *World Investment Report* (1994).

etical analysis of the mainsprings of economic growth, styled new (endogenous) growth theory, has also fed this enthusiasm for FDI. New growth theory emphasizes investment in human capital, learning by doing and learning by observing, increasing returns to scale and the major factors contributing to growth.[24] The transfer of human skills and spillover effects are also frequently emphasized characteristics of FDI.

The growth in international trade and investment in services offers unique opportunities for employment generation in developing countries with an educated labour force. Growth in trade and investment in services is itself a consequence of the dramatic developments which have occurred in information technology and of innovations in manufacturing. These innovations have resulted in the generation of a new set of service and manufacturing activities, which has implications for specialization and division of labour. Increasingly services are splintered from goods and services tend to be embodied in goods; when the design process for a car or its components is contracted out to specialized consultants this is an example of services splintering from goods, but when a music concert is embodied in a tape this is an example of services being embodied in goods.

Splintering of services from goods promotes scale economies and growth. Foreign firms can subcontract service activities to indigenous service producers, and many services can be labour-intensive components of the production process. Again, the embodiment of services in goods provides a unique opportunity for the use of skilled labour in developing countries. The services of software programmers and computer operators can be embodied in disks and traded. This creates employment opportunities for both high-skilled workers (in software programming) as well as workers with only a good basic education (as key-punch operators). Indeed, with the liberalization of trade in services there could be scope for temporary movement of skilled workers across national borders. The much publicized growth in exports of computer software from India, and the growth in demand for Indian software programmers, provide an illustration of the sort of employment generation that growth in trade and investment in services can generate. For example, some airlines and insurance companies now ship the data they need to analyse to India, where it is processed by Indian computer experts; the software they write is traded internationally; and Indian computer programmers and software experts undertake short tours of duty abroad on behalf of MNEs. The comparative advantage that countries such as India possess in this line of activity is due to the investments of the country in higher education, which has produced information technology experts in large numbers and given the country a competitive edge over others in terms of both efficiency and wage rates. This case again illustrates the vital importance of investments in human capital in the age of information technology.

Another relevant feature of the recent operations of MNEs is the integration of their activities across the globe. Simply put, individual functions (such as finance, procurement, research and development (and assembly) can be shifted to different locations as part of a global cost-minimization strategy. These functions are carried out by affiliates, subcontractors, joint-venture partners and other associates. Such integration of operations is reported to be frequent in information technology, bio-technology, and the automobile and new materials industries, all of which are characterized by high entry costs, scale economies and a rapid pace of technical change. The traditional farming out of components and parts manufacture is an elementary version of such integration, being usually confined to less technologically intensive industries; on the other hand, the complex integration schemes of recent years extend to the location in different geographical regions of not only the production of components but also various other segments of the value-added chain, such as finance and research and development. While the full implications of integrated production for employment in developing countries remain to be seen, it is likely that endowments of skilled labour and infrastructure facilities (including transport and communications networks) will be even more important as determinants of FDI in the future than in the past. This evolving feature of MNE operations may again favour a selected list of countries which are well endowed in these respects.

Emerging concerns over globalization

The rapid growth of world trade and flows of foreign investment, together with the rapid technical change that has been occurring simultaneously, have understandably given rise to a number of apprehensions over the implications of globalization. These apprehensions are basically twofold: the uneven distribution of the benefits among countries and problems of income redistribution within countries even when there are net benefits from globalization as a whole. The first of these derives from the observation that the least developed countries appear to have been excluded from the benefits of globalization so far and hence are in danger of being increasingly marginalized. This would aggravate problems of international inequality. The second apprehension derives from the fact that the costs and benefits from increased openness to the global economy are typically unevenly distributed among social groups within a country. A case in point is the concern that the social costs of structural adjustment in some developing countries have been borne disproportionately by poorer groups. Another concern is reflected in the highly topical debate in the industrialized countries over the impact of trade and investment relationships with lower-wage economies on employment and wage inequality. Specifically, the problem springs from the observation that low-skilled workers have been experiencing the highest incidence of unemployment, declining relative (and in some cases, absolute) wages, and reduced job prospects. The extent to which this can be blamed on trade and investment relationships with developing countries is a central issue of concern.

Cutting across these distributional issues is a third apprehension: that the rapid diffusion of new technologies, a major driving force behind the globalization of production, is causing massive job losses. This section will begin with a brief discussion of issues of international inequality and will then go on to review the debate on the impact of globalization on employment and wage inequality in the industrialized countries. This will be followed by a discussion of the impact of technical change on employment.

International inequality

Some observers fear that globalization has unleashed economic forces which tend to increase inequality in the global distribution of income. One reason that has been advanced is that the reduction of trade restrictions has been uneven. Tariffs and other barriers to trade have, on average, fallen quite sharply, but trade liberalization has proceeded more rapidly for goods and services of interest to the industrialized countries than for goods of interest to the developing countries. Restrictions on imports of clothing, textiles, footwear and agricultural products, for example, all of which are important exports from developing countries, remain high even after the recently completed Uruguay Round of the GATT.

Another reason that has been advanced is that globalization has tended to result in greater inequality because capital tends to be attracted to the already industrialized and to the rapidly industrializing countries, where the returns on investment are relatively high, and to bypass the poorest countries, where profit rates tend to be relatively low. This concentration of capital at the global level helps to perpetuate existing inequalities in productivity, incomes and material well-being. A particular concern is the marginalization of the least developed countries from the benefits of globalization. As discussed earlier, these countries as a whole have received only a tiny fraction of total flows of foreign direct investment and their share in world trade has fallen. The causes of, and possible remedies to, this marginalization are discussed in Part II of the Report.

A related concern is that the increasing transformation of knowledge into a private income-earning asset that can be sold or rented to the highest bidder is also a contribution to growing inequality between industrialized and developing countries. It is argued that there has been an enormous increase in the scope or coverage of copyright and patent protection as well as the length of time for which protection is granted, and that recently completed GATT negotiations have contributed to this process. Since developing countries are large net importers, potentially and actually, of knowledge from the developed countries, it is argued that they will find it increasingly difficult to gain access to productive knowledge and advanced technology. This will, in turn, accentuate inequalities at the global level.

Regardless of differences of opinion on how strong these disequalizing forces are, the apprehensions of developing countries on this score do raise serious issues for consideration. Growing inequality and the marginalization of the least developed countries would clearly be undesirable features of globalization and both international and national action to reduce these problems therefore deserve high priority. Among the areas for future international action are the granting of greater trade concessions to the least developed countries and new initiatives in international assistance directed at strengthening their capacity to share in the gains from globalization.

Employment in industrialized countries

Globalization has also given rise to fears in the industrialized countries that their standards of living are now under threat from low-wage countries, especially the newly industrializing countries. At the heart of these fears is the perception that the growth of cheap imports from developing countries, together with the relocation of production to these lower-cost production sites, has led to deindustrialization, job losses, and falling wages for unskilled workers in the industrialized countries. From this perspective, a continuation of current trends in trade and investment flows will depress industrialized countries' living standards to the levels obtaining in cheap-labour countries. Not surprisingly such perceptions have been at the root of the recent resurgence of protectionist sentiment in several industrialized countries.

As noted in the earlier discussion on the Uruguay Round, the move towards freer trade and investment flows will indeed entail transitional costs in many countries. It was argued, however, that the best response was positive adjustment, not protectionism. The underlying rationale for this was the dynamic gains from freer trade and investment flows which would confer benefits on all parties. In contrast, protectionist arguments implicitly assume that present trends in trade and investment flows will make it impossible for some to gain without inflicting losses on others. Hence the fears that the economic progress of the newly industrializing countries must invariably be at the expense of the industrialized countries.

Protectionist arguments typically focus in a one-sided way on short-run transitional costs and then provide pessimistic extrapolations based on these. They ignore the compensating benefits that have been reaped over the same period and, more importantly, the even more substantial benefits that will come once adjustment is complete. For example, present anxieties in the industrialized countries feed on the fact that there have been job losses in labour-intensive industries, that there has been a sharp rise in the incidence of unemployment among the unskilled, and that wage differentials have widened in favour of skilled workers. All or most of these phenomena are attributed to import penetration from low-wage countries and the relocation of industry there. It will be argued below that the magnitudes involved have been exaggerated and that, contrary to gloomy protectionist prognoses, both developed and newly industrializing countries will gain much from increased trade and investment flows.

Trade

A number of recent studies have attempted to calculate the effect of trade with the South on jobs and wages in the North. One study argues that the rise in imports from the South reduced the demand for unskilled workers in the North by no less than 20 per cent in the 30 years to 1990.[25] Three-quarters of that decline took place in the 1980s. In the United States, and also to some extent in the United Kingdom, this fall in demand has shown up as greater wage inequality, whereas in continental Europe it has been manifested in unemployment. The analysis finds a close relationship between increased imports from developing countries and the fall in manufacturing employment during the past two decades: the bigger the increase in imports, the bigger the drop in manufacturing jobs. The study also shows a strong correlation between increases in import penetration and increases in skill differentials: the bigger the country's increase in imports from the South, the sharper has been the increase in inequality.

The reasons for these trends, it is argued, lie both in the direct and the indirect effects of trade on employment. The South's exports are concentrated in labour-intensive sectors; the impact on employment is thus larger. And competition from imports can displace labour even when the actual import ratio is low, because in order to retain their market share firms respond to competition by cutting costs through labour-saving methods. The study calculates that only a quarter of the estimated 20 per cent drop in demand for low-skilled workers is due to the direct effects of trade on low-skilled jobs in manufacturing. The rest is mainly accounted for by labour-saving innovation induced by trade, and indirect effects on jobs in the service sector.

Another study finds that employment in the United States has fallen most sharply in industries with the highest proportion of unskilled labour. Imports from developing countries, it is argued, may have caused a 6 per cent reduction in demand for unskilled workers in manufacturing between 1978 and 1990. They have also contributed to a rise in wage inequality between skilled and unskilled workers, as wages in unskilled manufacturing have fallen or stagnated.[26]

All this seems to corroborate what the Stolper-Samuelson trade theorem would predict: that increased trade liberalization reduces the income of the factor of production used relatively intensively in imported goods sectors, and raises the income of the factor used intensively in exports. This tends to equalize factor prices across trading countries. In the case of Northern economies, then, the Stolper-Samuelson theorem tends to suggest that employment and wages among low-skilled labour (used relatively intensively in imports) would fall, while employment and wages would rise for skilled labour (used relatively intensively in Northern exports).

But these findings have been challenged. One well-publicized study[27] finds that, contrary to the expectations formed by the Stolper-Samuelson theorem, the relative price of unskilled labour-intensive manufactured goods in the United States in fact increased relative to skill-intensive goods during the 1980s. Furthermore, the study argues that if trade were to blame for widening wage inequalities, one would expect to see a fall in the ratio of skilled to unskilled labour in all manufacturing industries. The reason is that with a fixed supply of labour, the only way an economy can shift production towards the competitive sector (in the United States case, the skill-intensive sector) is if firms economize on more costly skilled labour. But the data presented in the study seem to indicate that the opposite has occurred in the United States: across all manufacturing sectors, the ratio of skilled to unskilled workers has risen. The study thus concludes that, if the demand for unskilled workers has fallen, it is because of some common factor that affects all sectors and not because of trade, since the latter would change the industry mix. That common factor is argued to be new technology. Indeed, there is a growing body of literature which blames the technological revolution of the past decade for causing the dwindling demand for unskilled workers and the decline in their real wages.[28]

The general evidence on the effect of advanced technologies on employment generation has been analysed by the OECD.[29] In the case of manufacturing, the (relatively small) gains in high technology and science-based employment were more than offset in these OECD countries by the decline in other manufacturing industries.[30] Especially serious was the decline in demand for unskilled workers.

A debate has consequently emerged on the possible "skill-biased" nature of recent technical change, particularly in relation to information and communication technology (ICT).[31] The latter is now recognized by an increasing number of economists to represent a pervasive, so-called "general purpose" technology,[32] which could imply significant increases in the demand for skilled labour. But regardless of whether or not technical change has been skill-biased, the diffusion of ICT will be characterized by a gradual increase in the "knowledge base" of economic production. In other words, the rapid diffusion of ICT has led, and is likely to continue to do so, to a substantial "exclusion" of large parts of the labour force, either unskilled or wrongly skilled and incapable of retraining. This bias in the demand for labour has only emerged over the last 10 or 15 years, but is likely to be much more pronounced in the rest of the 1990s. In this sense, therefore, it is new technology that is the basic cause of the problems faced by unskilled workers in industrialized countries. These problems will be there whether or not they are aggravated by trade with developing countries.

Whatever the final verdict is on this debate, two things are clear. First, it is unlikely that all the blame for the falling demand for unskilled workers can be placed on import penetration alone. Other factors are clearly at work. Secondly, manufactured imports from developing countries still account for a relatively small share of the OECD's total imports of manufactures (around 14 per cent in 1992)[33] and GDP (about 3.8 per cent). This sets a modest upper limit to the extent of the possible negative impact. It is not, however, unreasonable to conclude that trade with the South has been at least partly responsible for the loss of unskilled jobs and the widening wage differentials in the North. But this has to be set against compensating gains.

It is not only the South that has benefited in terms of larger markets for its exports and more jobs. The North has gained too, and will continue to gain from freer trade and faster economic growth in the South. Indeed, over the past two decades, the growing exports of developing countries to the OECD have been accompanied by a more or less equivalent increase in exports from the OECD to developing countries, particularly those in Asia. Perhaps even more important is the direct effect of North-South trade expansion on Northern living standards.

On the demand side, growth in the South provides countless new business opportunities for the North, and new customers for its products. For instance, one estimate suggests that the volume of the United States' exports to China and India could grow by 15 per cent per annum over the next decade. Indeed, increased exports will give the South more money to spend on imports. Most countries in the South spend all the foreign exchange they have on buying imports of capital equipment, commercial services and branded consumer goods from the North. Thus, higher output in the South is more likely to increase than to reduce output in the North. In addition, if increased FDI improves the South's growth, the benefits will rapidly filter through to the North.

On the supply side, the feedback effect comes in terms of greater competition, thus spurring productivity and innovation in the North. An increase in cheaper imports from the South is also likely to give consumers in the North a boost in real income. Already, in countries such as the United States, the average prices of goods such as shoes and clothing, the bulk of which come as imports from the South, have fallen by more than 20 per cent in real terms over the last ten years. Larger international markets will also allow Northern firms to exploit economies of scale fully – not just in production, but also in research and development. And fast-growing emerging economies in the South will offer savers in the North ever higher returns.

At a more fundamental level, free trade and the adjustment to comparative advantage increases world output and welfare. In the long run, North-South trade should have little impact on overall employment in the North; it will simply reallocate labour from low-skilled import-competing industries to high-skilled industries and services. This will lift the average quality of jobs and hence average wages.

The problem is in the interim: high-skilled workers in the North will gain, but redundant low-skilled workers will find it difficult to upgrade their skills and thus find productive employment at decent wages over the short run. The solution to these problems, however, lies not in protectionism, but in appropriate domestic policy responses. These policies will be discussed in Part IV of the Report.

Foreign direct investment

Two related concerns in Northern countries stem from increased foreign direct investment in the South. First, it is claimed that this has resulted in the relocation of production and jobs from the North to the South. This, it is argued, is "deindustrializing" the North, and thus reducing both the number of unskilled jobs and real wages of unskilled labour, as such jobs can be performed more cheaply in the South. Second, it is feared that this phenomenon has intensified through technology transfer via MNEs. It is argued that, while in the past, the North's higher real wages were justified by higher productivity, the lowering of foreign investment barriers has caused the technology that supports productivity to be transferred more speedily across borders. As Southern producers acquire Northern technology, they will become even more competitive – that is, increase productivity while maintaining low wages – thus wiping out even more jobs in the North.[34]

In reality, however, although capital inflows into the South have risen sharply in recent years, their actual level still remains modest: one estimate suggests that the entire net outflow of investment from the North since 1990 has reduced the North's capital stock by a mere 0.5 per cent from what it would otherwise have been.[35] Moreover, the impact on employment so far appears to have been limited. According to a recent UNCTAD study, of the 73 million persons employed worldwide by MNEs, only 16 per cent are employed in developing countries, the rest being in the North.[36]

But how much of this represents an actual relocation of jobs from the North to the South?

In France, where concerns over "delocalization" has been pronounced, a number of estimates of job losses have been put forward. One estimate claims that over a million jobs in France are threatened as a result of delocalization to Asia and Eastern Europe.[37] The estimate bases its claims on the fact that firms in electronics, clothing and footwear have cut their employment in France by 50 per cent over the last decade.

Other estimates, however, suggest that this is a vast exaggeration, and that, in fact, less than 5 per cent of French companies' FDI is accounted for by relocation in the strict sense. Affiliates of MNEs in South-East Asia employ only 5 per cent of workers employed abroad by French multinationals.[38]

Another recent study argues that although jobs have been relocated in a few specific industries such as textiles and electronics, the proportion of FDI which represents straight relocation from rich to poor countries is small.[39]

However, as in the case of trade, it is important to look beyond current numbers to the potential long-run mutual gains. Multinationals maximize profits on a world scale, typically shifting resources (technology, management, sales ability, capital) to areas where their returns are highest and buying inputs where their prices are lowest. In the host country, MNEs are likely to boost output, offer employment, pay taxes, and stimulate competition. But this is not a one-way process. In the home country, investment is likely to be boosted as profits flow in from overseas operations. Moreover, many of the common criticisms concerning the impact of outward FDI on source-country economies are founded on fragile grounds. For example, contrary to the belief that FDI substitutes for home-country exports, both theory and evidence suggest that FDI and exports may well in fact be complementary: FDI may generate increased exports of components and parts to affiliates of MNEs in the host countries. It may also generate exports of technology and know-how which yield return flows of royalties and technical fees. FDI is thus likely to be trade-expanding.

Moreover, where increasing returns to scale are present, the expansion of trade and foreign investment could lead to a generalized increase in factor productivities and incomes through a "lifting all boats" effect.[40] Furthermore, increased trade and FDI could, by promoting complete specialization in the production of a good, also result in a situation where the real wages of both skilled and unskilled labour would rise. The net effect could be to leave both skilled and unskilled labour better off under free trade than under autarky.[41]

A major argument against FDI is that it reduces domestic investment in the home country. But this is not necessarily the case. FDI tends to be industry-specific, and the decision on whether to invest at home or abroad is determined by alternatives available in a particular sector, not by the range of all possible investment opportunities. Investments are rarely mobile across sectors, not least because of the advantages accumulated in "intangibles" such as brand names, technical know-how and managerial skills, which are industry-specific. These advantages provide the basis for profitable expansion abroad when the home market is saturated. MNEs thus typically concentrate on exporting such intangibles which, however, represent low domestic opportunity costs. Hence FDI may occur without any corresponding decline in domestic investment.

Another explanation for mutual gains derives from product life-cycle theories that relate trade and investment to the same stimuli.[42] These theories, when applied to the operation of a multinational firm, explain why MNEs prefer to shift production of certain goods in the final stage of the product life cycle to low-wage, labour-abundant, developing countries. So long as product innovation continues in the industrial countries such relocation of production is a process that yields benefits to both capital-exporting and receiving countries.

Thus, in the long run, there are many gains to be had from FDI, as global welfare and efficiency are raised. And the net result should be a more efficient international division of labour.

Furthermore, while the industrial North may currently be losing out in terms of wages and employment in low-skilled manufacturing, such a distribution of gains should not be seen as static. As the global activities of multinationals result in an ever greater convergence of technical know-how, more and more industries are likely to become "footloose", driven by small new advantages that may be reaped from relocating production. The result, to quote Bhagwati, may be "kaleidoscopic comparative advantage, where one day I have comparative advantage in X and you in Y, and tomorrow it may be the other way around, and then back again: a sort of musical chairs".[43] In other words, FDI is likely to flow in both directions.

Indeed, FDI patterns in the East and South-East Asian region have already shown signs of such dynamism, involving a crisscrossing of investment flows across countries. Not only are the sources of FDI in the region predominantly intraregional, but new countries in the region are emerging as sources of FDI. During 1986-92, about 70 per cent of FDI inflows into the low- and middle-income countries in the region (China, Indonesia, Malaysia, the Philippines and Thailand) were from other countries and territories within the region, about 50 per cent coming from the four newly industrializing economies (Hong Kong, the Republic of Korea, Singapore and Taiwan, China), and 18 per cent from Japan. The share of European and the United States' FDI combined was about 20 per cent – less than Hong Kong's. In 1992, the new FDI surge into China was again mainly from Hong Kong, Singapore and Taiwan, China – resulting in inflows of more than US$11 billion.[44]

New technologies and employment

As signalled earlier, one of the apprehensions connected to globalization is that the rapid spread of new technologies is destroying a significant number of jobs. This, however, overlooks the fact that technical change is two-edged in nature: it both destroys old jobs and creates new ones. In general, economists have argued that the job creation effects have in the long run outstripped the job destruction effects, albeit accompanied by a steady reduction in working hours throughout the nineteenth and twentieth centuries. Nobody has claimed, however, that "compensation" is automatic, painless or instantaneous; the new jobs may not match the old ones with respect either to skill or to location. Where the mismatch is severe and/or prolonged economists speak of "structural unemployment" and the problems of "structural adjustment". The rapid increase and presently high rates of "long-term" unemployment or male "non-employment" in most developed countries is often cited as evidence for the existence of structural unemployment.

Schumpeter introduced the concept of "successive industrial revolutions" when new technologies were diffusing through the productive system.[45] In his long cycle theory such new technologies could give rise to major waves of new investment and employment in new industries and services which would stimulate expansion throughout the economy. When these expansionary effects began to diminish, a period of relative stagnation or depression would follow until a new impulse developed from a new set of technologies.

Whether or not they accept Schumpeter's long wave ideas, few economists or engineers today would deny the enormous worldwide impact of ICT. In fact, many commentators go even further and suggest that ICT is ushering in an entirely new era of "post-industrial" society. The extraordinary reduction in costs associated with microelectronics in successive generations of integrated circuits, of telecommunications and of electronic computers is having great effects on almost every branch of the economy, whether in the primary, the secondary or the tertiary sectors. Scientific and market research, design and development, machinery, instruments, production systems, marketing, distribution and general administration are all deeply affected by this revolutionary technology. Moreover, falling costs and prices in microelectronics, computers and telecommunications affect a widening range of products and services.

In attempting to assess the employment creation and destruction effects it is important to distinguish the direct from the indirect effects. The direct effects are the new jobs created for the production and delivery of new products and services. The indirect effects are the consequences elsewhere. Computer terminals are to be found everywhere, but it is not always clear whether they are displacing workers or creating additional new services and employment. To compare the balance of gains and losses is thus a difficult undertaking, as numerous empirical studies of the 1970s and 1980s confirm. The naive view of ICT as simply a process of automation and job destruction has its counterpart in the equally naive view of ICT as a purely positive source of new employment. Any sophisticated attempt to assess the employment effects must take into account both job destruction and job creation.

One such approach (change of "techno-economic paradigm")[46] stresses both the direct and indirect effects of ICT. It points to the rise of entirely new industries in the second half of this century, such as the software industry, the electronic computer industry itself, the microelectronic industry, the VCR and television industry. Each of these now employs millions of people but barely existed before 1950. Even more, however, it stresses the indirect effects of the ICT revolution.

The indirect effects of a major new pervasive technology such as ICT (i.e. the effects on other industries and services as well as on the ICT industries themselves) include job destruction as well as job creation. Whether the balance is positive or negative in a given national economy cannot be assessed by simply counting new jobs gained and old jobs destroyed. It has to be recognized that the expansionary effects on any national economy or the world economy as a whole paradoxically depend on rapid increases in labour productivity. What a revolutionary new technology can do is to create the basis for a virtuous circle of growth in which investment is high, and labour productivity grows fast but output grows even faster, so that there is a net growth of employment. Whether this virtuous circle can be sustained depends on macro-economic policies, employment policy and trade as well as on the new technologies. If there is a good match between technologies, policies and institutions, prolonged periods of full employment can result.

This was the happy situation in Europe, Japan and North America in the 1950s and 1960s, based on cheap oil, very rapid expansion of the automobile and other consumer durable industries, of steel and plastics and of many related services. Productivity growth was high but output grew even faster, so that there was also considerable growth of employment and very low unemployment. The virtuous circle achieved in the 1950 and 1960s in most OECD countries has again been achieved with the aid of new technologies, but this time in Asia. The "four tigers" of Eastern Asia and, more recently, some other economies of South-East Asia, have achieved remarkably high output growth, productivity growth and employment growth. These experiences illustrate that rapid and efficient diffusion of ICT, combined with global expansion strategies, could promote a worldwide boom and generate virtuous circles in many countries. The strong downward trends in costs and prices of ICT products and services will help to dampen any inflationary dangers.

Notes

[1] World Bank: *Global economic prospects and the developing countries* (Washington, 1994).

[2] UNCTAD: *Handbook of International Trade and Development Statistics*, various issues, and World Bank: *Data on diskette. World tables 1994* (Washington, 1994).

[3] Those countries where tariffs as a percentage of the value of imports (the average level of tariffs) were reduced between 1985 and 1988 included Côte d'Ivoire (26 to 25 per cent); Mexico (34 to 16 per cent); Republic of Korea (26 to 25 per cent); Uruguay (32 to 29 per cent); Chile (35 to 17 per cent); Costa Rica (92 to 62 per cent); Senegal (40 to 34 per cent); Sri Lanka (43 to 41 per cent); Turkey (43 to 40 per cent); Brazil (81 to 42 per cent); Colombia (83 to 48 per cent); Ecuador (50 to 49 per cent); Indonesia (20 to 18 per cent); Philippines (38 to 33 per cent) and Argentina (28 to 26 per cent), UNCTAD: *Trade and Development Report* (New York, 1989).

[4] These countries included Malaysia (where tariffs as a percentage of the value of imports was 14 per cent by 1985); Singapore (where the equivalent figure was as low as 0.3 per cent by 1985); Jamaica (17 per cent in 1985); and Bolivia (20 per cent in 1985) (ibid.).

[5] Countries which significantly relaxed non-tariff measures between 1985 and 1988 included: Bolivia, Côte d'Ivoire, Jamaica, Republic of Korea, Chile, Nigeria, Senegal, Sri Lanka, Turkey, Brazil, Colombia, Ecuador, Ghana, Kenya, Morocco, Pakistan, Philippines, Argentina (ibid.).

[6] These countries included Uruguay and Costa Rica, both of which had a frequency of application of quantitative restrictions of 1 per cent by 1985 (ibid.).

[7] Indeed, in a sample of 15 developing countries for which IMF data on real effective exchange rate movements are available over a comparable period of time, the real effective exchange rate index declined in 13 countries between 1985 and 1992. The two countries which registered increases in the REER between 1985 and 1992 were Côte d'Ivoire and Uruguay.

[8] Pharmaceuticals, construction equipment, medical equipment, steel, beer, furniture, farm equipment, spirits, wood, paper, toys.

[9] Participants will be free to implement the reductions in fewer stages or at earlier dates, if they wish (UNCTAD: *Trade and Development Report*, op. cit., 1989).

[10] See, for example, T.T. Nguyen, C. Perroni and R. Wigle: "The value of a Uruguay Round success", in *The World Economy* (Oxford, Blackwell), Dec. 1991; idem: "An evaluation of the Draft Final Act of the Uruguay Round", in *Economic Journal* (Oxford, Blackwell), Nov. 1993; and D. Greenaway and C.R. Milner: "The Uruguay Round: Global employment implications", background paper prepared for the World Employment Report.

[11] ibid.

[12] Nguyen, Perroni and Wigle, 1993, op. cit.

[13] A. Wood: *North-South trade, employment and inequality* (Oxford, Clarendon Press, 1994).

[14] Nguyen, Perroni and Wigle, 1993, op. cit.

[15] Wood, op. cit.

[16] C. Hamilton: "A new approach to estimation of the effects of non-tariff barriers to trade: An application to the Swedish textile and clothing industry" in *Weltwirtschaftliches Archiv*, 1980, pp. 298-325.

[17] C. Pearson: *Emerging protection in the footwear industry*, Thames Essay, 36 (London, Trade Policy Research Centre, 1983).

[18] Hamilton, op. cit.

[19] Pearson, op. cit.

[20] UNCTAD: *Trade and Development Report, 1994* (New York, 1994).

[21] Data reported in *The Economist* (London), 6 Aug. 1994, p. 65.

[22] S. Lall: "Policy options for improving the employment outcomes of FDI", mimeo (Geneva, ILO, 1994), p. 3.

[23] A. Parisotto: "Direct employment in multinational enterprises in industrialized and developing countries in the 1980s: Main characteristics and recent trends", in P. Bailey et al.: *Multinationals and employment: The global economy of the 1990s* (Geneva, ILO, 1993).

[24] P. Romer: "Increasing returns and long-run growth", in *Journal of Political Economy*, Vol. 94, Nos. 4-6, 1986, pp. 1002-1037; and R.E. Lucas: "Why doesn't capital flow from rich to poor countries?", in *American Economic Review*, paper and proceedings, Vol. 80, 1990, pp. 92-96.

[25] Wood, op. cit.

[26] J. Sachs and H. Schatz: *Trade and jobs in US manufacturing* (Washington, Brookings Institution, Brookings papers on economic activity, 1994).

[27] R. Lawrence and M. Slaughter: *International trade and American wages in the 1980s: Giant sucking sound or small hiccup?* (Washington, Brookings Institution, Brookings papers on economic activity, 1993).

[28] ibid., and Richard Freeman: *Is globalization impoverishing low skill American workers?* (Cambridge, Harvard University Press, 1993).

[29] OECD: *Technology and the economy: The key relationships* (Paris, 1992).

[30] OECD: *The OECD jobs study*, Part I (Paris, 1994), pp. 146-147.

[31] E. Berman, J. Bound and Z. Griliches: "Changes in the demand for skilled labour within US manufacturing: Evidence from the Annual Survey of Manufacturers", in *Quarterly Journal of Economics*, 1994, 109, pp. 367-397.

[32] E. Helpman and M. Trajtenberg: "A time to sow and a time to reap: Growth based on general purpose technologies", Working Paper No. 4854 (Cambridge, Massachusetts, National Bureau of Economic Research, 1994).

[33] OECD, op. cit.

[34] This fear is expressed by, among others, K. Schwab, President of the World Economic Forum, in a joint article with C. Smadja: "The new rules of the game in a world of many players", in *Harvard Business Review*, Nov. 1994. Schwab and Smadja argue that with increasing cross-border movements in capital and technology, it is possible for the South to have high productivity and high technology, but low wages.

[35] P. Krugman: "Does third world growth hurt first world prosperity?", in *Harvard Business Review*, July-Aug. 1994.

[36] Parisotto, op. cit.

[37] J. Arthuis: *Délocalisations et l'emploi: mieux comprendre les mécanismes des délocalisations industrielles et des services* (Paris, Ed. d'Organisation, 1993).

[38] *The Economist*, Survey of the Global Economy, 1 Oct. 1994.

[39] UNCTAD: *World Investment Report*, op. cit.

[40] For an elaboration on this point, see J. Bhagwati: "Free trade: Old and new challenges", in *Economic Journal*, Mar. 1994, pp. 231-246.

[41] Ibid. See also J. Bhagwati and V. Dehejia: "Free trade and wages of the unskilled: Is Marx striking again?" in J. Bhagwati and M. Kosters (eds.): *Trade and wages* (Washington, American Enterprise Institute, 1993),

in which the authors reject many of the assumptions of the Stolper-Samuelson theorem on the grounds that these do not hold in the real world. In particular, they assume that, first, production functions are subject to increasing returns to scale, and second, that they allow for factor intensity reversals. They conclude that free trade can then improve the shares of both factors of production compared with a situation where no trade exists.

[42] Product cycle theories of trade developed by Hirsch and Vernon argue that it is changing technology that determines trade. Initially, as new goods are being developed and first sold, the uncertainty over their production and marketability is met by flexibility which requires considerable inputs of skilled labour and proximity to the market. Since these are the same factors that stimulate innovation, there is a locational link between innovation and production: new goods will be produced and exported by rich and large economies. As the product matures, its basic technology and functional specification become standardized, making flexibility less important. World demand grows, making large-scale production feasible, and production costs become significant. In this second stage of the production cycle, comparative advantage shifts away from the innovating countries (which are typically high-cost locations) to other relatively wealthy capital-abundant countries. The final stage occurs when (if) technology and specifications become wholly standardized and universally known – which allows production to be broken down into a number of relatively unskilled tasks and stimulates competition and pressures to reduce costs. The comparative advantage finally shifts to low-wage, labour-abundant developing countries, which eventually become net exporters. Note that with international investment, the whole of the cycle could take place under the auspices of a single firm, and the final stage would represent production by an MNE in a developing country, with exports coming back to the home country. Note also that while the later stages of the cycle correspond closely to Heckscher-Ohlin theory, it is innovation which makes the difference. In the absence of innovation, trade would settle down to a Heckscher-Ohlin equilibrium pattern.

[43] Bhagwati, op. cit.

[44] World Bank: *East Asia's trade and investment* (Washington, 1994).

[45] J. Schumpeter: *Business cycles: A theoretical historical and statistical analysis* (New York, McGraw Hill, 1939).

[46] C. Freeman and L. Soete: *Work for all or mass unemployment: Computerized technical change into the 21st century* (London, New York, Pinter, 1994).

2 PART TWO
Developing countries

Employment trends

Divergent economic performance among groups of developing countries since the beginning of the 1980s has resulted in sharply contrasting employment trends. The worst performers in terms of economic growth have experienced negative employment trends, while those with high growth rates have seen significant improvements in their employment situation. The poor performers have experienced a slowing down in the growth of – or absolute declines in – modern-sector employment, a rise in open unemployment and underemployment, an increase in the share of precarious and low-productivity informal-sector employment, and falling real wages. In contrast, countries with high growth have experienced improvements in all these indicators.

Figure 5.
Growth in GDP and manufacturing jobs, 1981-90 (annual average change, percentage)

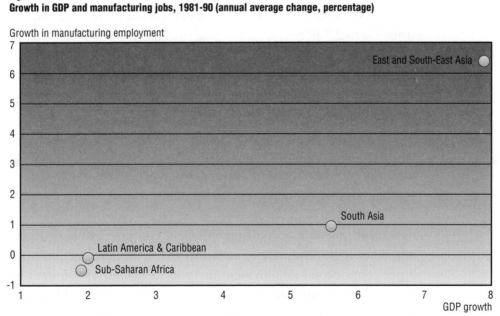

Source: ILO data for employment calculated from LABORSTA; World Bank data for GDP calculated from World Bank, World Tables.

The reason why the rate of growth of modern-sector jobs is crucial is because these are "good jobs" in the context of a typical developing country. They represent regular employment with wages which are often significantly higher than earnings from alternative employment in agriculture or the urban informal sector. They are also the only jobs to have fringe benefits such as pensions and medical benefits attached to them and they typically fall within the ambit of protective labour legislation. For all these reasons, the rapid growth of modern sector jobs has been a major objective of employment policy in developing countries.

From the standpoint of the economy as a whole, this was the route to higher productivity and overall growth, while for the majority of workers still locked into low-productivity employment it was the principal escape route to a better life.

As is well known, developing countries in Asia have outperformed those in sub-Saharan Africa and Latin America since 1980. There has been consistently spectacular growth in East and South-East Asia (with the exception of the Philippines) while growth in South Asia has picked up significantly from previous trends. This has resulted in clear improvements in the employment situation (table 4 in Part I).

In the rapidly growing economies of East and South-East Asia the salient facts are as follows:

- total employment grew rapidly in the 1980s, with a marked acceleration in the latter half of the decade. The growth rates ranged from 2.3 per cent in Hong Kong to 5.9 per cent in Singapore;

- as a result, unemployment fell between the mid-1980s and the early 1990s. The unemployment rates in the latter period were extremely low, ranging from 2.0 to 2.7 per cent;

- in some countries, such as Malaysia, Singapore and Taiwan, China, labour shortages emerged and there was significant immigration of labour from neighbouring lower-income countries;

- employment growth was spearheaded by the manufacturing sector. Manufacturing employment grew at a rate of over 6 per cent per annum during the 1980s for the dynamic economies of the region;

- as a result, the structure of employment continued to shift to manufacturing and other high-productivity activities in the modern sector rising from about 7 per cent of total employment in 1960 to around 18 per cent by 1994. This presented growing opportunities for those in low-productivity activities to move into better modern-sector jobs, thereby sharing in the gains from growth;

- at the same time real earnings grew steadily, with the rate of growth averaging a little over 5 per cent per annum during the 1980s (see table 12);

- the combined effect of these developments was a steady decline in levels of poverty and the region's noteworthy performance in terms of an equitable distribution of income. Indeed, an international cross-section of countries showing the proportion of people under a given poverty line and their relative per capita mean consumption level suggests that East and South-East Asia, with a per capita consumption level around 26 per cent lower than Latin America and the Caribbean in 1990, had, nevertheless, half the proportion of people living under the common poverty line: in 1990, around 15 per cent of the population in East and South-East Asia lived under the poverty line compared with 59 per cent in South Asia, 54 per cent in sub-Saharan Africa and 28 per cent in Latin America and the Caribbean (table 13).

These highly favourable outcomes were largely due to the successful development strategies followed by these countries. The main elements of these included the maintenance of macroeconomic stability, high levels of savings and investment, a liberal trading regime, an export-oriented industrialization strategy, and the successful attraction of foreign direct investment. Academic opinion remains divided on a number of specific aspects of this successful East Asian model such as the importance of state intervention in stimulating growth, but there is little disagreement that successful integration into the global economy was the main ingredient of the region's achievement.

From the standpoint of employment policy the East Asian experience confirms that rapid growth of labour-intensive manufacturing (and other modern-sector activities) is the key to achieving full employment and rising standards of living in developing countries. Such a pattern of growth results initially in the rapid reduction of surplus labour in traditional agriculture and the informal sector, and subsequently to rising real wages when surplus labour has been eliminated.

In South Asia, the changes in employment conditions have on the whole been positive although falling well short of the dramatic successes of East Asia. This has been due to the fact that growth, although faster than in the past, has not matched the rates reached in East Asia. The growth has also been of shorter duration, and South Asian countries have only recently embarked on economic reforms towards a more open and market-oriented economy. Moreover, these countries still have the vast majority of their labour force in agriculture and the urban informal sector, representing a considerable pool of labour to be absorbed by the modern sector. Understandably, therefore, employment trends in South Asia give a mixed picture, the highlights of which are as follows:

– there has been moderate growth in modern-sector employment, as in India where it grew by 1.6 per cent per annum in the 1980s;

– manufacturing employment grew at a little less than 1 per cent per annum for the region during the 1980s. The rate of growth recorded in Bangladesh and

Table 12. **Real earnings in manufacturing**

Region	Years	Average annual rate of growth (percentage)
Sub-Saharan Africa[1]	1975-80	–0.6
	1980-88	–12.3
Latin America and the Caribbean[2]	1971-80	–2.13
	1981-92	–3.13
East and South-East Asia[3]	1971-80	5.32
	1981-90	5.12
South Asia[4]		Index of manufacturing real earnings per employee (1987 = 100)
	1971	86.2
	1980	87.4
	1985	91.5

[1] Real annual earnings per employee in manufacturing, 1987 $. Source: World Bank, *African Development Indicators,* Washington, DC, 1992. [2] Source: UNIDO: Industrial statistics database (Vienna, 1994). [3] Comprises Indonesia, Republic of Korea, Malaysia, Philippines and Thailand. Source: UNIDO, op. cit. [4] Comprises Bangladesh, India, Pakistan, Sri Lanka. Source: UNIDO, op. cit.

Sri Lanka was 2.5 per cent per annum, but much of this was accounted for by an increase in the number of low-productivity self-employed workers;

– the structure of employment has been marked by a general move out of agriculture. Levels of poverty fell for the region as a whole during the 1980s, notably in Bangladesh, India, Nepal and Pakistan. The exception was Sri Lanka, which saw a marked increase in the incidence of poverty between 1978-79, when 19 per cent of the population lived below the poverty line, and 1986-87, when the figure was 27 per cent;[1]

– nevertheless, underemployment in rural areas remains high. In India 22 per cent of all male workers declared themselves available for additional work in the late 1980s, and this figure has been rising;

Table 13. **Estimates of poverty incidence: Per capita consumption levels in different developing regions, selected years**

Region/country	Year	Percentage population consuming less than $30.42 (per month; 1985 PPP)	Mean consumption $/person/month 1985 PPP	Index of distribution of consumption (Gini coefficient)
Sub-Saharan Africa	1985	53.48	45.76	
	1990	54.43	49.81	
Latin America & the Caribbean	1985	23.07	117.49	
	1990	27.77	109.66	
South Asia	1985	61.10	33.37	
	1990	59.00	35.12	
East and South-East Asia	1985	15.72	70.93	
	1990	14.71	80.26	
Indonesia	1990	21.72	56.14	0.332
Malaysia	1990	6.37	154.07	0.484
Philippines	1990	29.65	61.05	0.407
Thailand	1990	10.42	100.87	0.438
Brazil	1990	31.09	124.47	0.637

Source: Dipak Mazumdar and Priya Basu: *Macroeconomic policies, growth and employment: The experience of East and South-East Asia*, ILO/UNDP Paper No. 7 (Geneva, 1994).

–   there is a high proportion of employment in the urban informal sector: in India and Pakistan, for example, employment in the unorganized segment of the manufacturing sector was respectively 75 and 70 per cent of total manufacturing employment in 1990.

Employment trends in China were more dynamic than in South Asia, a direct result of the exceptionally high rates of growth sustained since the late 1970s. In particular:

–   agricultural employment decreased markedly from 77 per cent of the labour force in 1977 to 69 per cent in 1980 and further dropped to only 60 per cent in 1990. At the same time non-agricultural employment grew by an impressive margin of 58 per cent between 1977 and 1990;

–   total employment grew by 2.7 per cent per annum between 1982 and 1990.

Developments in sub-Saharan Africa were almost exactly the opposite of those in East and South Asia. Instead of highly dynamic growth there was economic retrogression. Instead of rapid industrial development, there was a collapse of the modern sector in many sub-Saharan countries.[2] The negative consequences of this for employment in the region are plain from the following facts:

–   there is strong evidence of a substantial decline in modern-sector employment since the mid-1980s in countries which experienced a sharp fall in GDP growth. Paid employment in manufacturing declined at a rate of 0.5 per cent per annum during the 1980s. This decline was especially severe in Ghana (by over half), Benin and Niger. In contrast, in countries such as Botswana and Mauritius which experienced the highest GDP growth in the 1980s, modern-sector employment continued to expand;

–   rural-to-urban migration remained high. This, together with the decline in modern-sector employment, led to an expansion of low-productivity urban informal-sector activities. On average, the informal sector is now believed to employ over 60 per cent of the urban labour force;

–   urban unemployment has increased and now ranges between 15 and 20 per cent compared to around 10 per cent in the mid-1970s;

–   real wages in manufacturing fell sharply throughout the 1980s. Of the 15 countries for which data are available, real wages fell in 12. The mean rate of decline was 12.3 per cent per annum during the 1980s.

The picture for Latin America is, on the whole, also negative, although there have been distinct signs of improvements in the past few years. In the first half of the 1980s the effects of the debt crisis led to an economic collapse which reversed previous progress on the employment front. The subsequent recovery, albeit still mild in most countries, has led to definite indications of improvement in the employment situation. There are, nevertheless, a number of negative features:

–   there was a steady fall in modern-sector employment between 1980 and 1992, with paid employment falling at a rate of about 0.1 per cent per annum during the 1980s. This reversed the trend of the previous three decades, when steady economic growth had led to a significant expansion of modern-sector employment;

–   over the same period the share of employment in the urban informal sector increased from 13.4 per cent of the labour force to 18.6 per cent;

–   in most countries the average real wage (across all sectors) fell during the 1980s, recovering in only a few countries towards the end of the decade. The extent of the decline varied across sectors, ranging from 5 per cent in industry to 20 per cent in agriculture. The minimum wage was also estimated to have fallen by an average of 24 per cent in real terms across the region, while average earnings in the informal sector declined even more sharply (by 42 per cent).

This synoptic survey of employment trends in the main developing regions shows that apart from East Asia, the rest of the developing world now faces the major challenge of employment creation. This is most acute in sub-Saharan Africa, where the economic retrogression still remains to be stemmed. Without economic recovery, the adverse employment trends that have prevailed for over a decade cannot even begin to be reversed. The gravity of the employment problem is compounded by the fact that the region has by far the highest rates of population and labour force growth as well as high rates of rural-to-urban migration. The labour force in sub-Saharan Africa grew by 2.4 per cent per annum in the 1980s and is projected to grow by around 2.5 per cent per annum for the rest of the 1990s. This means an additional 6 million jobseekers every year. Given the still predominantly rural structure of African economies, most of these new entrants should be absorbed in the rural economy, yet African agriculture exhibited a limited ability to retain labour in the 1980s in spite of reforms which have favoured the sector. Unless production conditions in agriculture are improved, "push" factors are likely to lead to a continuation of high rates of rural-to-urban migration. This in turn will lead to a further swelling of the already large urban informal sector and an intensification of urban poverty and squalor. The consequences of this are likely to be frightening; a further rise in crime,

Table 14. **Rates of unemployment in Latin America and Asia, selected years (percentages)**

		1970	1980	1985	1990	1992
Latin America and the Caribbean						
Argentina	National urban unemployment rate	4.9	2.6	6.1	7.5	6.9
Bolivia	National unemployment rate			5.8	9.5	6.8
	Urban unemployment rate (in La Paz)		7.5	15.0		
Brazil	National unemployment rate (a)		4.9[1]	3.4	3.9[4]	
	Unemployment rate in major metropolitan areas		6.3	5.3	4.3	5.9
Chile	National unemployment rate (b)		19.6[2]	12.1	5.6	5.3[3]
	Santiago metropolitan area unemployment rate		11.8	17.0	6.5	5.0
Costa Rica	National unemployment rate (b)		9.4[2]	6.8	4.6	5.5[3]
	National urban unemployment rate	3.0	6.0	6.7	5.4	4.3
	National underemployment rate		16.3	16.1		
	Visible underemployment rate		17.3	17.7[6]		
	Hidden underemployment rate		12.0	14.7[6]		14.3[3]
	Agricultural unemployment rate		3.9	5.5[6]		3.2[3]
	Visible agricultural underemployment rate		23.5	27.6[6]		15.6[3]
	Hidden agricultural underemployment rate		15.4	25.2[6]		29.4[3]
Ecuador	National unemployment rate		6.7[1]	9.8	11.4[4]	
	National urban unemployment rate			10.4	6.1	8.5[3]
El Salvador	National urban unemployment rate				10.0	8.0
Guatemala	National unemployment rate		2.2	12.9	6.4	6.5[3]
Honduras	National average unemployment rate		8.8	11.7		
	National urban unemployment rate			11.7	6.9	7.6[3]
Jamaica	National unemployment rate (c)		27.6[2]	25.0	15.7	
Mexico	National urban unemployment rate (d)		4.2[2]	4.4	2.8	2.6[3]
Nicaragua	National unemployment rate (a)			3.2	11.1	14.0[3]
Panama	National unemployment rate (d)		8.4[2]	12.3	16.3[5]	
	Panama City metropolitan unemployment rate			15.7	20.0	18.0
Paraguay	National unemployment rate		4.6	8.0	7.5	
	Unemployment rate in major urban areas			5.1	6.6	6.0
Peru	National unemployment rate		6.6[2]	7.1	8.3	9.4
	Unemployment rate metropolitan Lima (c)		7.1	10.1	8.3	5.9[3]
	National rate of underemployment		28.0[2]	42.6[6]	73.1	75.9
	Non-agricultural unemployment rate	8.3	10.9	17.6		
Uruguay	National unemployment rate				8.5	
	Unemployment rate in Montevideo	7.5	7.4	13.1	9.3	9.3
	National rate of underemployment				7.0	
Venezuela	National unemployment rate	6.9	5.9	13.0	9.2[5]	
	National urban unemployment rate	7.8	6.6	14.3	10.5	8.0
Asia						
China	Urban unemployment rate			1.8	2.5	2.3
Hong Kong	Unemployment (excluding unpaid family work – one or more hours) (d)			3.2	1.3	2.0
Republic of Korea	National unemployment rate (d)		5.2	4.0	2.4	2.4
Pakistan	National unemployment rate (a)			3.7	3.1	6.3
Philippines	National unemployment rate (d)		4.8	6.1	8.1	8.6
Singapore	National unemployment rate (d)		3.0	4.1	1.7	2.7
Sri Lanka	National unemployment rate (a)				14.4	14.1

[1] 1983; [2] 1982; [3] 1991; [4] 1988; [5] 1989; [6] 1986.
(a) persons 10 years or older; (b) persons 16-66; (c) persons 14 years or older; (d) persons 15 years or older.

Source: de Jainvry (1994) for Latin America; ILO for Asia.

and social and political unrest, could occur given the large numbers, including many educated young people, who face faint prospects of advancing into modern-sector jobs.

In South Asia a significant challenge remains because of the widespread poverty and underemployment that still exists in spite of some progress in alleviating these problems over the past decade. Much hinges on the successful management of the economic reforms that have only recently been initiated. If the higher growth rates of the past decade are maintained or even exceeded then employment trends should continue to improve. Nevertheless, it could take a few decades before the substantial labour surplus is eliminated. Not least of the reasons is the continuing high rate of population and labour force growth. The labour force in South Asia is projected to grow by 2.1 per cent per annum for the rest of the decade and is likely to remain at this level even further beyond. This implies the influx of a little over 10 million jobseekers a year until the end of the decade. The magnitude of the task of labour absorption that this represents can easily be appreciated when we observe that total employment in the modern sector stood at about 60 million at the end of the 1980s.

In China the outlook is better in spite of the similarity to South Asia in terms of the sheer size of its rural population. This is because GDP growth rates have been more than double those of South Asia, while rates of increase of population and labour force are substantially lower.

In Latin America the picture is mixed. While the majority of countries have achieved macroeconomic stability, significant economic restructuring and growth rates of over 3 per cent, problems remain in other countries. Brazil, Ecuador, Peru, Uruguay, and Venezuela still had inflation rates of over 30 per cent in 1992. At the same time four countries (Brazil, Jamaica, Nicaragua and Peru) had growth rates which were either negative or below 0.5 per cent per annum. Thus the recovery has not spread fully, although a few countries achieved very high growth in 1991 and 1992. An added problem is the backlog of underemployment that arose from the recession in the 1980s; this has to be reduced over and above catering for normal labour force growth. As in South Asia the prospects for improvements in the employment situation are crucially dependent on the successful implementation of economic reforms and a sustained return to higher rates of output growth.

The impact of globalization on employment

The new context

The world of the 1990s is very different from that of the 1950s, when issues of employment, income inequality and poverty in developing countries first attracted the attention of policy-makers. The world at mid-century was not closely integrated.

Today globalization has triumphed. The world economy is more closely integrated than ever before: the market is rapidly superseding government controls and planning as a mechanism for allocating resources; and liberal ideas about economic management and social policy have acquired a near monopoly in intellectual circles. Thus the context in which employment, income inequality and poverty are discussed has changed beyond recognition.

Globalization has had two consequences which deserve emphasis. First, it has created opportunities for material betterment. By enlarging national markets to encompass the global economy, it has expanded the dimensions of the market enormously, encouraged greater specialization and division of labour, and thereby created conditions which facilitate the growth of incomes and output. The effects of globalization go far beyond the potential benefits arising from a reallocation of resources and the exploitation of static comparative advantage. The benefits include the creation of new markets, the transfer of technology across national borders and the creation of new technologies, the movement of finance capital on a huge scale, and the stimulation of investment. In other words, much more is at stake than a simple change in the composition of output in response to a change in relative prices.

A second consequence of globalization is that it has weakened the ability of individual States to manage their economies. At the macroeconomic level, the mobility of finance capital has reduced government control over interest rates and the exchange rate; the flexibility of multinational enterprises has reduced the ability of government to affect the level of investment and its geographical location; and the international mobility of technical and highly skilled labour has made it more difficult for governments to impose progressive income and wealth taxes and to sustain high levels of public expenditure.

The impact of globalization on labour demand

These changes have affected employment policies and outcomes both positively and negatively. To begin with, the relative growth of international trade has increased pressures on governments to manage their economies so as to facilitate trading success. Among other things, this has made the real exchange rate (a joint product of the nominal exchange rate and domestic inflation relative to that of the rest of the world) an extremely important variable, constraining governments' freedom of action with respect both to the nominal exchange rate and to policies bearing upon inflation.

Competition among developing countries for foreign investment similarly restricts their macroeconomic freedom. There is ample evidence that private investment is deterred by macroeconomic instability and that the developing-country governments most successful in attracting investors have been those giving priority to macro stability. The convergence in thinking about policy includes a far wider recognition than formerly of the importance of prudent fiscal and monetary policy stances, and the high cost of rapid inflation.

Globalization thus constrains governments to give macro management a higher priority than they might otherwise have chosen. The key issue is what implications this has for the promotion of employment. In important respects the implications are positive. There is an obvious imperative for countries faced with a binding foreign exchange constraint to give priority to strengthening their balances of payments. There is a similar imperative upon countries with low savings and/or investment rates to avoid discouraging both by rapid inflation. Their exemplary records of macroeconomic management are regarded as a major reason for the economic (and employment) successes of the East Asian "miracle" economies and there is a good deal of evidence from elsewhere of the positive growth effects of macro stability.[3]

These considerations suggest that the premium placed on macro management due to globalization is beneficial for employment creation. However, it is necessary to qualify such a conclusion. For one thing, when an economy is characterized by inflationary and balance-of-payments pressures, it is difficult, in the short run, for a government to restore stability without short-term losses of output and employment. Thus, there arises an intertemporal trade-off.

A further qualification to the conclusion that stability is good for employment is that, in practice, stabilization often takes forms which have adverse and sustained effects on investment levels (and therefore on the potential for job creation). This, for example, is a finding of most studies of the economic effects of International Monetary Fund and World Bank adjustment programmes.[4] These effects occur because governments find their capital budgets easier to cut in times of financial stringency and because private investment tends to remain low, despite the improved policy environment, owing to heightened uncertainties generated by the programmes and the negative effects of reduced public infrastructural spending. This result helps to explain another: Bank and Fund-sponsored adjustment programmes are generally not associated with significant changes in economic growth, at least in the short to medium term.

All in all, therefore, there is a long-run tendency for a positive effect, but there are pitfalls along the way.

Happily, there are a number of policy areas upon which it is possible to report more positively. Perhaps the most important of these relates to the relative prices of labour and capital which exert a strong influence on the employment elasticity of an economy's growth path. There seems little doubt that globalization encourages developing-country governments toward policy choices favourable to employment, i.e. which tend to raise the cost of capital relative to labour. This rise occurs first through the necessity to avoid currency overvaluation, which would lower the price of imported capital goods in terms of local currency. It may be useful to point out in this context that a number of developing countries in East and South-East Asia and Latin America have lowered their real effective exchange rates considerably since the mid-1980s (see figure 6). The increase in the relative cost of capital occurs also through the relaxation and rationalization of import restrictions which have accompanied the opening-up of economies. There has been a near-universal tendency within protectionist regimes to place the highest trade barriers on finished consumer goods (to protect local manufacturing) and the lowest on imported capital goods – thus

Figure 6.
Real effective exchange rates, 1979-92

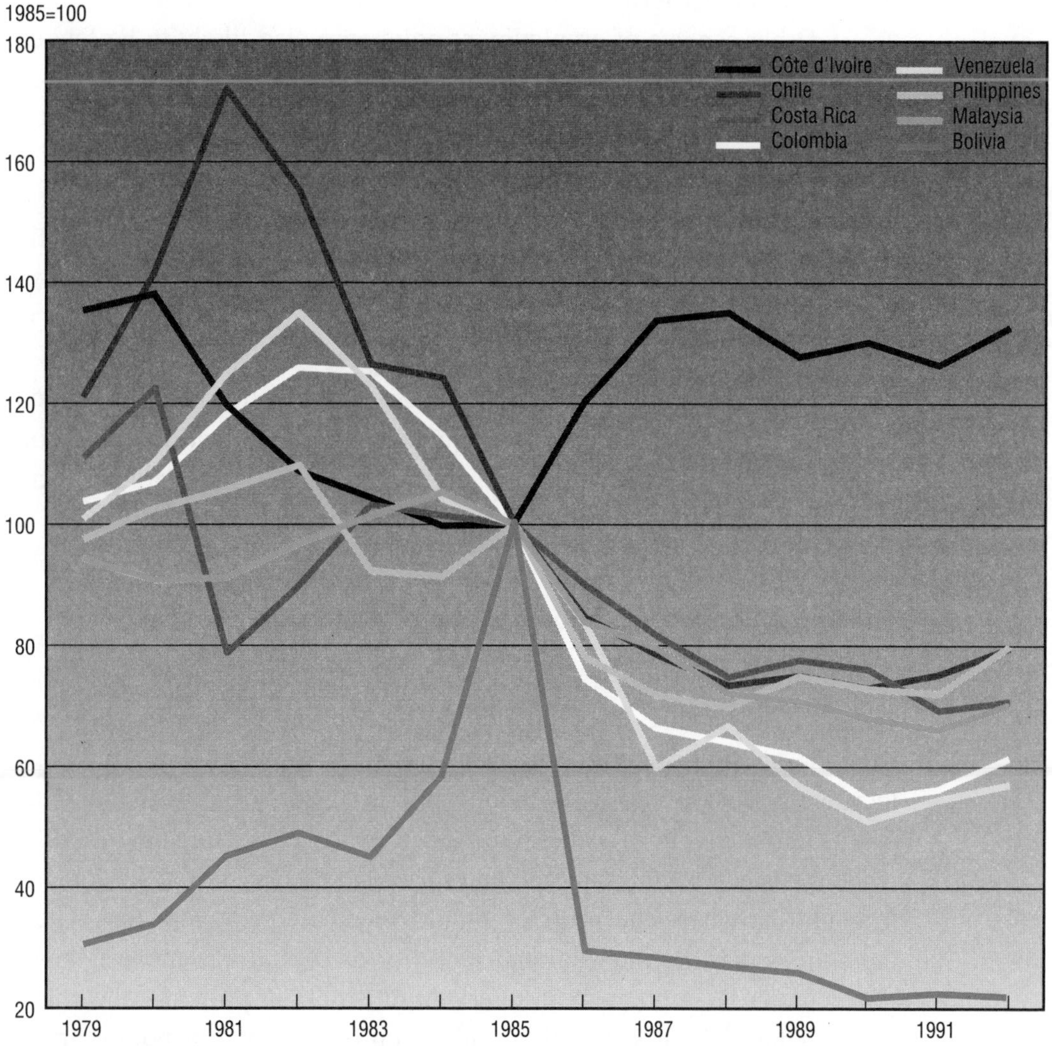

1985=100

REER based on relative consumer prices.

Source: International Monetary Fund: *International Financial Statistics Yearbook* (various issues).

lowering the effective local-currency cost of capital. Furthermore, financial sector liberalization, also integral to the opening-up process, helps to ensure that the cost of capital reflects its scarcity value in capital-scarce countries, removing or reducing state-imposed ceilings on interest rates and other aspects of "financial repression".

On balance, then, the association of globalization with liberalization in many developing countries is to be viewed positively as a policy shift favouring sustained growth of output and employment. However, in countries with industrial sectors which grew up behind high trade barriers there remains a rather acute short- to medium-term problem of transition to international competitiveness, with dangers of sometimes large-scale job losses in industries that cannot make the transition, or can do so only on the basis of substantial layoffs. Again, this reflects a trade-off between the shorter and longer terms.

Other aspects of employment policy are also likely to be favourably affected by globalization trends. They are likely to reinforce policies for the development of the rural economy, and to alleviate rural-urban inequalities by creating productive work opportunities in rural areas and so reduce incentives for rural-to-urban migration, with its attendant problems of urban unemployment. Such reinforcement is likely to come from the relaxing of industrial protectionism just discussed, from higher producer prices for agricultural and agro-industrial exports (via changes in exchange rate and tax policies), and from the greater priority given to agricultural development in the new consensus on policies.

Overall, then, the net effect is very sensitive to the time-frame employed. In the shorter term, the adverse consequences of adjustment probably dominate; in the longer term, the positive effects are more likely to prevail, especially if macro stabilization and liberalization have their predicted beneficial effects.

The impact of globalization on labour standards

However, in several important respects globalization has made it harder for governments to raise labour standards. The reason for this is that government interventions, say, to raise minimum wages or improve working conditions, almost always increase the cost of employing labour and shift the distribution of factor incomes against profits and in favour of wages. Globalization, by increasing the mobility of firms, has made it easier for multinational enterprises to escape these consequences by moving to countries where the costs of employment are relatively low. The other side of the coin is that the international mobility of capital has made it more difficult for governments to implement an interventionist labour policy of the conventional type.

Thus, labour legislation and its enforcement is a policy area in which the forces of globalization are likely to have adverse consequences, tending, therefore, to erode the quality of formal-sector employment. This tendency largely arises from pressures to compete successfully on world markets for manufactured goods and from competition to attract foreign direct investment, and has to be set against the additional jobs that are created as a result of such endeavours. There is evidence that foreign investment decisions are sensitive to the content and implementation of labour market legislation. The desire to attract investment therefore gives governments an incentive to dilute, or fail to enact, measures intended to protect the welfare of workers, or to turn a blind eye to infringements of legislation with this in mind.

These fears concerning the dilution of labour standards in the face of trade liberalization and increased competition for foreign investment surfaced sharply in the controversy about labour conditions in export processing zones (EPZs). These zones are free of trade controls and often provide an institutional framework tailor-made for foreign investors. In the worst cases, trade unions are banned, or strongly discouraged; wages are very low; working hours are exceptionally long; and various other safeguards, e.g. with respect to health, safety and holidays, either do not apply or are not enforced.[5] Sometimes, the laissez-faire environment leads to actual human rights abuses. Firms can infringe workers' rights without serious risk of legal consequences.

However, conditions in EPZs vary a lot between countries. Experience shows that they also change as they develop, with unionization rates rising, the proportion of women workers declining and real earnings increasing (steeply in East Asia), admittedly from a low base. It is also easy to attribute too much to the forces of international competition: the quality of employment is poor in low-income countries characterized by excess labour supply, so it makes more sense to compare conditions in EPZs with those prevailing elsewhere in the domestic economy than with conditions in more developed economies. Such comparisons have tended to show that wages and working conditions in EPZs are often equal to or higher than in comparable jobs outside them.

Within the framework of the ILO's Tripartite Declaration on Multinational Enterprises and Social Policy of 1977, a voluntary international code of conduct for MNE operations, triennial surveys are undertaken of the effect given to this code in member States. The most recent, the Fifth Survey of 1992, refers to experience under the code during the years 1989 through 1991.[6] This indicated that the Declaration's principles were fairly widely observed. MNEs were generally found to comply with national legislation, and often applied standards relating to wages, benefits, conditions of work, and occupational safety and health which both exceeded statutory requirements and those practised by domestic firms.

However, workers' organizations in particular identified a number of concerns arising from the widespread restructuring and reorganization of production, some of which may be associated with the trend toward more integrated global strategies within MNEs. Thus, while MNEs were generally positively assessed in their avoidance of arbitrary dismissal, workers' organizations identified substantial concern with job insecurity. Similarly, some respondents pointed to restrictions on freedom of association and the right to organize and bargain collectively. The introduction of new patterns of labour-management relations emphasizing "firm-centric" cooperation were associated by a few respondents with subtle union-avoidance strategies or the more explicit promotion of company unions. In addition, a few respondents recorded difficulties arising from the properly multinational nature of MNEs. Access to relevant information for bargaining purposes, or to "real decision-makers" was cited by a few respondents. A few workers' organizations also noted difficulties in obtaining information from MNE affiliates in other countries or in establishing cross-border consultations with such affiliates. The evolution toward more globally integrated strategies can be expected to keep such concerns alive.

On export processing zones, respondents stated that national labour laws, including those relating to industrial relations, applied in the EPZs. A few governments and worker organizations nevertheless reported instances where investment incentives had included restrictions on freedom of association and the right to organize, coupled with the lack of adequate mechanisms and support for dispute resolution.

While EPZs still remain a minor part of the overall employment picture in developing countries, they can nevertheless be seen as precursors of the types of problems over labour standards that are likely to arise on a much larger scale as globalization intensifies. For reasons set out earlier, these problems cannot be adequately addressed through national action alone. International action is clearly required to safeguard against a competitive debasement of labour standards in the drive to improve shares in world trade and attract foreign investment. This debasement is undesirable both on humanitarian grounds and because it provides protectionist interests within industrial countries with a weapon to reestablish discriminatory barriers against imports from developing countries.

The underlying problem is not a new one. Indeed, it was an important part of the rationale for establishing the ILO in 1919. Its Constitution mentions that:

> ... the failure of any nation to adopt humane conditions of labour is an obstacle in the way of other nations which desire to improve the conditions in their own countries.

While the basic framework for cooperative international action to safeguard and improve labour standards is in place, a fresh impetus is required in the face of the increased scale and intensity of the current process of globalization. Without this new impetus there is a real danger that much of the progress achieved over the past 75 years will be undone. Worse, the process of globalization itself, which promises much in terms of material progress, can be undermined by growing inequality and social conflict within and between countries.

The specific form which this new impetus should take remains a matter of controversy, as evidenced by the current debate over the inclusion of a social clause in international trade agreements. But this debate over form should not obscure the fact that there is a substantive underlying problem to be solved and that inaction would be harmful for economic and social progress globally. The issue should therefore be given the highest priority in international efforts to develop a more effective institutional framework to regulate the new global economy. An exclusive focus on economic issues such as trade, investment and finance, ignoring or underemphasizing their social implications, is unlikely to yield satisfactory and sustainable outcomes.

Policy responses to globalization

Provided that an effective solution is found to the problem of labour standards, countries are likely to do better on the employment front if they adopt policies that respond positively to globalization, and that are designed to take advantage of trading and other opportunities that are resulting (as against passive or defensive responses, based on a generalized distrust of globalization, that place the domestic economy at a competitive disadvantage). The most successful developing economies, in terms of output and employment growth, have been those that have best exploited emerging opportunities in the global economy. This has been true in terms of exploiting potential export markets and of gaining a place in emerging networks of global production fuelled by the growth of foreign direct investment. In contrast, countries which have failed to respond to the new opportunities created by globalization

Figure 7.
Manufacturing exports and employment,1980-90 (annual average growth rate, percentage)

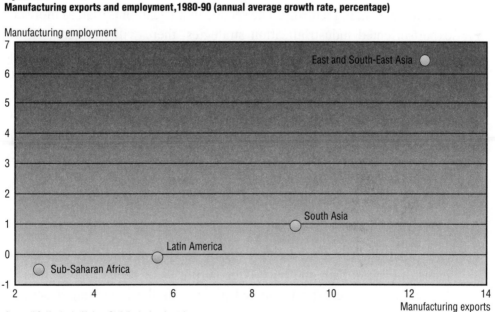

Source: ILO: *Yearbook of Labour Statistics* (various issues).

have performed poorly and, in many cases, have experienced economic retrogression. It is evident from figure 7 that East and South-East Asia, which experienced by far the highest rate of growth of manufacturing exports during the 1980s, also had the highest employment growth. At the other extreme was sub-Saharan Africa with its low manufacturing exports growth and negative employment growth in that sector.

Two important means of capturing the potential gains from globalization in terms of higher growth of output and employment are the adoption of export-led industrialization policies and the attraction of FDI. As seen in Part I, by far the fastest growth in developing country exports in the past three decades has been in manufacturing. Barring any resurgence of protectionism in industrialized countries, an expansion of manufacturing exports should continue to be an effective means of reaping benefits from globalization. Similarly, countries which have succeeded best in attracting FDI have experienced rapid growth in manufacturing output and exports.

However, two important qualifications need to be made immediately. The first is that not all developing countries currently have comparative advantage in manufacturing.[7] Countries which are land-abundant, rich in natural resources and with low levels of human resource development are more likely to have comparative advantage in primary production than in manufacturing. For these countries, the adoption of open economic policies would mean greater specialization in primary production. The employment creation gains from trade could, in these cases, be increased through diversification of primary exports and greater domestic processing of primary products. Even in these countries, however, the longer-term strategy should be to increase the skill level of the labour force in order to acquire comparative advantage in manufacturing. The second qualification is that, as more countries adopt export-oriented industrialization strategies, there will be increased competition in world markets for manufactured exports. This will tend to reduce the terms of trade for exporters of manufactures but it is unlikely that this will eliminate the advantage of specializing in manufactured exports in countries with comparative advantage in such production. It is relevant to note in this connection that early starters in export-led manufacturing such as the Asian NICs have since shifted up from labour-intensive to more skill-intensive production, thus liberating markets for labour-intensive exports to late starters.

Trade and industrialization

An export-oriented policy regime is vital in countries that are starting on the industrialization path and have large surpluses of cheap labour. It is also important to maintain strong export-oriented policies as the industrial structure matures and grows more complex. Export orientation provides the discipline that both firms and policy-makers need to ensure that industrial policy leads to a competitive industrial sector rather than to a protected and technologically slothful structure that provides neither growth nor employment.

The most direct way of ensuring export-oriented industrialization is to follow a strategy approximating free trade. In countries that cannot, or do not wish to follow such a strategy, export incentives and facilities (like EPZs and bonded status to export-oriented firms outside such zones) can provide an effective means of creating employment. Most countries in East and South-East Asia have used export incentives of this type, often backed by other measures to promote (even force) export growth, such as subsidized credit, access to import licences for domestic production, tax credits, information provision and so on.[8] These measures have been used to offset the protection given to infant industries being fostered to the countries' long-term comparative advantage. They have permitted spectacular growth in the exports of simple manufactured goods in the early stages of their industrial development. However, as long as market failures exist in product markets (newcomers to industry cannot face the full force of competition from established producers in activities with complex technologies and long, risky learning periods) and factor markets (skills, technology, capital and so on), a policy of non-intervention can hold back the industrialization process. The lesson from South-East Asia is precisely that, where selective interventions are well designed and implemented, and directed at remedying these market failures, the results are startling rates of growth, diversification and technological prowess. In contrast, economies that have liberalized rapidly and without adequate provision to overcome market failures have failed to reproduce this sort of performance, even if they have been very open to FDI. The case of Chile, with the longest experience of liberalization in the developing world, is very relevant here. Its manufacturing export growth has been relatively weak (3.3 per cent per annum over 1980-88), and the growth has come mainly from resource-based activities that have "natural protection" and relatively short learning periods. Despite two decades of liberalization and its large human resource base Chile's manufacturing exports per capita are only $96 compared to $3,500 for Taiwan, China.[9] Clearly, the real issue is how interventions can be well designed, implemented and integrated between the trade and supply-side variables.

In any case, "classical" forms of import-substituting protection should be avoided. Such policies, involving wholesale and indiscriminate protection to manufacturing industry, can inhibit dynamic growth. They often fail to address the market failures that hold back development in industrial newcomers, because they are not selectively applied and their duration is not geared to the "learning" period needed to absorb new technologies. They do not tackle the basic incentive problem created by import protection, that protection itself takes away the need to invest in the difficult, expensive and prolonged process of building up the new capabilities needed to master new technologies. In addition, the granting of protection in classic import-substituting economies has not been integrated with measures to remedy failures in factor markets (especially for skills, information, credit and infrastructure).

If infant industry protection is given, this should apply only to a few activities at a time. These activities should have the potential to be fully competitive in a reasonable period of time, should involve difficult technologies that need time and effort to absorb, and be in the country's long-term comparative advantage. Protection should be limited in duration and offset by strong incentives to invest in upgrading capabilities, e.g. measures to promote exports. It must be complemented by measures to provide the specific skills, the financing and the technological support needed to achieve competitiveness. Infant industry protection should be constantly monitored and administered flexibly, so that mistakes can be rectified quickly. And it should draw upon the considerable experience of such industrial policy in South-East Asia. Only then can industrial employment be promoted in the long term, based on a competitive and dynamic industrial sector.

Thus, while a thrust towards export orientation is desirable, this is not equivalent to a rejection in principle of all forms of trade intervention. There is a danger of going too far in the direction of reducing interventions. Indeed, there is neither theoretical nor empirical support for complete lack of intervention when market failures abound. Many activities, especially those involving high levels of skill and technology and extensive supply linkages, may need a period of temporary protection to get established at any depth in a developing country.

Foreign direct investment

Recent experience has shown that the successful attraction of FDI can be a powerful spur to rapid industrialization and employment creation. Indeed, adopting effective policies to this end is an important means of gaining access to the benefits of globalization. MNEs offer many advantages that other forms of capital inflow cannot: equity flows are often a safer way of financing than fixed debt, the growth of international production is inexorable in certain activities, and MNE investment often represents the easiest and most efficient way to gain access to advanced technologies and skills as well as export markets. The presence of MNEs may be particularly important for countries at early stages of development when indigenous entrepreneurial and technological skills are scarce and factor markets are highly imperfect. It also becomes especially significant at more advanced stages of industrial development when state-of-the-art technologies are needed that local sources cannot supply.

Apart from factors that policy cannot directly affect (like location, size, resource base, external shocks or the political system), important variables affecting the inflow of FDI are economic and policy stability, a favourable attitude towards private enterprise in general, good infrastructure and macroeconomic management, clear and transparent policies towards investors, and a trade and industrial regime that allows MNEs to operate in internationally competitive conditions.[10] There is general consensus that large tax and other incentives to foreign investors are not a good way to attract FDI. Serious investors pay more attention to the underlying long-term economic situation rather than to tax concessions that run out in a relatively short time.

It may be desirable to target or promote foreign entry into sectors or activities that benefit employment creation in developing host countries. In Asia, MNEs have been particularly effective in raising employment levels in labour-intensive assembly activities aimed at world markets, like garments, semiconductors, other electronic and electrical products, toys and shoes. However, because of technological progress and automation, some of these activities no longer offer the possibilities of employment creation that they did two decades ago. This is particularly true of semiconductor assembly. Nevertheless, others continue to remain labour-intensive, in particular garments and shoes, and the assembly of certain types of consumer electronics.[11] At low levels of industrialization, such FDI can be very useful for creating employment and opening the economy to international markets; there may be some entrepreneurial skills created in simple activities like garments (as has happened in Bangladesh). Moreover, in some cases, as in Malaysia, the investors may strike deeper roots and invest in more capital-intensive technologies as wages rise.

However, the attraction of such investments is not easy. It needs not only cheap labour (many sub-Saharan countries, for instance, have lower wages than most Asian countries but are failing to attract export-oriented labour-intensive investments), but also a certain level of literacy, worker discipline, physical infrastructure and a stock of local technical and managerial talent. Moreover, after assembly operations start, it is necessary for the host economy to invest in building up new skills and infrastructure to enable foreign investors to upgrade their facilities. The need for proactive policies by the host government to promote the deepening of the industrial structure is constant and universal. No economy is insulated from competition from other low-wage countries seeking to attract export-oriented investors into labour-intensive activities, and countries have to upgrade continuously in order to maintain their locational advantage.

Just as important is the need for policies to secure entry to new, more demanding industrial and service activities so as to diversify the industrial structure, increase local linkages and find new sources of comparative advantage. This is crucial to the creation and maintenance of employment in the longer term, and to the raising of its quality. Dependence on a few simple assembly products is unlikely to drive the process of structural transformation that development involves. Thus, MNEs have to be encouraged to invest in more complex technologies and activities over time, and local supply capacity has to be improved in order to capture more value added for the economy and to diffuse skills. This requires policies to create incentives (direct incentives to MNEs as well as trade and industrial policies more generally) and to favourably affect supply-side variables. Some countries have encouraged structural transformation by offering infant industry protection to complex activities and by enforcing local content provisions. Others target foreign investors that can offer more advanced technologies of interest to the government and encourage them to buy locally and/or conduct more technological activities in the host country. Others still restrict

MNEs to activities that local enterprises are unable to undertake, and invest in building up the technological capabilities of the latter to internationally competitive levels. There are success stories for each approach.

The correct set of policies on the sectoral composition of FDI depends very much on the level of development of the host economy and the strategic approach of the government. The objectives of raising the quantity of employment, improving its quality over time and maintaining the momentum of growth and competitiveness of the productive sectors can be pursued in several different ways. Each calls for proactive policies by the host government, but the nature of the measures may differ.

In general, carefully designed and evaluated incentives can help to achieve certain objectives and overcome particular market deficiencies. The ideal incentives are those that guide economically desirable investments into activities and areas in the country's interest that would not be adequately promoted by market signals alone. In the employment field, these could be incentives to enter activities that are employment-intensive, areas that suffer from high unemployment, and technologies that are particularly demanding of skills, and to set up local facilities for labour training and technological development. Needless to say, the incentives should not be excessive in relation to the benefits sought, and they should not attempt to distort long-term economic forces. In fact, it is important to ensure that market distortions are removed to the extent possible before granting incentives. The incentives themselves should not discriminate between firms (say, between local and foreign firms); their main aim should be to remedy market failures that impede healthy development.

Adjustment measures

The adoption of these trade liberalization, export-oriented industrialization and investment promotion policies will for many countries amount to a far-reaching programme of economic reform. As pointed out earlier, many developing countries still have to undertake a serious adjustment effort before they are able to reap the potential gains from globalization. These are countries which still suffer from macro-economic instability and a burden of external debt,[12] which still have high levels of protection in their trade regime and where other economic reforms remain to be implemented. The agenda for reform clearly needs to be pursued but the manner in which the transition to a more open and liberalized economy is managed is a critical determinant of success.

Two key, and interrelated, elements are measures to facilitate the redeployment of labour from declining activities to new ones and the minimization of the social costs of adjustment. The interrelationship between these two elements arises from the fact that effective measures to facilitate redeployment will reduce the extent and duration of transitional unemployment and hence lower the social costs of adjustment. Similarly, measures to reduce these costs by moderating the pace of adjustment will mitigate the severity of the labour redeployment problem.

An important lesson from the initial round of stabilization and structural adjustment programmes in the wake of the debt crisis in the early 1980s is that instantaneous adjustment is neither economically feasible nor socially sustainable. The economic problem arises from the fact that the structure of production and institutions can adjust only with significant time-lags. This is not only because of the gestation periods inherent in implementing new investments and in retraining labour. It is also because in the context of low-income countries supportive measures such as improving basic infrastructure, increasing the availability of credit, and strengthening both market institutions and the administrative capacity of government are often important determinants of the capacity to respond to new incentives. Without such measures supply responses to new economic incentives created by economic reforms will be slow. It would hence be desirable to allow sufficient time for supportive measures to be put in place in drawing up programmes for economic reform.

Another powerful argument for avoiding a precipitate implementation of reforms is that the capacity to adopt effective measures for labour redeployment and to provide social safety nets is typically weak. Labour administrations have virtually no experience in coping with mass redundancies through retraining and other active labour market programmes that are common in industrialized countries. Similarly, social safety nets are often non-existent or highly inadequate. For both these reasons it is desirable to avoid a large and sudden increase in redundancies and the abrupt adoption of measures such as the removal of consumption subsidies which will reduce the living standards of the poor. Again it is important to make adequate advance preparations within the reform programme for providing both redeployment assistance and a social safety net.

The redeployment and safety net measures need to be adapted to circumstances prevailing in developing countries. For example, where the modern sector is small and dominated by public-sector employment it may not be feasible to redeploy all retrenched workers to alternative modern-sector jobs. In such cases there will be only limited scope for measures such as retraining, and adjustment assistance will have to take other forms such as the promotion of self-employment and the organization of public employment programmes. Such direct employment creation programmes are also an important means of providing basic income support for the poor who are adversely affected by the adjustment programme. In low-income countries there is likely to be a continuous need for such measures even in the absence of the additional hardships created by economic reforms. (Issues relating to such schemes are discussed in more detail in a following section.) The essential point is that in the context of adjustment they should be geared up to meet additional needs generated by the process of adjustment.

The likelihood that developing countries will successfully implement appropriate redeployment and safety net programmes can be increased in various ways. Within the government, the first requirement is to strengthen the capacity of ministries of labour to either design and execute redeployment and safety net programmes directly or oversee the implementation of such programmes when they are entrusted to special agencies or to non-governmental organizations. This will ensure that concern over the social costs of adjustment is backed up by a real capacity to implement programmes. The second requirement is to give ministries of labour a stronger role in the formulation of structural adjustment programmes, among other things involving them in negotiations over policy conditionality where this is an important element. The reason for this is that labour ministries usually have a clear social mandate and hence their involvement in the formulation of economic policy would help to ensure that social dimensions are duly taken into account.

But more is required than just government action. The social partners, too, should be consulted on the design and implementation of adjustment programmes. This is important for at least two reasons. The first is one of principle, namely that those most affected by economic reforms should be consulted. The second is of a practical nature in that such consultations are necessary for building essential support for the reform programme. Since economic reforms have far-reaching effects on the structure of production, on the level and structure of wages, and on the organization of work within enterprises, their success depends to an important extent on the support that can be mobilized from the main protagonists, i.e. workers and employers. Without such support reform efforts in areas such as wages policy, labour legislation and enterprise restructuring can be thwarted by industrial unrest and the obstruction of change.

In order to make tripartite consultations substantive and of real value it will be necessary to strengthen the capacity of trade unions and employers' organizations to analyse and discuss economic policy issues. This involves training officials and ensuring that the organizations have access to relevant information. A fundamental prior requirement, however, is respect for basic rights such as freedom of association, for, without this, representative and viable organizations of workers and employers cannot develop. Such development is important not only for promoting socially sustainable adjustment programmes but also for the more basic reason that they are essential for the attainment of social justice and the development of democratic societies.

The formulation of a sound adjustment programme should also be guided by policies to promote the growth of productive employment and the reduction of poverty. Such policies will, of course, need to be pursued whether or not a formal structural adjustment programme is necessary in the initial period. Even in countries that are not burdened by problems of macroeconomic imbalances and external debt, there is often much that remains to be done to raise the rate of employment creation. The main characteristics of desirable employment promotion policies are therefore discussed in the following sections.

Labour market regulation

Labour market deregulation has often featured as an element of structural adjustment programmes. It is argued that excessive government intervention in labour markets through public-sector wage and employment policies, minimum wage fixing and employment security rules is a serious impediment to adjustment and should therefore be removed or relaxed. On this reasoning, in order to adjust successfully to globalization, developing countries should implement substantial deregulation of their labour markets.

In support of this argument a contrast is often drawn between the extent of labour market regulation in Latin America and the newly industrializing countries in Asia. It has been argued that the over-regulation of the labour market in Latin America has both entrenched labour market dualism between a highly protected urban formal sector and a largely unprotected informal sector and has impeded labour market adjustment to changing market forces. In contrast, it is argued that labour markets are only sparsely regulated in the Asian NICs and that this has been an essential factor behind the successful implementation of export-led development strategies. Moreover, it has been contended that, far from abstaining in labour markets, Asian governments actively repressed the independent activities of trade unions, particularly in their wage-setting role, at the formative stages of the export-led development strategy.

Two questions arise in this connection. Was the repression of trade unions a component of the Asian development model? If so, was it necessary for economic success?

On the first point, two observations can be made. First of all, trade union freedoms were indeed curtailed in many Asian countries, originally for political reasons, and subsequently for economic ones.[13] Second, the patterns of trade union organization, industrial relations, and the restrictions applying to both are substantially different across Asian countries, so much so that it begs the question of whether one can refer to "an" Asian model of labour market policy. For example, while the Republic of Korea, Singapore and Taiwan, China, have severely controlled the activities of trade unions, Hong Kong, with its British tradition of voluntarism, has not. Furthermore, while the Republic of Korea at times took a variety of ad hoc measures to control or repress trade union activities, Singapore and Taiwan, China, have consistently attempted to ensure the control of a single political party over a single official trade union. Intervention in the wage-setting process has been virtually non-existent in Hong Kong, but moderate to strong in the Republic of Korea although, as will be noted below, now of declining significance; in Singapore, such intervention has for long been part of a corporatist arrangement in which the trade union movement, through its involvement in the tripartite National Wage Council, has been able to exert some influence on economic and social policies within the admittedly narrow framework imposed by the State. In the 1970s, such corporatist mechanisms kept real wage growth considerably below the growth of real GDP; at the end of the decade, a policy of "wage correction" sought to resolve the resulting problem of labour shortage while encouraging industries to move up to more skill-intensive production.

It can thus be argued that, within the general market orientation of these economies, considerably more – or considerably less – than the free market was at work, and that the region itself seems characterized by greater diversity than is usually attributed to it.

Were these various patterns of control of labour market behaviour necessary for economic success? Here, an affirmative answer is doubtful. First, since so much else accounts for the success of export-led development in these economies, it would be hard to isolate the independent weight of labour market policy factors. As the World Bank observes: "workers are generally more willing to accept flexibility of wages around a rapidly rising trend because downward adjustment implies a slower rate of increase rather than an absolute decline in real earnings."[14] Second, the style and degree of repression varied across these countries, while their economic success was uniform: there would seem no obvious correlation between the diverse patterns of labour market and industrial relations policy in the region and the economic success enjoyed by these economies.[15]

In any case, the increasing role of both protective legislation and, in some settings, the growing maturity and independence of labour market institutions in these countries since the 1980s do not appear to have impeded continued growth. Considerable progress has been made in both the Republic of Korea and Taiwan, China, with regard to trade union rights. The negotiation of wage guidelines by the central employers' and workers' organizations in Korea in 1993 and 1994 mark a departure from the more pervasive influence of the State in the 1980s. Innovations in the flexibilization of wage policy under the aegis of Singapore's National Wage Council are an indication of social consensus on wage determination. As to the growth of protective legislation, additional statutes now add to the underlying welfare orientation apparent in many of these countries. Even in laissez-faire Hong Kong, for example, government provision of housing has been widespread, and there has more recently been an expansion of laws covering the employment relationship and occupational safety and health, along with that of a highly efficient labour inspectorate. Minimum wage legislation was introduced in the Republic of Korea in the late 1980s, and has a longer tradition in Thailand and Taiwan, China. The Republic of Korea will put in place an unemployment insurance system in 1995.[16]

These policy developments in Asia thus highlight the fact that neither a totally deregulated labour market nor labour repression is indispensable for success in export markets.

In the case of Latin America, there can be little doubt that these countries entered the decade of structural adjustment in the 1980s with a pattern of labour market regulation belonging to an earlier era – highly protected urban workers in the modern sector and a burgeoning and unprotected informal sector consisting of economic activity largely in services in agriculture, to which labour market regulation did not extend. Nor can there be any doubt that high levels of worker protection that apply to only a minority of the labour market create rigidities there and incentives for employment to expand in the unregulated sector. The historical pattern of labour market regulation in the region that developed during the era of import substitution therefore required reform.[17]

Yet this does not necessarily imply that labour market regulation was the sole or main cause of poor economic performance. To isolate the inappropriateness only of labour market regulation is to ignore impediments of more fundamental significance in the economic restructuring of the region. The collapse of the import-substitution model exposed rigidities in the labour market, but also laid bare an uncompetitive industrial structure and inappropriate macroeconomic and industrial policies. Reforming the latter has been the major challenge, and one that is con-siderably more basic than the mere obsolescence of a pattern of labour market regulation.

Another reason for believing that labour market regulation was not the main cause of poor economic performance was that formal rules were easily cir-cumvented. During the 1980s, the changes arising from structural adjustment policies made labour markets more flexible *de facto*. Formal regulations changed little but a process of "underground flexibilization" occurred. The informal sector grew at more than double the rate of formal-sector employment. At the same time, the shares of part-time, temporary, and subcontracted employment increased relative to full-time jobs. Within the formal sector, employment growth was greatest in the small-firm sector (10 employees or less) which accounted for over 40 per cent of formal-sector employment growth during the decade. A pronounced trend for large-firm sub-contracting to small firms in both the formal and the informal sector also became apparent.[18]

Wages were also severely affected, and, by the end of the decade, as a con-sequence of downward real wage flexibility, the erosion of real minimum wages and the devaluation of exchange rates, labour costs in Latin American manufacturing had declined sharply relative to the Asian NICs. The labour-cost advantage that all of the dynamic Asian economies had relative to Latin America in 1980 had eroded substantially or disappeared altogether by 1990. While such indicators of labour market flexibility have been everywhere apparent, the cost of this largely unregulated flexibility is also apparent in widening inequality, rising poverty, and continued unemployment and underemployment.

Since the 1980s, and with the return of democratic rule, the reform of labour legislation and some strengthening of trade unions and industrial relations are evident in Latin America. Many have amended regimes of employment security protection, either by broadening or easing the grounds under which dismissals can occur or by facilitating recourse to temporary forms of employment. The reform challenge is to establish reasonable and realistic standards which are applicable to all segments of the labour market. While inducing greater flexibility in the labour market, regulation ought also to aim at extending protection to larger segments of it. Constraints previously imposed on trade unions and collective bargaining have been lifted, and industrial relations, including tripartite consensus at the national level, have in some countries played a growing role in the solution to problems caused by adjustment.

This is perhaps most evident in Mexico, where major tripartite agreements include the Economic Solidarity Pact of 1987, which has been subsequently revised on several occasions and includes an anti-inflationary policy and a comprehensive incomes policy; the Pact for Stability and Economic Growth of 1988, which was aimed at promoting competitiveness and employment; and the National Accord for Raising Productivity and Quality. In addition to these tripartite agreements, a major programme of poverty alleviation (the National Solidarity Programme) targets the most vulnerable in the adjustment process.

In contrast to a national tripartite approach to regulatory adjustment stands Chile, which, following a period of repression of trade union rights during the 1970s, embarked on an extensive programme of labour market deregulation during the 1979-90 period. Industrial relations during this period were tightly controlled and confined to the enterprise level, and the right to strike was severely curtailed. At the outset of the reform process in the early 1980s, the relative absence of selective labour market policies or a social safety net resulted in high costs borne by substantial groups of the labour force. Unemployment was the direct result as public-sector employment contracted and inefficient private-sector firms shed jobs. As measured in terms of employment creation, the reduction of open unemployment and real-wage growth, the results of Chilean economic restructuring have begun to bear fruit since the mid-1980s. The return to democratic rule, moreover, has been accompanied by an expansion of protective labour legislation.

As in the case of Asia, therefore, these developments with respect to labour market regulation in Latin America do not provide any confirmation of the view that it is necessary to have an essentially unregulated labour market in order to be internationally competitive. While the experience has highlighted the importance of reforming inappropriate regulations it has also shown the value of avoiding totally unregulated flexibility. In particular, there have been positive examples of the benefits of tripartite consultation and a sound industrial relations systems in solving problems caused by adjustment.

Reducing underemployment and poverty

Adopting policies that respond positively to globalization is the key to achieving sustained growth and productive employment creation in developing countries. But for many countries this in itself will not be sufficient to reduce the massive underemployment and poverty that currently prevail. A successful shift to a more open economy and the acceleration of industrial growth and exports will undoubtedly boost employment creation through both its direct and its indirect effects. However, given the large proportion of the labour force that is still engaged in low-productivity activities, even a high rate of labour absorption into the modern sector will not solve problems of underemployment and poverty fast enough. Development strategies should therefore also aim to raise productivity in traditional agriculture and in the urban informal sector where large numbers will still have to find a livelihood for many years to come.

The magnitude of the problem can be illustrated using a few figures. In sub-Saharan Africa 70 per cent of the labour force were still employed in agriculture in 1992. In South Asia the corresponding proportion was 65 per cent. Even the larger countries which had enjoyed rapid growth for over a decade, such as China and Indonesia, had shares of 60 and 65 per cent respectively. In Latin America only four countries have more than 50 per cent of the population living in rural areas, but the urban informal sector is large: in 1992, 32 per cent of non-agricultural employment, equivalent to about a fifth of total employment, was in that sector. If we add to these the numbers employed in traditional agriculture then an average of one worker in three is employed outside the modern sector. Thus even in middle-income countries with high levels of urbanization, employment outside the modern sector is still substantial.

The problem is compounded by low productivity, substantial underemployment and a high incidence of poverty in the agricultural and urban informal sectors. In sub-Saharan Africa, for instance, the rural poor represent between 80 and 98 per cent of the total poor in a sample of countries for which data are available. In Latin America rapid urbanization has caused the incidence of poverty to shift increasingly to the urban areas: in 1990 35 per cent of the urban population were estimated to have been living in poverty. Moreover, underemployment in agriculture was estimated to be between 60 to 70 per cent in Peru, 39 to 47 per cent in El Salvador, and 29 per cent in Brazil.

These problems worsened over the 1980s in sub-Saharan Africa and Latin America. In sub-Saharan Africa indirect indicators point to a worsening of poverty: per capita calorie availability dropped significantly from an already low level in a majority of countries, while both the rate of increase in life expectancy and the decrease in infant mortality slowed down. In Latin America too, average poverty levels increased during the 1980s and average consumption per capita fell (table 13). Over the same period income inequality also increased: the Gini coefficient rose from 0.51 to 0.57.

These figures indicate that, while responding to globalization is now a strategic new concern, the "classical" development agenda defined in earlier decades still remains relevant. In order to reduce underemployment and poverty it is essential to ensure that allocation of investment is not biased against the agricultural and urban informal sectors. This can be achieved through appropriate public investment as well as institutional reforms to improve the access of producers in these sectors to capital markets. Apart from this there will be a need for programmes to raise productivity in the rural and urban informal sectors as well as direct for poverty alleviation programmes.

Investment

Those developing countries that have adopted policies to encourage a high rate of investment have succeeded in attaining rapid growth; those that have enjoyed rapid growth, in turn, have succeeded in creating employment opportunities, reducing

Figure 8.
Gross domestic investment and savings rates, 1970-91

Gross domestic investment rate　　　　　　**Gross domestic savings rate**

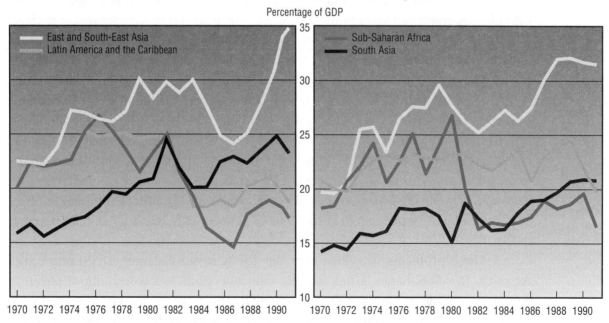

Source: World Bank, *Global Economic Prospects and Developing Countries* (1994).

the rate of unemployment and raising the real wages of low-skilled labour. It is evident from figure 8 that East and South-East Asia clearly saw the highest rates of investment and saving among the developing regions. Their growth and employment performance has also been the most buoyant. In addition, they have succeeded in creating income-earning opportunities and promoting more secure livelihoods for those not engaged in wage employment. Almost always this has been accompanied by some reduction in poverty and, in some cases, by reductions in inequality. Growth is thus necessary for a rapid decline in poverty, although not sufficient.

Physical capital formation remains a necessary condition for rapid economic growth, and the growth success of the low-income countries is due to the fact that they have allocated a larger share of their GDP to investment than have the OECD countries. In 1991, for example, the rate of investment in the low-income countries was 27 per cent of GDP – with rates of 36 per cent in China, 35 per cent in Indonesia and 20 per cent in India – as compared to 21 per cent in the OECD countries on average.

It is also important to invest in human capital. The most successful developing countries have not only had a high rate of physical capital formation; they have also given priority to human capital formation.

Investment in human capital – particularly in basic education, primary health care, nutrition and population programmes – can enjoy rates of return that are at least as high as the returns on conventional investments. Indeed, one of the characteristics of the highly successful East Asian economies is the priority given to human capital formation. Emphasis on human capital in countries such as China, Japan and the Republic of Korea has contributed not only to rapid growth but also to an employment-intensive growth pattern; this has resulted in an exceptionally fast increase in the real wages of working people and a dramatic decline in poverty.

Investment in human capital is often complementary to expenditures on physical capital. Where this occurs, it can help to raise the productivity of investment in physical capital and thereby provide an additional stimulus to growth. Moreover, investment in human capital tends to result in a more equitable distribution of wealth and hence is an effective way to redistribute assets in favour of the poor and thus improve equality.

It is not enough, however, to have a high rate of investment; it is just as important to allocate investment efficiently so that each unit of investment adds as much as possible to net income. It is here that many developing countries compare unfavourably with developed ones, and there is clearly scope for policy initiatives to raise the productivity of investment. If carried out, such initiatives would raise rates of growth and, more importantly, have a highly beneficial impact on employment, poverty alleviation and income equality.

A fundamental reason for the insufficient productivity of investment in developing countries is poor or no access to formal-sector credit leaving large sectors of the economy starved of financial support. Small urban businesses have much difficulty in obtaining credit; agriculture and livestock breeding are undersupplied, and small farmers obtain virtually no credit from banks; fishermen and rural artisans cannot obtain loans from commercial banks; the informal sector as a whole has little access to credit; and new enterprises in any sector are rarely able to obtain start-up capital. Most people in developing countries are either self-financed or use the informal credit market: money-lenders, traders, landlords, friends and relatives. Most formal-sector credit, in effect, is reserved for large, well-established, urban enterprises. The consequence of this huge capital market imperfection is that many potentially highly profitable private-sector enterprises fail to get established and many small but established enterprises are unable to grow rapidly for lack of capital.

There is, then, an opportunity for policy makers to improve the functioning of the capital market – by institutional innovation, by better regulation of the banking sector, by supporting credit programmes targeted at specific groups such as women, informal-sector entrepreneurs and small farmers, and by increasing the supply of "venture capital". An improvement in the allocation of capital within the private sector could contribute much to employment generation, to creating more income-earning opportunities for the self-employed and to a reduction in the incidence of poverty. The emphasis should be on encouraging new private-sector enterprises to emerge (preferably those which are small in scale and labour-intensive) and on enabling small private-sector enterprises to expand, innovate and penetrate new markets (including export markets).

In addition to instituting reforms to ensure wider access to credit it is also important to remove distortions which artificially reduce the cost of capital. Relative factor prices have a strong influence on the degree of mechanization, the labour intensity of production and the amount of employment created per unit of investment. If finance capital is "cheap" relative to the cost of employing labour – either because real interest rates are well below the opportunity cost of capital or real wage rates are above the opportunity cost of labour – methods of production will be excessively mechanized (i.e. the capital-labour ratio will be above the optimum), employment per unit of output will be below the optimum and, most importantly from the point of view of long-term growth, the number of new jobs created as a result of investment activities will be smaller than would otherwise be the case. Relative factor price distortions can arise from a malfunctioning either of the labour market or the market for credit. Whereas once it was thought that labour market imperfections were at the root of relative factor price distortions – i.e. that formal-sector workers received too high a wage – today it is widely accepted that the problem arises in the capital market, and specifically in many developing countries interest rate policy is strongly biased against the employment of labour. Figure 9 shows real interest rates in the Republic of Korea, Malaysia and Thailand, compared with Argentina, Ghana and Mexico. The contrast is remarkable. In the East Asian case, low inflation and flexible financial policies kept real interest rates positive, and within a narrow range. For the comparators, a combination of nominal interest rate controls with high and unstable inflation led to negative, and wildly fluctuating, real interest rates, thus biasing factor choice in favour of capital.

The problem is that interest rates in the commercial banking system are often too low, while they are often too high in the informal credit markets, assuming that credit is available at all. The result is that capital-intensity is raised in the formal sector, reducing the number of jobs created there. At the same time, capital-labour ratios outside the formal sector are too low and the productivity of labour is depressed. People may be employed, but their average incomes may leave them in poverty. There is thus a strong case on efficiency and equity grounds for lending to the poor, not by providing subsidized credit but by increasing the quantity of credit available at rates of interest determined by the market.

Figure 9.
Real interest rates: Examples from East and South-East Asia and other selected countries, 1970-87

Real interest rate (percentage)

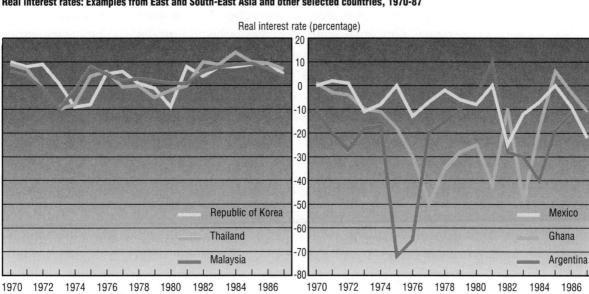

Source: World Bank, World Tables.

It was once thought that high transaction costs, absence of collateral and high risks of default precluded lending programmes for the very poor. The enormous success of the Grameen Bank in Bangladesh, however, which devised highly innovative credit schemes in rural areas, particularly among poor women, has shown that these problems can be overcome. The example of the Grameen Bank is spreading to other countries, e.g. Bolivia and Indonesia, but the surface has only been scratched and many unexploited opportunities exist to create employment and reduce poverty by reallocating finance capital in favour of the poor.

The urban informal sector

In many countries formal-sector employment has grown slowly or even declined, especially after the poor economic performances of the 1980s. It is the informal sector that has been absorbing the additional labour and, consequently, this sector is becoming increasingly important as an object of government policy. In the 1960s, when formal-sector employment was buoyant, the prevailing attitude towards the informal sector was one of indifference or even hostility; in contrast, the impact of structural adjustment policies in the 1980s has caused many governments to turn, often over-optimistically, to the informal sector for viable alternative employment opportunities.

While the long-term solution to the employment problem is to restore higher rates of growth to modern-sector employment, there are nevertheless several benefits in promoting the informal sector. Many of its activities are labour-intensive and use simple technology, and so provide a relatively easy way to create and expand employment. It also provides a form of "safety net" income for poor households, and is especially important as a source of subsistence income during recessions.

The range of informal-sector activities is vast. In rural areas cottage industries and homeworkers produce traditional handicrafts and implements of simple design, such as basic furnishings and agricultural tools, which are aimed at low-income consumers. In urban areas the variety is greater, spanning from the archetypal shoe-shine boys and cigarette-sellers to innovative metalworking enterprises with hired labour and apprentices, formal-sector subcontracts and product design.

The informal sector typically consists of both dead-end survival activities and small-scale activities with the potential for growth and technical upgrading. The main aim of policies should therefore be to increase the modernizing element of the sector. This requires both better supply conditions (capital, technology, skills, etc.) and improved demand conditions, which depend not so much on the sector itself but on developments in the rest of the economy.

In general, a prosperous and dynamic formal sector is an important condition, necessary but not sufficient, for the development of a modernizing informal sector; a depressed formal sector may increase the numbers in the informal sector, but these are likely to be in the "sponge" subsector and not the modernizing one. Consequently, while the informal sector may provide a safety net for workers who fall from the formal sector when the latter is depressed, it is unlikely to provide an alternative source of growth in that context.

The ultimate objective of policy should thus be to draw surplus labour into productive employment through rapid industrialization and growth. This would reduce the "sponge" component and lead progressively to an informal sector dominated by dynamic small-scale enterprises that interact and compete with the formal sector. In Africa informal sectors are still dominated by low-productivity survival activities. In

Latin America the informal sector is more urban-based, exhibiting both "sponge" and dynamic employment. It is among some of the successful economies of East Asia that a thriving base of small-scale enterprises has been created.

However, even in the absence of a rapidly growing modern sector there is still a case for adopting measures directed at promoting the dynamic segment of the informal sector. For instance, it is widely agreed that "access to credit rather than the cost of credit is the bottleneck for small-scale enterprises".[19] Very small enterprises face special problems because of a lack of collateral, so successful credit schemes must by-pass normal collateral requirements and substitute alternatives such as group guarantees. Upgrading technology and providing information about efficient and appropriate technologies is also an important aspect of promoting modernization in the sector. Because of poor channels of information, government or NGO support for technology development and dissemination institutions is often needed.

In many economies official regulations present a considerable handicap for the sector by requiring complex administrative procedures and excessively high standards of products and processes, and by limiting location. Complex regulations can hamper the sector's flexibility: in Peru, the acquisition of a licence to operate a street kiosk takes 43 days and costs five times the minimum monthly wage.[20] Such regulations encourage the development of an illegal sector which avoids the regulations, but also damages the informal sector's operations. The appropriate policy response is to support informal-sector activities by bestowing secure property rights to the land, squatter housing and other productive assets assembled by the poor; and by removing administrative obstacles and controls which prevent the growth of micro-enterprise and small-scale businesses and inhibits entrepreneurship.

The provision of infrastructure is typically biased against the informal sector: problems with power, telecommunications, water and transport all make modernization especially difficult. Well-located and appropriate infrastructure is an important aspect of improving the supply conditions in the sector.

Rural employment

The process of adjustment to the global economy creates potential benefits for the agricultural sector. As noted earlier, the implementation of the Uruguay Round will create new opportunities for agricultural exports from developing countries. Moreover, economic reforms have often improved the terms of trade for agricultural producers. For example, in several sub-Saharan African countries the dismantling of the State's procurement and marketing of products, together with the reduction of taxes on agricultural products, has resulted in higher prices for producers. Similarly, in several Latin American countries, especially Chile, Ecuador and Mexico, export promotion policies have led to a surge in agricultural exports such as fruit and vegetables.

So far, however, the response of the agricultural sector to these new opportunities has been disappointing in most countries. Of the 26 sub-Saharan African countries on which there is data for both food and export crops, 77 per cent experienced falling food production per capita and 81 per cent falling exports per economically active person in agriculture. The median of all countries was an 8 per cent decline in food production per capita and a 20 per cent decline in agricultural exports per economically active person during 1987-91. Food production has not been able to keep up with population growth, and the productivity of labour in export agriculture has also been falling. In Latin America agricultural GDP per capita fell in 11 out of 19 countries between 1980 and 1990; the simple average decline for all countries was 0.3 per cent per annum. There was also an increasing share of employment in the traditional agricultural sector accompanied by falling average farm sizes, increased landlessness and falling real wages.

A major reason for the negative performance of sub-Saharan African agriculture in spite of improved price incentives has been the disengagement of the State. This has involved the termination of subsidized sales of inputs and distribution programmes, making it more difficult for farmers to raise their productivity by obtaining inputs such as improved seeds, animal traction and fertilizer. State credit programmes have also been cut back and private credit has not as yet moved in to fill the void. Thus, even where the use of fertilizer and other inputs has been profitable at the higher new prices after the withdrawal of subsidies, the non-availability of credit has been a serious obstacle. In addition, fiscal pressures, brought about by the economic decline and the reform process itself, have led to reductions in public investment in infrastructure. The consequent deterioration of the rural infrastructure has increased the costs of processing, storage, marketing and transport for agricultural producers and hence has decreased the net returns to farmers. This has severely limited the response of agricultural producers to the change in the terms of trade in their favour.

Similar problems have arisen in Latin America and India. In some Latin American countries the historical marginalization of peasant farms was exacerbated in the 1980s by the reduction of programmes to support small farmer integration. In particular, the involvement of small farmers in export agriculture has been marginal because they have been unable to overcome the handicaps of inadequate scales of production and high capital requirements for most export crops. In India, concern has been expressed over the likely impact of the New Economic Policy on agricultural development. The specific fears are over the reduction in public investment, state withdrawal from the provision of agricultural credit, and the reduction of extension services; all of these are likely to weaken the productive capacity of small farmers. If these changes are introduced then, together with improved incentives to agribusiness as a result of liberalization, they could well undermine the survival of small farms. The upshot could be the uprooting and proletarianization of small farmers and a reduction of employment as a result of an increase in capital-intensive and mechanized production.

This brief review of recent developments serves to highlight the importance of continued state support to the small farm sector. This is desirable on both equity and efficiency grounds. In the first place, to neglect the small farm sector would be to aggravate problems of rural poverty and underemployment. The poor who are concentrated in that sector would face reduced prospects for raising their productivity and incomes. This is especially harmful since it is unlikely that better alternative employment opportunities can be generated for all those who are displaced by falling incomes or the growth of capital-intensive and mechanized agriculture. Moreover, withdrawal of state support is unlikely to be justified on efficiency grounds since, with adequate support services, the small farm sector can be competitive; experience has shown that investment there yields high economic and social returns.

The main objective of rural policies in countries where there is still substantial employment in the small farm sector should therefore be to upgrade production in that sector and to increase its integration into the economic mainstream. This will require public investments to upgrade rural infrastructure, policies to improve the access of small farmers to credit; and extension services to support the adoption of new plant varieties and better farming methods. In the context of trade liberalization it will also be important to emphasize measures to increase the capacity of the small farm sector to benefit from new export opportunities. This includes assistance in meeting grading and quality control requirements for export markets, in developing marketing channels, and in strengthening cooperation among producers. The promotion of rural non-farm employment should also remain an important element of rural employment policies, since it has significant potential for absorbing surplus rural labour at relatively low investment costs.

Poverty alleviation

Even if all the policies discussed so far are implemented in earnest they will not be sufficient to solve problems of underemployment and poverty. The reason is the massive backlog of underemployment and poverty referred to earlier. This basic problem is compounded if the initial conditions are also characterized by a high degree of inequality in the distribution of income and productive assets.

Most developing countries are characterized by an abundance of labour relative to natural and physical capital. As a result the wages received by low-skilled labour (and the incomes of many of the self-employed) tend to be low. The combination of high income inequality and low wage rates means that poverty will be widespread.

Thus, even if everyone is fully employed, the problem of poverty among labouring households will remain as long as labour is abundant. It is not enough to create employment; in many countries the result would be to enlarge the class of the working poor engaged in low-productivity employment.

Moreover, even under the best of circumstances there is likely to be considerable slack in the labour force in both rural and urban areas. This can take the form of year-round or seasonal unemployment or part-time employment with lengthy periods of joblessness. Programmes to create employment for the unemployed and the underemployed are thus important for poverty alleviation. A number of countries have experimented with labour-intensive public works programmes and their experience suggests that a guaranteed employment scheme could be a viable and valuable policy initiative in many other developing countries. In the state of Maharashtra, India, a successful employment guarantee scheme has been in operation since 1975. In Bangladesh there has been a large food-for-work programme for about three decades. Labour-intensive schemes to construct basic infrastructure facilities have also been created under Indonesia's Kapupaten programmes, the Republic of Korea's Saemul Undong movement, Bolivia's emergency stabilization programme and in many African countries.

A guaranteed employment programme should concentrate on building up productive assets that can be expected to raise output and incomes in future. It should not be regarded as a short-term measure to provide relief in an emergency or as an income transfer or welfare programme. Rather, it should be seen as a mechanism for mobilizing otherwise unused resources for physical capital formation and growth. In other words, its main purpose should be to generate employment and reduce poverty and inequality by accelerating labour-intensive investment and thereby promoting faster growth.

A programme of guaranteed employment should act as a residual source of employment, at a wage no higher than the going market wage for landless agricultural labourers. It would thereby become a safety net for those capable of productive work.

The participants would receive two types of benefits from an employment scheme. First, they would receive subsistence wages during the period when they work. In Maharashtra, for example, more than three-quarters of the beneficiaries are landless workers or small farm households and about 40 per cent of those employed are women. The subsistence wages in some cases account for between one-third and two-thirds of total household incomes. Thus the direct benefits accrue largely to the poor and are not negligible when seen from their perspective.

Second, to the extent that the assets created under the scheme generate a permanently higher demand for labour, the workers should in future enjoy higher market wages or more days of employment, or both. Most of the benefits, however, are likely to accrue to landowners in the form of lower costs (e.g. if road construction reduces the cost of transport), higher output (e.g. from irrigation projects), higher land rents and hence higher land prices.

One way to overcome this problem would be to transfer ownership of the assets created by unemployed workers to the workers themselves. Not all assets created by a guaranteed programme could be managed in this way, but considerable scope exists for simultaneously transforming idle labour into physical capital and workers into shareholders in cooperative enterprises. For instance, a cooperative could be organized around an irrigation project where water is sold to farmers; a timber, firewood or fruit cooperative could be organized around a tree-planting project; a toll-charging company could be organized around a bridge-building project; a fishing or duck-raising cooperative could be based on an artificial pond, and so on. These individual cooperatives could then be grouped into multi-purpose cooperatives that would have overall responsibility for managing the collectively constructed assets. Such an approach could combine job creation and poverty alleviation with an improvement in the distribution of wealth.

Over and above such schemes of direct employment creation, it will be important to provide at least a modicum of economic security for poor people in poor countries. As mentioned earlier, the poor do not have easy access to capital markets (and hence cannot borrow when income temporarily falls below sub-sistence expenditure), nor do they have access to insurance markets (and hence cannot protect themselves against, say, incapacitating illness or crop failure). The poor are disproportionately affected by this "market failure"; consequently, there are grounds for the government in effect to act as lender and insurer of last resort. The non-poor also face market failures, but their means are greater and consequently their ability to cope and provide for themselves is greater. Hence public measures to provide economic security, if they cannot be universal, should focus on the poor.

A number of developing countries have, in fact, given priority to expend-itures on economic security. Among these are Sri Lanka, Costa Rica and, in India, the states of Kerala and Tamil Nadu. In each of these cases public expenditure has contributed to impressive gains in human development and in none has expenditure on economic security resulted in unacceptably slow rates of growth. If there is any conflict at all between growth and economic security, it must be very mild. Indeed it is likely that a well designed programme to increase economic security – by lowering risk, encouraging investment and reducing the desired number of children per household – would actually increase incomes and growth.

These programmes should be directed at giving the poor improved access to basic social services such as education, health care, sanitation and welfare assistance. The problems of funding them can often be eased by diverting expenditure away from lower-priority items such as defence and by correcting patterns of expenditure which mainly confer benefits to the better-off. Effective targeting of expenditures to the poor can also contribute to the more efficient use of scarce resources, thereby easing funding constraints.

The marginalization of Africa

The policy framework set out in the previous section assumes that certain institutional preconditions are in place and concentrates on the types of policies that need to be implemented to respond successfully to new opportunities in the global economy. The institutional preconditions include the existence of a stable framework of property rights and mechanisms for enforcing contracts that provide the necessary conditions for investment to take place. This applies to both domestic investment and the attraction of foreign direct investment. Other important preconditions include a stable framework of policy rules and the capacity to formulate and implement the required policies.

In many of the least developed countries some of these preconditions are absent and this basic handicap needs to be overcome before policies to raise rates of investment, and output and employment growth can begin to be successfully implemented. Many countries in sub-Saharan Africa suffer from this handicap, a fact which probably constitutes a significant part of the explanation for Africa's growing marginalization in the world economy. This section therefore examines the factors causing African marginalization and the main actions that could help to overcome it.

Africa has been increasingly marginalized in the world economy over the past two decades. Its share of world trade and investment has declined to negligible proportions and its economies have become more inward-oriented during a period in which all others have become more integrated into the world economy. The only international economic dimension in which Africa has become non-marginal is aid. Not only does Africa receive more aid than other regions, but the international economic institutions that are currently concerned with Africa are overwhelmingly donor agencies.

This marginalization would not be so disturbing if African countries were growing rapidly. However, as is well known, African growth has fallen far short of that in all other areas of the world and in per capita terms has barely even been positive. To date, no region has grown rapidly while becoming disconnected from the world economy. Indeed, recent studies have established a clear econometric causal relationship running from enhanced export performance to enhanced growth.[21] We do not yet understand why this relationship holds, although there are several conflicting explanations, but that Africa's marginalization in trade and investment is an important cause of its slow economic growth is highly likely on present evidence.

Africa's share of world exports has fallen steadily. However, since this partly reflects adverse price effects, a more telling statistic is the growth in the volume of exports relative to that of other regions. In the decade 1970-80 Africa's exports grew at 2.8 per cent per annum as against 12.2 per cent per annum for East and South-East Asia. During 1984-89 African export growth picked up somewhat, growing at 2.4 per cent per annum but East and South-East Asia's export growth accelerated to almost

14 per cent during that period, and the developing country average rate of growth of exports was 7.3 per cent per annum. The performance of exports from sub-Saharan Africa was significantly better in 1990, but this was almost entirely accounted for by the performance of oil-exporting countries. Moreover, African export growth decelerated to –2.8 per cent per annum for the period 1991-94. The rest of Africa has not participated in the otherwise global phenomenon of export volumes rising more rapidly than national output. An index of the degree of outward orientation of the economy shows sub-Saharan African economies to be less outward-oriented than those of any of the other four developing regions, as described in the previously mentioned study by Dollar. Indeed, the gap between Africa and the next most inwardly oriented (the Middle East) is much greater than that between the Middle East and the most outward-oriented (East Asia).

African exports are highly concentrated and have remained so. The share of primary commodities in exports was 83 per cent in 1970 and was still 76 per cent in 1992. Indeed, there were some indications of increased concentration: the share of agricultural export earnings coming from the two main crops, coffee and cocoa, averaged 35 per cent in the 1960s but was 40 per cent by 1989-90, despite record low prices for coffee.[22] If we turn from trade to investment, direct private investment into developing countries in general has increased enormously over the last decade and is now around $200 billion per annum; the share going to Africa, however, has shrunk to negligible proportions. Current estimates are that less than one per cent of this flow is going to sub-Saharan Africa. The absolute amount in 1992 (the most recent data) was even less in real terms than the inflow in 1985, the nadir of economic crisis for much of the continent. By contrast, Africa has become central to aid programmes. For some African economies, aid and remittances are now their main participation in the world economy. Sub-Saharan Africa receives around five times the amount of net official transfers per capita as does South Asia. These transfers account for 9.3 per cent of African GNP as opposed to 2.1 per cent for South Asia. Net transfers have approximately doubled as a proportion of GNP from the early 1970s to the early 1990s. By 1991 sub-Saharan Africa was receiving around a third of global net aid transfers.

Explaining marginalization

Until the late 1980s it was straightforward to explain Africa's marginalization in terms of domestic policies which were hostile both to the private sector in general and to the export sector and foreign capital in particular. Sometimes this was reflected by uncompensated nationalizations, as in Ethiopia, Tanzania and Uganda and sometimes by compensated nationalizations, as in Senegal. These phenomena were accompanied by the creation of parastatal enterprises and subsidies on imported capital by means of an overvalued exchange rate attained through restrictions on consumer imports. This overvaluation strategy in turn taxed exports and so precluded the development of manufactured exports. Unfortunately, both the small scale and the uncompetitive environment in which manufacturing firms were operating made this strategy highly costly.

During the 1980s, usually under the auspices of structural adjustment programmes, these policies were to an extent reversed. Trade and exchange rate policies were liberalized, other markets deregulated, and some parastatals privatized. Manufactured exports remain, however, a very small component of the economy.

The most straightforward explanation of this failure of response is thus to argue that the policy reforms have not gone far enough. While the most egregious impediments have been removed, African governments are competing with other governments which continue to place a higher value upon exporting manufactures and which positively welcome foreign investment. On this view, while the reforms of the 1980s have narrowed the gap, a gap remains and marginalization reflects merely the existence of a gap rather than its magnitude. Location decisions therefore continue to reflect the presence of this gap, partly caused by continuing policy discrepancies such as higher rates of corporate taxation, and partly by the legacy of previous policy disparities such as the neglect of infrastructure for the productive, as opposed to the social, sector.

It is likely, however, that more basic factors than just a gap in policy reforms are at work. One is the higher degree of risk in African economies and the other is a deficiency in the institutional preconditions for investment. With regard to the first factor, Africa is subject to two types of common risk to an unusual degree, namely policy change and shocks. All governments change economic policies from time to time. To an extent these changes are predictable because the government is following a policy rule (such as inflating the economy in the year before an election) and so do not generate much risk. Those policy changes that generate risk are where the policy rule is itself subject to change. In Africa the economic reforms of the last decade have constituted just such a rule change. This would not in itself have increased risk were the new policies expected with confidence to remain in place. However, the political context in which reform has been introduced has not made it fully credible. Usually the policy changes have not been freely chosen by the government but have been negotiated through donor conditionality. Policy conditionality thus increases policy uncertainty. The uncertainty over policy reversal is compounded by the very wide range within which policy is conducted. For example, in the past decade Nigerian trade policy has swung from intense foreign exchange rationing, indicated by a parallel market premium of over 300 per cent, to a completely free market, and back to even more intense rationing.

In addition to policy uncertainty, African economies are more subject than other economies to economic shocks arising from terms of trade and the climate. Africa and Asia obviously share the same movements in world prices, but African countries are more dependent upon a few primary commodities for export. Further, as

Neary has recently shown, trade restrictions actually increase exposure to external shocks.[23] Hence, Africa has had both larger shocks and is more vulnerable to them.

Both shocks and policy change alter relative prices. Hence, relative prices are more volatile in Africa than elsewhere. This in turn discourages irreversible investment. Various studies have shown empirically that price volatility reduces investment.[24]

In addition, severe deficiencies in the institutional structure deter investment. The African formal sector suffers from weak judicial and accountancy professions which make formal insurance more costly to provide. Further, firms face high risks because their fixed assets are illiquid. This in turn is because secondhand markets for capital goods are thin as a result of the small scale of production and the low level of investment, and because of the near impossibility of selling firms as going concerns. Proximately, a minor reason for this is the near absence of equity markets, with the exception of South Africa and Zimbabwe. More fundamentally, the unreliability of audited accounts, and the difficulty of establishing and enforcing legal title, preclude a firm being valued as a multiple of its present profits. As Besley shows in the context of investment in Ghanaian agriculture, where assets are less marketable, investment is lower.[25]

In Africa both the civil legal system and the audit system have deteriorated, in many cases, to the point where there is a sufficiently high probability of malfunction that the basis for transactions is undermined. Legal title to ownership of assets becomes increasingly contestable. In several African countries banks report that foreclosure on assets is now such an unreliable process that assets are losing their capacity to function as collateral.

In much of Africa accountancy standards are extremely low, there is little professional self-regulation, and audited accounts convey little more information than unaudited accounts. Prospective purchasers of equity, notably investment (or development) banks, have consequently either had very poor records of returns on their money or have been unable to place it.

The deterioration of the judicial and accountancy professions in Africa thus weakens or removes the key agencies of restraint which private agents use for asset transactions. Without these agencies, credit becomes restricted to trade finance. Investment must be financed out of the resources of the owners. Yet in committing resources to investment the owner lacks an exit route for his capital since firms cannot be sold as going concerns. Investments are thus highly illiquid and so unattractive.

These explanations for African marginalization, namely insufficient reform, high risk and weak restraints, are interrelated. To date, virtually all emphasis has been placed on policy reform as opposed to the other factors. While policy reform is surely a necessary condition for the reversal of marginalization, experience to date suggests that it is probably not enough.

Reversing marginalization

Africa's marginalization from the world economy will ultimately be solved by Africans.

Apart from dealing with issues of policy reform the basic weaknesses in terms of uncertainties surrounding the policy environment and the obstacles to investment will need to be overcome. Without this comprehensive approach it is unlikely that Africa can stimulate the rise in domestic and foreign investment that is necessary to initiate a reversal of its marginalization.

The rest of the world can either assist or hinder African efforts. The two main international interventions are the provision of aid and policy conditionality. Each of these interventions affects the prospects for reversing Africa's marginalization. For example, the resource transfer achieved by aid alters the incentive regime while donor conditionality influences the extent of policy reform. To date both of these interventions have had some deleterious affects and may even have been deleterious overall. However, there is a role for the international community both in the provision of resource transfers and in enabling African governments to lock in to policy choices. The international community should not detach itself but rather redesign its interventions.

For example, aid as currently conceived has unintended negative side-effects which need to be corrected. Since aid is an inflow of foreign exchange to the public sector, it appreciates the real exchange rate, reducing the incomes of those who produce tradable goods. Moreover, it raises public expenditure both absolutely and relative to GDP. These two features of aid alter the incentive regime facing the private sector. Through appreciating the real exchange rate, aid acts as an implicit tax on the export and import-substitute sectors. The exchange rate appreciation caused by aid directly contributes to the marginalization of Africa in the world economy since it reduces African exports. It might additionally cause marginalization through less direct mechanisms.

If the export sector has substantial externalities for the rest of the economy, then its contraction would rebound upon the growth rate. Moreover, quite aside from these detrimental implications of aid for economic performance, the exchange rate appreciation effect of aid is also morally problematic for donors. A transfer ostensibly intended to help the entire society has the effect of plunging an important component of it into poverty. Between them, these considerations suggest that Africa's high aid inflows may have been much less conducive to growth than the scale of the resource transfer might imply. In addition, the way policy conditionality has been appended to aid flows may have exacerbated the process of marginalization. Conditionality has been intrinsically forward-looking; that is, it has concerned itself with promises of policy reform. By being prospective rather than retrospective it has failed to reward past policy performance and so governments have little incentive to acquire reputation. The only mechanism for donors to enforce conditionality has been very short-term suspensions of aid if intra-programme targets are breached. In this case, a new programme might be negotiated before the date when the aborted programme would have ended. The new programme will again be forward-looking. With this structure, governments have an incentive to agree to more than they then implement, in the hope that breaches will either be ignored or suffer only short-term punishment. This is likely to give rise to policy volatility. More drastically, by paying for reforms, donors create an incentive for governments to raise the price as high as possible, exaggerating the political and economic costs of reforms and thereby slowing the reform process. In short, this process of policy conditionality increases policy uncertainty, which is both the predominant non-commercial risk and the predominant deterrent to foreign investment.

These features of current aid programmes and policy conditionality are not, however, exclusively due to intervention by aid donors. The weakness of Africa's internal capacity to impose restraints upon opportunistic private and public behaviour, and the small scale of its export industries, both suggest that more appropriate forms of intervention might be welcomed. The resource transfer could be redesigned so as to assist rather than implicitly tax the export sector. Most aid should be transferred to the private sector in general and the export sector in particular through a reduction in taxation. By contrast, donor conditionality is actually being used to induce heavier explicit taxation over and above the implicit taxation caused by real exchange rate appreciation. Conditionality could be redesigned to be retrospective rather than prospective, eliminating the reputation-destroying process under which governments are tempted to make promises which they fail to keep, and replacing it with a strong incentive for governments to build reputation. As governments build reputations, non-commercial risk would be reduced.

Notes

[1] According to data from SAARC (1992) as cited in T.S. Papola: *Employment in South Asian countries: Trends, prospects and issues* (Bangkok, ILO/ARTEP, 1993), paper presented to the Fifth Meeting of Asian Employment Planners, Bangkok, 1993.

[2] While the figure for the region as a whole suggests an increase in the share of manufacturing in total GDP over the last three decades, much of this is explained by a handful of more successful and fast-growing sub-Saharan countries such as Botswana, Cameroon and Côte d'Ivoire.

[3] See, for example, World Bank: *Economic growth and public policy* (Oxford, Oxford University Press, 1993); *The East Asian Miracle: Economic growth and public policy* (Oxford University Press, 1993); Mazumdar and Basu, op. cit.

[4] For evidence on the investment effects of World Bank programmes see P. Mosley, J. Toye and J. Harrigan: *Aid and power: The World Bank and policy-based lending* (London, Routledge, 1991), and L. Serven and A. Solimano: *Striving for growth after adjustment: The role of capital formation* (Washington, World Bank, 1993).

[5] ILO and United Nations Centre on Transnational Corporations: *Economic and social effects of multi-national enterprises in export processing zones* (Geneva, 1988).

[6] "Report of the Working Group entrusted with analysing the Reports Submitted by Governments and by Employers' and Workers' Organizations", Committee on Multinational Enterprises, ILO Governing Body document, 254/MNE/1/4 (Geneva, Nov. 1992). Responses to the survey were received by a mix of governments, and workers' and employers' organizations from 73 countries. While the information obtained is not scientific, it does constitute the broadest sample of opinion available on the social aspects of multinational enterprises. Through its Multinational Enterprises Branch, the ILO has published a variety of research findings on the social aspects of MNEs both at the sectoral level and in different countries and regions of the world.

[7] For a fuller discussion of the points in this paragraph, see A. Wood: "Trade and employment creation: Possibilities and limitations", paper for the OECD Development Centre Workshop on Development Strategies, Employment and International Migration (Paris, 11-13 July 1994, mimeograph).

[8] On the experience of Japan, the Republic of Korea and Taiwan, China, see UNCTAD: *Trade and Development Report 1994* (Geneva, 1994).

[9] S. Lall: "Industrial adaptation and technological capabilities", in T. Killick (ed.): *The flexible economy* (London, Routledge, 1994).

[10] See D.T. Lecraw: "Factors influencing foreign direct investment by transnational corporations", in P. Buckley and J. Clegg (eds.): *Multinational enterprises in less developed countries* (London, MacMillan, 1991). UNCTAD: *Trade and Development Report 1993* and *1994*, op. cit., has good descriptions of desirable FDI regimes and evolving requirements. See also L.E. Preston and D. Windsor: *The rules of the game in the global economy: Policy regimes for international business* (Boston, Kluwer Academic Publishers, 1992).

[11] See A. Mody and D. Wheeler: *Automation and world competition: New technologies, industrial location and trade* (London, Macmillan, 1990).

[12] The 27 low-income countries classified by the World Bank as "severely indebted" (with debt to GDP ratios of more than 50 per cent being an indicator of this) face particularly acute problems. For these countries, further progress on debt relief is probably necessary before adjustment can be successfully implemented. These countries account for about 10 per cent of the developing world's population and all but four of them are in sub-Saharan Africa.

[13] R. Freeman: "Does suppression of labor contribute to economic success? Labor relations and markets in East Asia", International Institute for Labour Studies, unpublished paper for seminar (Geneva, Nov. 1992). The author argues that the degree of repression of trade union rights and freedoms correlates with the strength of the Communist threat to political stability across countries in the region.

[14] World Bank (1993): *The East Asian Miracle*, op. cit..

[15] G. Fields: "Changing labor market conditions and economic development in Hong Kong, the Republic of Korea, Singapore, and Taiwan, China", in *World Bank Economic Review*, Vol. 8, No. 3.

[16] R. Plant: *Labour standards and structural adjustment* (Geneva, ILO, 1994), p. 83.

[17] A. Bronstein (1994): "Réglementation du marché du travail et relations professionnelles en Amérique latine: évolution et tendances récentes", unpublished background paper for the present report.

[18] V. Tokman (1994): "Generación de empleo en un nuevo contexto estructural", unpublished background paper for the present report.

[19] R. Meier and M. Pilgrim: "Policy-induced constraints on small enterprise development in Asian developing countries", in *Small Enterprise Development* (London), June 1994, pp. 32-38.

[20] H. de Soto: *The other path: The invisible revolution in the Third World* (New York, Harper and Row, 1989).

[21] D. Dollar: "Outward-oriented developing countries really do grow more rapidly: Evidence from 95 LDCs, 1876-1985", in *Economic development and cultural change* (Chicago), Apr. 1992, pp. 523-544; S. Edwards: "Openness, trade liberalization and growth in developing countries", in *The Journal of Economic Literature* (Nashville), Sep. 1993, pp. 1358-1393; and W.R. Easterly: *The African growth tragedy* (Washington, World Bank, 1994).

[22] Manufacturing exports from sub-Saharan Africa did show an improvement in the late 1990s, particularly for the period 1987-90, and African manufacturing exports in 1990 accounted for 15.1 per cent of total exports of Africa, and around 10 per cent of sub-Saharan Africa's total exports. But most of this increase in sub-Saharan Africa's market share is attributable to three countries: Mauritius, Côte d'Ivoire and Cameroon which, together, accounted for one half of the region's manufactured exports.

[23] P. Neary: *Trade shocks* (London, Centre for Economic Policy Research, 1994).

[24] See, for example, D. Fielding: "Determinants of investments in Kenya and Côte d'Ivoire", in *Journal of African Economics*, pp. 299-328.

[25] T. Besley: "Investment and liquidity in Ghanaian agriculture", in *Journal of Political Economy* (forthcoming).

3 PART THREE

Transition economies

Introduction

The analysis of employment outcomes associated with the transition process in the economies of East and Central Europe is a particularly difficult undertaking. The process of a wholesale transformation of centrally planned economies into market economies has never occurred before and "we have no general theory of the transformation, no optimal paths or well-defined endpoints".[1]

A particular difficulty arises from the fact that in a transition economy rapid change is occurring simultaneously on a wide front, in the goods, factor and money markets, in the external flows of commodities, etc. All these changes have to be managed simultaneously and in a coherent way. That is why, even more than in other economies, it is very perilous to analyse a particular problem, implicitly considering the whole system to be more or less stable. For example, an exclusive focus on the labour market is unlikely to yield meaningful conclusions. More than in any other economic context, a global analysis is essential in such economies. This does not mean that there should be no analysis of specific problems, but such an analysis has to be supported by a constant comparison and validation of specific issues with the global pattern of adjustment.

The issue we are mainly concerned with, namely the emergence of high and long-term unemployment, is a crucial one for many reasons. Not only does high unemployment cause the loss of income and undermine the most important means of social integration, it also jeopardizes the success of the whole transition process by generating social tensions. Thus, while labour market issues cannot be properly understood without taking into account strong linkages with the transition process as a whole, neither should overall issues such as the speed and sequencing of reforms be examined without reference to developments in the labour market. For example, political constraints generated by higher unemployment and greater economic insecurity can impose strong limitations on the pace of privatization and restructuring, and compromise the credibility of the reform process. There is thus a subtle equilibrium to be found between social sustainability and an adequate level of economic restructuring. In this connection, the implementation of adequate social safety nets will play a major role in maintaining social consensus in the context of growing unemployment and the dismantling of the former mechanisms of social security.

Moreover, the labour market has also to play a more direct role in the transition process: the reallocation of human capital is a fundamental aspect of successful restructuring. Of course, the market will ensure a large part of this reallocation of skills and talents from less to more efficient activities. But labour market policies will obviously also have a major role to play in the context of huge changes in the level and structure of both the supply and demand for labour.

Employment trends

The initial years of the transition process have been characterized by sharp falls in output. Output in the transition economies as a whole fell continuously during the period 1990-93, with falls of over 10 per cent per annum in the last three years of that period. This average figure, of course, subsumes differences between countries in terms of the extent and timing of the falls in output. Nevertheless, output fell in all countries in 1991 and again in 1992 except in Poland. In Eastern Europe, only Poland and Slovenia experienced falls of less than 10 per cent in 1991, while in the former USSR more than half of the republics had falls of over 10 per cent. In 1992, output started to grow in Poland while the fall in output became smaller in most other Eastern European countries. At the same time, the fall in output increased to calamitous proportions in the former USSR. By 1993 the relative improvement continued in Eastern Europe, with four out of eight countries (Albania, Poland, Romania and Slovenia) showing positive growth for the first time since 1989. Output stagnated in the Czech Republic but declined in Bulgaria, Hungary and Slovakia. In the former USSR output continued to fall without exception in 1993, although somewhat less than in 1992. Preliminary data for 1994 indicate that output increased in Eastern Europe, with the exception of Bulgaria; stabilized or even recovered in the Baltic States; and that there was a deepening of the recession in the Commonwealth of Independent States (CIS).

There are several competing explanations of the fall in output. One is that apparent falls in output are largely statistical artifacts. It is argued that the level of output was overstated in the previous statistics of centrally planned economies, and that during the transition period it has been underestimated because of the difficulties of measuring the emerging private activities. The former net material product concept used in centrally planned economies does not provide an accurate measure of the growth in services, which has been the most buoyant since the beginning of the transition process. But the "statistical artefact" explanation can surely not explain losses of 20 to 30 per cent in output. So the fall in output has to be considered as real.

Another explanation is that the fall of output is the direct and inevitable result of the transition process, representing the shedding of activities which have become uncompetitive. This argument implies that the pattern of change can be expected to follow a "J-curve" pattern, with unavoidable large falls during the first stage of a transition period.[2]

Table 15. **Annual percentage change in GDP, 1990-94, selected transition countries**

	1990	1991	1992	1993	1994, January-June	1994, forecast
Eastern Europe						
Albania	–10.0	–27.7	–9.7	11.0	n.a.	8.0
Bulgaria	–9.1	–11.7	–5.7	–3.8	–0.3[1]	–1.0/–3.0
Czech Republic	–1.2	–14.2	–6.6	–0.3	2.2	2.5
Hungary	–3.5	–11.9	–5.0	–2.3	n.a.	2.0
Poland	–11.6	–7.0	2.6	3.8	4.5	5.1
Romania	–5.6	–13.7	–15.4	1.0	n.a.	1.0
Slovakia	–2.5	–14.0	–7.0	–4.1	4.4	4.0
Slovenia	–4.7	–8.1	–5.4	1.3	5.0	3.0
Selected countries of the CIS						
Belarus	–3.0	–1.0	–9.6	–9.5	–31.0	n.a.
Russian Federation	n.a.	–12.5	–19.2	–12.0	–17.0	–15.0/–16.0
Ukraine	–3.4	–12.0	–16.8	–14.2	–26.5	n.a.
CIS	n.a.	–11.5	–17.8	–11.5	–20.0	n.a.
Baltic States						
Estonia	–8.1	–10.0	–14.4	–7.8	5.7[1]	n.a.
Latvia	2.9	–8.3	–33.8	–19.9	–2.5	n.a.
Lithuania	–5.0	–13.1	–39.3	–23.6	0.8	n.a.

n.a. = not available.
[1] First quarter only.

Sources: National statistical publications and statistical office communications to the ILO, United Nations Economic Commission for Europe: *Economic Bulletin for Europe*, Vol. 46 (1994), Nov. 1994.

A third explanation is that the fall in output was caused by factors exogenous to the transition process, mainly related to trade. The collapse of trade within the Council for Mutual Economic Assistance (CMEA) caused huge decreases in exports and a sharp deterioration in the terms of trade. The latter was mainly due to the transition to dollar pricing in Soviet trade, especially the increase in the price of Russian oil to almost international levels. This represented a large loss of income. A study by Rodrick[3] argued that this trade shock accounted for the entire drop in output in Hungary, for most of it in the Czech Republic and between a quarter and a third of it in Poland. But the reality is that exports to the West from most Eastern countries rose immediately and by almost as much as the loss in exports to the CMEA (but after a while, because of the recession in Western Europe and the implementation of non-tariff barriers in the EC, the drop in exports to the West is likely to have deepened the recession). Moreover, the transition process itself, involving restrictive stabilization policies and the complete removal of the whole centrally planned process of production, would obviously have played a major role in the reduction of output. The dislocation of the whole system of central planning of resource allocation before the institutions of a market economy began to function correctly has been held responsible for a large part of the decrease in production. As stressed by Jackman, "inflexibilities in the linkages between enterprises can create domino effects whereby production problems in one sector can reduce production both of its suppliers and in the enterprises using its product as an intermediate input".[4] A convincing explanation thus appears to be that the fall in output was the result of a "combination, the weights differing among countries, of excessive monetary contraction (beyond that needed for stabilization, at least if devaluation had not overshot) with the inadequacy of supply response (itself due to inadequate micro foundations, e.g. unchanged property rights, weak lending discipline, lack of competitive practices, old management methods . . .) in the face of shifts in demand that required reallocation".[5]

This different pattern of output declines can to a large extent be explained by differences in initial conditions and in the time of the initiation of transition. In general, Eastern Europe embarked on the transition ahead of the former USSR, a fact which partly explains the different timing of the worst falls in output. In addition, some Eastern European countries, such as the Czech Republic, Hungary, Poland, and Slovenia, had more favourable initial conditions than the rest in terms of either their pre-transition record of economic reform or their relative macroeconomic stability and degree of indebtedness.

Employment, labour force and the emergence of mass unemployment

In industrialized market economies such performances would have produced labour market outcomes worse than the Great Depression of the 1930s, and in some countries of the region comparisons with that era are already apt. Unemployment increased rapidly and had reached, by 1994, double-digit rates in almost all transition countries (see table 18), the only exceptions being the Czech Republic and Russia. But compared to the huge losses in output, the increase in open unemployment appears rather small. This can mainly be explained by two factors.

First, the decrease in employment has been much smaller than the decrease in output, thus inducing a worrying fall in productivity, especially at a time when successful restructuring requires its rapid growth to start closing the enormous gap between Eastern and Western Europe. This "labour hoarding" has generally been explained by the relatively slow pace of restructuring: the maintenance of a "soft budget constraint" on enterprises,[6] has allowed loss-making enterprises to continue to operate. In addition, as emphasized by Boeri,[7] the adjustment has often been implemented through a reduction of working hours instead of through a reduction in employment.

Second, a large decrease in activity rates has been recorded. Therefore, in most countries of the region, falls in employment have exceeded rises in officially measured unemployment. In the previous centrally planned economies, activity rates had been maintained at very high levels compared to Western standards. As clearly explained by Burda, "employment was a mechanism of social integration and protection".[8] While social insurance against insecurity and inequality is achieved through an explicit system of taxes and transfers in Western economies, state enterprises were given those social functions in the former socialist economies:

Table 16.   **Annual percentage change in employment, 1990-94, selected transition countries**

	1990	1991	1992	1993	1994, Q1[1]	1994, Q2[1]
Eastern Europe						
Albania	−0.7	−5.8	−16.6	−6.8	n.a.	n.a.
Bulgaria	−6.1	−13.0	−8.1	−6.0	−4.0	−3.5
Czech Republic	−1.0	−5.4	−2.6	−0.1	n.a.	n.a.
Hungary[2]	−3.1	−9.6	−9.3	−5.9	−3.0	−2.6
Poland	−4.0	−5.9	−4.2	−0.6	−1.6	−1.2
Romania	−1.0	−0.5	−3.0	−3.8	n.a.	n.a.
Slovakia	−0.8	−7.9	−5.3	−0.4	n.a.	−0.8
Slovenia	−3.9	−7.8	−6.6	−3.0	−2.6	−2.0
Selected countries of the CIS						
Belarus	−1.0	−2.5	−2.6	−1.9	−2.0	−1.9
Russian Federation	−0.3	−2.0	−2.4	−1.8	−1.3	−1.3
Ukraine	−0.6	−1.2	−4.0	−2.3	n.a.	n.a.
CIS	0.1	−1.2	−2.7	−2.1	n.a.	n.a.
Baltic States						
Estonia	−2.1	0.4	−14.7	−4.0	n.a.	n.a.
Latvia	0.1	−0.8	−3.7	−5.9	−4.5	−3.2
Lithuania	−2.7	2.4	−2.2	−4.2	−2.9	−2.2

n.a. = not available.
[1] Percentage change over the same period of preceding year, Q1 means first quarter, Q2 second quarter.   [2] Since 1992 data refer to the end of the year.

Sources: ILO: *Year Book of Labour Statistics*, various issues: national statistical publications and statistical office communications to the ILO: United Nations / Economic Commission for Europe: *Economic Bulletin for Europe*, Vol. 46 (1994), Nov. 1994.

employment was guaranteed, wages were low but so was the wage dispersion, and employment involved the payment by the enterprises of pensions, sickness allowances and family benefits. These features of the system ensured that the participation rate was very high, especially among women and elderly workers. A large part of the decrease in participation rates can therefore be linked to the changing role of enterprises with respect to the provision of social benefits. A second, and more worrying, explanation of the decrease in participation rates is that in some countries low or non-existent unemployment benefits have discouraged some of the unemployed persons from registering. Instead, they have simply left the labour force, quite often to join the "black economy". This appears to be especially the case in Russia. In Croatia, employment fell from 1,618,200 in 1989 to 1,243,600 in 1993, whereas unemployment rose only from 139,200 to 250,800. In Moldova, employment fell by 61,000 between 1989 and 1993, while unemployment rose only by 14,000.

A detailed study of four countries (the Czech Republic, Hungary, Poland and Slovakia) shows the amplitude of the relative effects of the decrease in employment and the drop in activity rates. Table 17 shows that the decrease in employment between 1989 and 1994 has ranged from 11.5 per cent in the Czech Republic to 28 per cent in Hungary. A drop in productivity occurred in the Czech Republic (−7.7 per cent) and Slovakia (−2.6 per cent) where employment did not adjust completely to the change in output. In contrast, productivity has started to increase again in Hungary (+8.6 per cent cumulated since the beginning of the transition) and Poland (+14.2 per cent). For these latter two countries, the productivity change

Table 17.   **Labour force, employment, and unemployment in selected transition countries, 1989-94**

Variation between years 1989 and 1994, Q1	Czech Republic[1]		Slovakia		Poland		Hungary	
	Absolute variation	Per cent variation	Absolute variation	Per cent variation	Absolute variation	Per cent variation	Absolute variation	Per cent variation
Labour force	−454	−7.9	−194	−7.2	−1 386	−7.5	−1 054	−19.2
Labour force of active age[2]	−180	−3.5	−45	−1.8	−698	−4.1		
Labour force of post active age	−273	−52.7	−148	−76.4	−666	−46.3		
Employment	−657	−11.5	−527	−19.6	−4 087	−22.2	−1 513	−27.7
Unemployment (ILO definition)	204		332		2 701		457	
Labour productivity		−7.7		−2.6		14.2		8.6

Levels	1989	1993-94	1989	1994	1989	1994	1989	1994
	End-year	Winter	End-year	Q1	End-year	Q1	End-year	Q1
Participation rate	70.3	63.5	68.2	63.1	65.3	60.9	66.7	57.1
Participation rate, active age	86.5	81.4	82.4	80.7	72.3	71.1	85.0	
Participation rate, post active age	24.5	11.6	21.2	5.0	30.4	15.2	18.9	
Unemployment rate	0.0	3.6	0.0	13.4	0.1	15.9	0.4	10.9

[1] Data for 1989 and 1994 are not strictly comparable. Data for 1989 refer to regular statistical yearbook series, while data for 1994 originate from labour force sample surveys.   [2] Men aged 15-59, women aged 15-54. For Poland, men aged 15-64, women aged 15-59.

indicates that employment has more or less adjusted because it has continued to decline in spite of the recent recovery in output. The second factor influencing unemployment rates was the change in participation rates. The main change has been the drop in the participation rate of workers of post-active age (men over 59 and women over 54). Before the transition, their participation rate was high: 20 per cent to 30 per

Table 18.   **Unemployment rates, 1990-94, selected transition countries[1]**

	1990	1991	1992	1993	1994
Eastern Europe					
Albania	9.5	9.1	24.2	19.5	17.0 (June)
Bulgaria	1.7	11.1	15.3	16.4	13.3 (June)
Czech Republic	0.8	4.2	2.6	3.5	3.1 (Nov.)
Hungary	1.7	8.5	12.3	12.1	11.0 (June)
Poland	3.5	9.7	13.3	15.7[2]	16.9 (June)
Romania	n.a.	3.0	8.4	10.2	10.8 (June)
Slovakia	1.5	11.8	10.4	14.4	14.4 (Oct.)
Slovenia	4.7	8.2	11.5	14.4	14.3 (Sep.)
Selected countries of the CIS					
Belarus	n.a.	n.a.	0.5	1.4	1.8 (June)
Russian Federation	0	0.1	0.8	1.1	2.0 (Oct.)
Ukraine	0	0	0.3	0.4	0.4 (June)
Baltic States					
Estonia[3]	0	0.1	1.7	1.9	2.3 (Sep.)
Latvia	0	0.1	2.3	5.8	6.2 (Oct.)
Lithuania[4]	0	0.3	1.0	4.4	3.8 (Oct.)

[1] End of period. Data refer to the registered unemployment.   [2] Since December 1993 a new labour force estimate has been used to calculate the unemployment rate, which is 16.4 per cent.   [3] Data refer to the unemployed receiving benefits.   [4] Since December 1993 a new system of report of the number of registered unemployed has been introduced.

Sources : ILO: *Yearbook of Labour Statistics*, various issues, national statistical publications and statistical office communications to the ILO; United Nations Economic Commission for Europe: *Economic Bulletin for Europe*, Vol. 46 (1994), Nov. 1994.

cent, while it was negligible in Western countries. During the first five years of transition, it dropped by approximately 15 percentage points in these four countries. Therefore, the reduction in total labour force was equivalent to between a quarter and a third of the employment losses, thus exerting a major attenuating effect on the rise in unemployment.

Long-term unemployment and disparities in unemployment

An emerging labour market issue, which should be influential in shaping both domestic policies and foreign technical and financial assistance, is the growing evidence of massive long-term unemployment, that is, lasting for a year or more. There is a strong likelihood that many of those drifting into long-term unemployment will become detached from the labour force and the mainstream of society.[9]

In Poland in early 1994, 44 per cent of the registered unemployed had been looking for a job for more than a year. In Bulgaria, data from the December 1992 Census showed that no less than 6 per cent of the whole labour force – 50.4 per cent of all registered unemployed – had been unemployed for more than a year, and many of those had drifted off the unemployment register, if they had ever been on it.[10] Elsewhere, the picture was not much more cheerful. In Slovakia, for instance, in 1993 about a third of the registered unemployed had been out of work for more than a year. In Hungary, by 1994 a majority of the unemployed, according to the official labour force survey, had been out of work for more than six months.

Another issue of concern is that with the growth of unemployment, various socio-economic disparities have been emerging. These threaten the political stability of the new nations, bring the risk of social discord much closer and undoubtedly contribute to a substantial worsening of socio-economic inequality. Regional disparities have widened considerably. Levels of unemployment of ethnic minorities have risen more sharply than the average. There is also mounting concern that women are being particularly adversely affected by labour market trends. A similar and equally disturbing trend has been experienced by disabled workers. Throughout the region, youth unemployment has been rising sharply and it is worrying that a vast number of teenagers and those in their early twenties could drift into a debilitating period of long-term unemployment. Another group hard hit by restructuring and rising unemployment consists of older workers in their fifties and sixties.

The growth of poverty

The worst aspect of economic restructuring is the appalling growth in the number of people living in poverty. In every country for which there are data, the proportion of the population living below some measure of a poverty line has grown, in most cases drastically. Thus – although the situation is certainly even worse in some other countries for which information is less reliable or up to date – the number of households in poverty has risen sharply in Bulgaria, the Czech Republic, Poland, Romania and Slovakia, and it is widely believed that the actual number exceeds those recorded in official statistics.

In Bulgaria, according to such statistics, by mid-1992 nearly 73 per cent of all households had incomes below the official social minimum, up from 42 per cent two years earlier.[11] In Poland over 40 per cent of all households were classified as living in poverty in 1991, again up sharply from two years earlier, and by mid-1992 official estimates (Central Statistical Office) indicated that over 50 per cent had incomes below the poverty line.

Worse, in the countries of the former USSR, according to unofficial estimates by prominent economists, by the end of 1991 about 100 million people were living below the official poverty line, with average real family incomes in some areas being 26 per cent below their levels at the beginning of the year.[12] In 1992, after price liberalization and slackening of monetary policy that unleashed hyper-stag-flation (consumer prices rose by over 2,500 per cent during 1992), the Russian Government's State Statistical Committee *(Goskomstat)* estimated that 80 per cent of the Russian population had incomes that put them below the designated poverty line.[13] By late 1992 commentators in Moscow were referring to living standards being in "free fall", with the average household spending over 75 per cent of its income on food, twice as large a percentage as a few years ago.[14] In 1993, poverty continued to be extraordinarily widespread, owing in part to the very sharp decline in the real value of the minimum wage.[15]

Whatever the criteria for measuring poverty, it seems to be increasingly related to labour market status and experience. Although many of those suffering declines in living standards have been those cut off from the labour force, such as pensioners, many more have been impoverished as a result of their changing labour force position. Many have been pushed into precarious, low-income jobs, others have suddenly found themselves unprotected by minimum wages, either because these have not been applied or because enterprises have been unable to pay them, as in Bulgaria, where the real value of the minimum wage was halved in 1991.

Possibly worst of all, those cut off from the formal economy have typically lost access to many forms of social payments and welfare provided through the enterprise, on which the distribution of social welfare was traditionally based.

As an example of the poverty explosion, table 19 presents the percentage of households of different types having incomes per capita below the official "low income" level in Poland.[16] As can be seen, the sharpest relative deterioration occurred for worker households. One can appreciate the gravity of social marginalization highlighted in table 20, which shows that nearly eight out of every ten households depending wholly on social transfers perceived their situation as bad or very bad; the situation has further deteriorated since 1989-90.

Table 19. **Percentage of households with income per person below the "low-income" level,
by household type, Poland, selected years, 1981-90**

| Year | Household type | | | | |
	Total	Worker	Worker-peasant	Peasant	Pensioner
1981	14.2	10.6	16.4	16.9	23.3
1989	16.3	13.7	12.3	22.3	26.4
1990	33.2	33.2	28.3	41.8	32.2

Source: Central Statistical Office, Warsaw; Kordos, op. cit., p. 7.

Across Eastern and Central Europe, millions of workers in the state sector
have joined the "new working poor", whether through cuts in real wages, loss of social
benefits traditionally provided by employing enterprises, shortened working time
or periodic bouts of prolonged unpaid leave, the latter having been a very common
response of managements in Bulgaria, Romania and Russia, and probably elsewhere
as well.

A process of socio-economic stratification has appeared to accompany the
evolution of labour markets. While the real level of average wages has typically
fallen by large amounts, the real minimum wage has fallen by much more, while the
earnings of a privileged élite have multiplied.

Meanwhile, young people been drifting into poverty through prolonged non-
access to jobs, or by being pushed into low incomes in the "informal", often illegal,
economy. And very many older workers have been impoverished by having been
dismissed from jobs and pushed into even earlier retirement than corresponded to
the early retirement ages prevailing in the region.

Poverty has continued to worsen in all countries in the region for which there
are available data and reports. There is also no evidence that this situation is being
reversed. That is the background against which to assess labour market trends.

In conclusion, four major labour market features should be highlighted:

— since the "relatively" low level (compared to the decrease in output) of unemployment has been achieved mainly through "labour hoarding" and through
a huge reduction in the labour force, the amount of "hidden" unemployment
can be assumed to be high. This will be revealed sooner or later. Therefore,

Table 20. **Percentage of households assessing their economic situation as bad or very bad,
by household type, Poland, 1989-90**

| Year | Household type | | | | | | | |
	Total	Worker	Worker-peasant	Peasant	Pension	Only benefits[1]	Private	Self-employed
1989	22.5	19.6	12.6	14.2	36.6	76.6	18.5	5.4
1990	28.8	25.8	16.1	22.2	41.5	79.2	23.4	11.3

[1] Persons employed outside state sector; "Only benefits": those dependent on state transfers.

Source: Central Statistical Office, Warsaw; Kordos, op. cit., p. 7.

even with a strong recovery, unemployment is not likely to decrease; without this recovery, the prospects are for a further increase in unemployment;

–   long-term unemployment will continue to be a major problem and this could worsen without economic recovery;

–   the reduction in the economically active population will have strong social and fiscal implications. The continuous decrease in activity rates among the population past working age can be explained by either voluntary departures or by early retirements imposed on older workers, who are not entitled to receive unemployment benefits. In both cases, adequate pensions schemes should be implemented. But the increase in dependency ratios will further burden the already overwhelmed pension systems;

–   large changes in the structure of employment will continue to occur with the shift in production and the induced reallocation of resources.

In this context, labour market policies will have to play an increasingly important role. The main challenges will be to cope with the structural changes in the labour force and in employment through training and retraining, to provide assistance for reintegration into work of the long-term unemployed, to develop adequate unemployment benefit and pension systems and to strengthen active labour market policies.

Employment policies

Overall framework

The crisis of mass unemployment will ultimately be solved only by the expansion of output and the creation of jobs in new activities in line with the comparative advantage of these economies. The transition process will have to continue to shift production out of uncompetitive capital goods and "high-tech" industries that were able to survive only through subsidies and insulation from world market forces. The shift will have to be towards more labour- and skill-intensive industries where there is genuine comparative advantage. Recent export trends indicate that the most rapid growth has been in industries such as textiles and garments, foodstuffs and resource-based products. With further progress towards market-determined price signals and the removal of production subsidies a clearer picture will emerge of competitive production opportunities in both the domestic and world markets.

In the same way as industrialized and developing countries, the transition economies too will need to adjust to new opportunities in the global economy. The challenge they face is great because of the extremely distorted initial production structure and their late entry into the global economy. As a result of this they lag seriously behind developing countries of comparable income levels in terms of shares of world trade and foreign direct investment flows. For example, "total extra-merchandise exports from Eastern Europe and the former Soviet Union in 1993 did not surpass those of the Republic of Korea alone".[17]

A key element of adjustment is to raise rates of investment. This is necessary in order to upgrade physical infrastructure and to create productive capacity in new activities. Unfortunately, since the initiation of the transition process domestic fixed investments have fallen in the wake of the collapse of output. At the same time initial optimism about the inflow of foreign direct investment has turned out to have been misplaced. "Since 1990 the total inflow has been under $10 billion (for nine countries). Moreover most of the investment is concentrated on just a few countries: the four 'advanced' transition economies have received over 90 per cent of the total since 1990, with most (80 per cent) of it going to Hungary and the Czech Republic. Negligible amounts, if any, have gone to other transition economies in the former Soviet Union."[18] This is in sharp contrast to the surge in foreign direct investments that has occurred over the same period in the newly industrializing countries of Asia and Latin America.

It is imperative to improve on these investment trends if the problem of mass unemployment is to be overcome. This will require the completion of reforms to create a system of property rights and enforceable contracts as well as a stable macroeconomic environment and well-functioning capital markets. Unless this is done, investment, both domestic and foreign, will continue to be deterred by a perception of high risks surrounding the security of assets and future economic prospects. In addition, improvements in physical infrastructure are essential for the successful attraction of FDI. A major effort will also be required in training and retraining in order to adjust the mix of skills to the requirements of the new structure of production. A skill mix that was appropriate to the old uncompetitive structure of production is unlikely to fit the requirements of new industries seeking to gain a niche in the global economy.

Trade liberalization, privatization and enterprise restructuring will obviously have to proceed in order to bring about a shift in the structure of production that is more in line with comparative advantage. Thus far trade liberalization has been marked by abrupt shifts in policy. In Poland, Russia and Hungary, for example, initial far-reaching import liberalization has been reversed by the reintroduction of quantitative restrictions and the selective raising of tariffs. In addition, export controls, including the compulsory surrender of foreign exchange earnings, remain in place in many countries. Overall only the Czech Republic and Slovenia among the transition economies are subject to GATT disciplines. Privatization and enterprise restructuring have proceeded at different paces and taken different forms. While the share of private-sector production and employment has grown significantly, much remains to be done in most countries.

A central policy issue with direct implications for the employment situation is the pace at which trade liberalization, privatization and enterprise restructuring should proceed. Proponents of rapid change argue that anything less would thwart the whole transition process. The removal of soft budget constraints and the strict enforcement of bankruptcy laws are seen to be necessary both for restoring macro-economic balance and eliminating industries which make a negative contribution to total output. In addition, it is argued that a rapid shake-out of labour from un-competitive industries is essential for releasing labour to the private sector, for restraining wage increases and hence inflation, and for strengthening work effort within enterprises.

But there are strong arguments against adopting this approach. Foremost among these is the fact that it will impose intolerable social costs. With unemployment levels already in the range of 10 to 15 per cent in most countries a further sharp increase would be socially catastrophic. Living standards have fallen sharply and poverty has increased. Another massive wave of unemployment would lead to further falls in real wages that would exacerbate the increase in income inequality and poverty that has already occurred. All this would surely threaten the social sustainability of the transition process and breed political instability. Another important consideration is that parts of the reform process cannot, intrinsically, be accomplished at a stroke. The creation of effective new institutions and the restructuring of product and labour markets requires a time horizon of at least a few years even in the best of circumstances.[19] To push for widespread bankruptcy before a functioning market system and the correct incentives to guide economic agents are in place would not necessarily lead to clear gains in efficiency. Finally, it does not appear to be true that a further aggravation of mass unemployment is necessary either for supplying labour to the private sector or for containing inflationary pressures. Most of the recruitment to the private sector has in fact been directly from those in employment, not from the pool of the unemployed. On the containment of inflation, it has to be noted that a high proportion of the current unemployment has become long term. Since the long-term unemployed are not in the pool of effective jobseekers it is doubtful whether a further increase in their numbers will do much to dampen inflationary pressures.

There is therefore a strong case to be made for adopting a more gradual approach to trade liberalization, privatization and enterprise restructuring. This case is further strengthened by the fact that there exist policy instruments which make it feasible to temporarily slow down the process of restructuring while still ensuring that change occurs in the right direction. This contradicts the view that the only choice is an all-or-nothing one between instant restructuring or no progress at all towards transition.

The gradual approach should not rely on a continuation of indiscriminate and unconditional protection through soft credits to state-owned enterprises or the imposition of import quotas. Such measures would indeed freeze necessary progress in restructuring. Instead, temporary assistance should be provided through transparent fiscal measures and be targeted to enterprises that show promise of future viability. The assistance should also be time-bound, be conditional upon progress in restructuring, and be structured around a phased reduction of support. If these features are steadfastly adhered to then it will be feasible to achieve a gradual restructuring that still proceeds on the correct path. At the same time this will yield immense social and political benefits for the reform process.

A gradual strategy has been followed by several of the European transition economies, notably Romania, the Ukraine and the Czech Republic, in all of which wage employment fell by substantially less than GDP between 1989 and 1992.

However, in some cases the gradual approach has been a substitute for reform rather than a conscious part of it. This is the case in Romania, for instance: subsidies have kept inefficient enterprises alive and the process of restructuring has hardly started; in 1991 33 per cent of the State's unemployment fund was spent for support for the "technically unemployed", still on the books of enterprises. In the Ukraine, too, official loans to state enterprises at negative real interest rates, in addition to subsidies and enterprises' loans to each other, have kept the annual rate of decrease in state and collective sector employment as low as 3 per cent between 1990 and 1993, a period when real GDP was falling at an annual rate of 14 per cent. Unpaid leave and short-time working, which affected 40 per cent of employees in the fourth quarter of 1993, have been the means of avoiding mass redundancies – a form of social and economic compromise. In the Czech Republic, on the other hand, the relatively low rate of decrease in state sector employment has not apparently involved subsidies, but has been due, rather, to delays in privatization and to wage restraint. This is a deliberately gradualist approach to reform rather than its avoidance or postponement.

Among other European economies, Poland and Hungary have probably taken the toughest line on lay-offs and bankruptcies, while Slovenia (where subsidies were cut and lay-offs occurred but successive governments have not felt able to close down lossmakers) and Slovakia have been in an intermediate position.

Labour market policy developments

Regardless of the choice of overall reform strategy, labour market policies will have to figure prominently in Eastern and Central Europe in the next few years, in view of the prevalence of mass unemployment. Already the rhetoric has run ahead of the reality, and there are few governments that have not pronounced themselves intent on promoting an "active" labour market and social policy. Budgetary constraints and other factors have made the outcomes rather modest so far.

Labour market policies will be expected to cut unemployment, reduce labour market segmentation and the increasingly disadvantaged position of vulnerable groups in society, promote geographical, occupational and industrial labour mobility and raise productivity.

In the initial phases of the reform process in many countries of the region, the primary response of governments was to pass comprehensive "framework" employment laws. The importance of these laws is that they created a legal and administrative basis for the development of a wide array of labour market policies, making commitments on such diverse issues as the "right to freely chosen employment", income transfers to public works and labour market training and retraining schemes. They represented the first steps on the road to the creation of a regulated labour market.

This development has led to unresolved tensions over the degree to which policy responsibility should be centralized or decentralized, and the extent to which the government alone should be responsible, rather than relying on some tripartite mechanism or the partial privatization of social and labour policy. These are familiar debates in Western Europe, but have a particular intensity and a long future in Central and Eastern Europe.

The emerging mix of labour market policies designed to respond to unemployment and the patterns of labour market restructuring highlight the considerable challenges that will have to be faced in the next few years.

(a) The emergence of employment services

To function adequately in a modern industrial economy, all human resource policies must be backed by an adequate services network, which means in practice a network of employment exchanges and support services. Nowhere in Central and Eastern Europe has such a network existed. In the past three or four years, considerable effort – backed in most cases by substantial international financial assistance – has been devoted to rectifying this. The most substantive programmes so far have been in the former German Democratic Republic, Hungary and Poland. In the latter two, huge World Bank-funded employment services projects were launched in 1991 and 1992 respectively.

Throughout the region, the development of basic employment services should receive high priority for some years. Not only did the old employment offices fill a different role from that expected of employment services in a well-functioning labour market, but the number of offices and staff were minimal, if they existed at all. Thus, in Czechoslovakia, employment offices only started to operate in November 1990; in Poland, in 1991, there were only about 400 offices for a population of over 35 million, in Hungary there were only about 160 in a country with a population of over 10 million. At the end of 1991, Poland had 49 labour offices at the *voivodship* (county) level and 356 at the local (district) level, employing a total of 7,630 staff. As there were then 2.2 million unemployed, that implied one official for every 321 unemployed.[20] By 1993 a typical employment bureau official in Bulgaria and Hungary had to be responsible for dealing with well over 200 unemployed applicants. Currently, in Western Europe there is probably an average of one employment service official for every 1,000 workers; in Central and Eastern Europe, it is a little over one per 10,000. In Russia in early 1993 there were 2,400 employment offices for a labour force of over 80 million. These figures give some idea of the depth of the problem and point to the difficulty of operating an efficient or equitable set of policies.

(b) Vocational, labour market and on-the-job training

In Central and Eastern Europe an enormous emphasis is now placed on training.[21] Undoubtedly, there is a need for training and retraining, although some politicians and analysts surely place too much faith in the capacity of training to reduce unemployment, increase labour mobility, raise productivity and reintegrate disadvantaged groups into the labour force.

First, as far as general and vocational education is concerned, it is widely argued that in most of the region levels have been respectable and in some cases even high by international standards. Perhaps that picture is deceptive. Some observers question the quality of vocational education, and in the late 1980s there were clear signs of falls in the numbers covered. Most strikingly, there has been a long-standing decline in Russia.[22]

The prevailing systems have also been criticized for being excessively rigidly oriented to available jobs, whereas what is required for the restructuring period and for the international labour market of the 1990s is a broadly based and flexible educational structure.

Second, enterprise-based training, including retraining, will have to be boosted throughout the region, since it may enable many workers to shift out of moribund industries and enterprises into new avenues of employment. However, the reality in Central and Eastern Europe in 1991-93 was that very many large industrial enterprises cut back on training, as a relatively easy way of responding to the growing financial pressures they were facing. In Russia this pattern of cuts has accentuated a long-standing decline in training generally. Many enterprises have cut the funds allocated to training, and many have shut the training institutes that they traditionally operated. Thus, in the ILO 1992 labour flexibility survey, one in five industrial enterprises that had operated a training institute in 1990 had closed it by mid-1992.[23]

In such circumstances, it is vital that governments should intervene more directly, perhaps by detaching training institutes from industrial enterprises and running them directly, or by encouraging local groups of enterprises to fund them jointly with government authorities, perhaps on a tripartite basis, so that the views and capacities of workers are adequately taken into account. In 1991 the German authorities began to do that through their privatization agency, the Treuhandanstalt. Other countries would be advised to follow this route, since huge centralized training institutions are out of tune with the more flexible labour market needs of the 1990s.

Third, labour market training, i.e. schemes for providing training and re-training for those out of employment, are seriously undeveloped. Although data are scarce, it has been estimated that in 1990 only 1 per cent of the registered un-employed in Poland participated in training schemes; in Hungary the corresponding figure was better, but still low, 8.7 per cent; in Czechoslovakia in early 1991, such schemes covered a mere 0.4 per cent of the registered unemployed, in Bulgaria the corresponding figure was 3.9 per cent. Little seems to be known about drop-out rates or the placement record of trainees. But the neglect of such training has been pervasive.

There is no evidence of any rapid growth of labour market training in 1991 or 1992, despite a stated commitment to its expansion. In 1991, as well as in 1990, in most countries less than 1 per cent of the registered unemployed participated in training courses, the exception being Hungary, but even there the per cent enrolled in state-sponsored training courses fell from 8.7 per cent in December 1990 to 2.9 per cent in June 1992, when about 17 per cent of unemployed school-leavers were participants.

There are many reasons for the minor role attained by such schemes. Perhaps, most importantly, the uncertainty about economic restructuring has made it hard to determine what workers should be retrained for, a point often made by observers in Poland, but elsewhere as well.

Finally and most conspicuously, an insignificant number of the growing number of Russians becoming registered as unemployed are being directed to such training schemes, and the financial squeeze there as elsewhere is making growth in labour market training increasingly hard.

In short, there is a worrying gap between the stated commitments to training and the realities, in spite of the overwhelming emphasis placed on it by foreign donors.

(c) Public works

Another labour market policy on which perhaps excessive hopes are placed in Eastern and Central Europe is direct job creation through short-term public works. A commitment to public works has figured prominently in legislative reforms, as in the USSR's Employment Law of 1991 and in the Polish Employment Acts of 1989 and 1991.

However, there has been a failure to develop major public works programmes in the past two years, which is ironic, given the long tradition of community work and non-production work by workers in the region.

Certainly, there is ample scope for social and infrastructural improvements in all the countries of the region, especially in the ecological sphere, and public works schemes might be a useful form of regional adjustment policy. Yet there has been little use of them in practice in most of the countries, partly because of underdeveloped institutional procedures and shortage of public finance.

(d) Other demand-side measures

Among other measures attempted or considered in Eastern and Central Europe to boost employment in response to the labour market restructuring crises have been the usual batch of subsidies and credit for the establishment of small-scale enterprises, including self-employment. Certainly, among the obstacles to the growth of new enterprises have been the lack of credit, marketing skills and entrepreneurial experience. But it would be wrong to claim that there has been a lack of entrepreneurial flair, especially as there was a flourishing "second economy" in most of the countries of the region for many years under the old systems.

Since 1989, most governments have provided aid and basic technical assistance to the development of new businesses, and there has been a large growth of small-scale enterprises. A problem is that much of those seem to be in low-productivity services, in work of dubious legality or in insecure forms of work that result in a high rate of business mortality. The mafioso economy is spreading rather easily, alongside the much welcomed "kiosk economy". The reality is that a very large part of emerging informal economic activity consists of survival activities on the roadside, yielding remarkably little.

Another popular policy has been the use of wage subsidies, primarily to keep workers in jobs to slow the pace of employment dislocation. Thus, in 1991 the Polish Government introduced an incomes policy that, among other things, encouraged the preservation of low-paid employment, and in Bulgaria in 1992 the authorities proposed giving subsidies to state enterprises as long as they maintained the previous level of employment. In some countries workers have reluctantly accepted pay cuts or paid or unpaid leave in return for keeping jobs in their enterprise, which the State has subsidized. This has paradoxically boosted the extent of hidden unemployment, as has been the case in Poland and Bulgaria. For workers, that option has been quite attractive, since at least they have retained entitlement to enterprise-level benefits.

As a transition measure, wage subsidies may slow the spate of redundancies required by restructuring and perhaps slow the predicted growth of mass emigration. The cost to the government is less than it seems, to the extent that unemployment benefits would have to be paid to many of those who would otherwise have been displaced and to the extent that by earning higher income at least some of the employed would pay income tax and social insurance contributions. Particularly promising are schemes that combine subsidies with retraining or enterprise-creating measures.

Yet all employment and wage subsidy schemes have drawbacks, most notably "deadweight" effects (subsidizing jobs that would have existed in any case) and "substitution" effects (resulting in the displacement of those in regular jobs by those in subsidized positions). Critics would say that these schemes are a market distortion, impeding essential changes in the labour market, and that they weaken discipline in wage bargaining. In short, they are no panacea.

(e) Supply-reducing measures

Across the region, as in Western Europe during its restructuring crises of the 1970s and 1980s, among the most popular responses to the labour market difficulties of the "transition" have been measures to cut aggregate labour supply or at least that of particular groups. Thus, there have been schemes to increase youth enrolment in educational institutions, to persuade women to extend maternity leave and to induce workers in their fifties to take earlier retirement.

Among women, the effective labour force participation rate has been reduced by various indirect means, such as by the closure of enterprise-based or funded child-care facilities.[24] Women have also been encouraged to take longer maternity leave, thereby reducing the measured unemployment rate, as has been the case in Czechoslovakia.[25]

As for older workers, early retirement schemes have long been established in Eastern and Central Europe, and have accounted for a high share of expenditure on pensions – one-third in the case of Poland, for example. There is relatively little scope for resorting much more to that policy. An objection to such measures is that they legitimize discrimination against workers in their fifties and even forties, worsening their already fragile standard of living and discouraging any policy for retraining them.

By contrast, policy-makers could usefully consider measures to increase older workers' labour supply and employment prospects, as an anti-poverty measure and as a rational long-term policy. As in other industrialized countries outside the region, in the longer term raising the labour force participation of older workers will be essential, given the "greying" of the population and the fiscal imperative of reducing the rise in the dependency ratio.

(f) Human resource development and social protection

Human resource development and redevelopment strategies cannot be divorced from the overall structure of social security provision. In this regard, the legacy in Eastern and Central Europe is distinctive. Essentially, social policy was comprehensive, centralized and linked firmly to employment in state enterprises, which were the primary distributor of social benefits, from child care and health to training and pensions. Benefits were distributed as worker rights and, formally at least, not linked to labour market performance.

The biggest change in the past three years has been the widespread adoption of a policy to curtail such benefits and their replacement by a so-called "social safety net", promoted by the concerted advocacy of the Bretton Woods financial institutions. This has affected social and human resource development policies in numerous and far-reaching ways. The idea is that, in order to cut public expenditure and to reduce the budget deficit, social benefits should be "targeted" on the poor, essentially providing benefits only to those deemed to be deserving and needing them. Unfortunately, this is not as simple as it seems.

Essentially, the safety net approach involves increased selectivity in social protection and greater reliance on means tests. The approach has been adopted for most forms of social protection, but here we will focus on the application of that principle to unemployment benefits and other labour market policies connected with human resource development. The basic fear is that a highly targeted approach to income transfers, based on complex conditions and systematic means tests, may not be consistent with the establishment of an effective social safety net. In addition, it is not clear that targeting is feasible in circumstances of high and unpredictable inflation, at least not without serious administrative difficulties and adverse consequences for social equity.

As far as unemployment benefits are concerned, most new governments introduced fairly generous schemes at the outset of the reform process, although in some cases there was an over-hasty adoption of some Western scheme that was malfunctioning in its parent country and was demonstrably inappropriate for a country undergoing a major restructuring process. In any case, pressures from foreign advisers and imposed fiscal constraints led successive authorities to reshape their schemes, mostly through a tightening of conditions that had to be satisfied for benefit receipt. The resultant problems are familiar. As more conditions, means tests, behavioural tests and limits on entitlement have been imposed, so the numbers of unemployed failing to receive benefits have grown and the number needing (though not necessarily receiving) social assistance has also grown.

As in so many other ways, Poland has been the harbinger in this respect, and the changes have undoubtedly resulted in further intensification of poverty associated with unemployment. Even in 1991, before the first of the major changes were introduced, about 93 per cent of all families affected by unemployment had incomes below the social minimum, or poverty, level.[26] Yet at the time a justification for advocating a reduction in the level of benefits and a tightening of conditions for receipt was that they were acting as a disincentive to work. In August 1991 the average unemployment benefit was 53 per cent of the average wage, and according to official estimates only about two-thirds of the registered unemployed received benefits.[27]

Then, under the Employment Act introduced in December 1991, entitlements were severely restricted. The registered unemployed could only receive benefits for up to 12 months, and not at all unless they had been employed for at least 180 days during the previous year; exceptions were made in the case of school-leavers, for whom a three-month waiting period was introduced, those leaving military service and women returning from maternity leave. The level of benefits was cut to 36 per cent of the average wage in the previous quarter of the year, which in an inflationary climate means less than a third of the current average wage. Henceforth, if workers leave jobs voluntarily or are dismissed for disciplinary reasons, they are denied benefits for three months, as are unemployed persons who refuse any job offered. As a result of these measures, particularly the one placing a limit of one year on receipt of benefit, it was officially expected that the share of the registered unemployed eligible for the meagre benefits would fall to about 40 per cent after November 1992.[28]

In fact, over 400,000 unemployed people lost their right to unemployment benefits at the end of 1992, and as an immediate result 48 per cent of the registered unemployed no longer received unemployment benefits.[29] This disentitlement process continued through 1993, and may have had some effect on the general election results.

Besides the dire implications for the unemployed in Poland, it is worth noting that the Russian labour policy authorities have been attracted by the revised Polish system of unemployment benefits, and indeed all countries of the region have been moving in a similar direction.

With the rapid growth of long-term unemployment, a declining proportion of the unemployed are likely to receive benefits. This highlights the approaching crisis. Demands on the funds allocated for unemployment benefits have been growing, leading governments to tighten conditions and raise contribution rates, which has encouraged employers and workers to find ways of evading payments. At the same time, a high and growing number of unemployed are not being entitled to benefits and those who are have been receiving an increasingly inadequate amount.

Thus, in 1990 about a third of total expenditure devoted to unemployment in Poland consisted of funds for labour market training, public works and other such measures; by 1991 and 1992 that share had dropped to one-fifth, on the grounds that they had been "crowded out" by the need to pay unemployment benefits. Thus, in Bulgaria in mid-1992 transfer payments comprised 91 per cent of all expenditure in the "vocational training and unemployment" fund, and "active" measures only 1.5 per cent. In Hungary, in 1992 and 1993 all "active" measures combined (including labour market training, public works, job subsidies and crisis management measures) comprised merely 14.6 per cent of public expenditure on unemployment, compared with 69.2 per cent in 1989 and 62.2 per cent in 1990.[30]

It is part of the problem that the authorities and many advisers to ministries of the countries in the region seem to see training and related measures for the unemployed as competing with the provision of adequate income protection. Human resource development policies should be treated separately, as the essential complement to social security. Unless this is recognized, the contradictions and resultant underdevelopment of labour market policies cannot but intensify.

(g) The role of industrial relations in the transition process

The new industrial relations systems of the transition economies are still in the process of formation. Since the beginning of the transition period, the main form of industrial relations in the countries concerned has been that of tripartite consultations and negotiations at the central level. One important reason for this is that – because of the long tradition of central control and because of the intrinsic difficulties of the transition process – the governments of many transition economies wanted to exercise a relatively tight control over economic and social development. Such control is almost impossible in a context of completely decentralized industrial relations systems. Moreover, there was no middle alternative to completely centralized industrial relations, since the emerging employers' organizations were generally not in a position to act as effective partners at the industry-wide or regional levels. Another important reason is that the experience of Western European countries had shown that tripartite consultations and negotiations had often eased social tensions in a period of difficult adjustment. It was hoped that such consultations and negotiations would equally facilitate the transition process in Central and Eastern Europe by mobilizing support for the political and economic changes under way and by promoting acceptance of the social costs involved: if all parties were associated in the taking of decisions, the outcomes of the process would indeed stand a greater chance of being perceived as equitable by all concerned and of being effectively implemented.

In most transition economies – including the Russian Federation, the Ukraine, Hungary, Bulgaria and the Czech Republic – national tripartite consultations and negotiations take place within bodies especially set up for this purpose. Important consultations and negotiations of this type have, however, also taken place outside such bodies, the most prominent example being those that have led to the signature of the Polish State Enterprise Pact in 1993.

The main areas in which national tripartite consultations and negotiations have played a role are the preparation of labour legislation, the design of wage policies, the formulation of public policies on other economic and social issues and, more occasionally, the settlement of important labour disputes. In this latter area, the example which comes immediately to mind is the settlement, in October 1990, by the Hungarian tripartite body, of the taxi and truck drivers' blockade, which is probably the most dramatic labour conflict to have occurred in the country concerned in recent years. In the other areas, tripartite dealings more often than not take the form of consultations of the social partners by the government. However, in a number of instances, they have also led to genuine decisions or agreements. For example, the Hungarian tripartite body decides on guaranteed minimum wage levels. Wage issues have also frequently been the subject of tripartite negotiations in a number of Central and Eastern European countries – notably Bulgaria, the Czech Republic, Hungary and Poland. These agreements have essentially sought to strike a balance between the need for wage moderation and the need for acceptable workers' incomes, while at the same time attempting to gradually abolish government-imposed wage control measures. A number of important agreements dealing with a broad range of non-wage issues and aiming particularly at the introduction of active labour market policies and the social protection of workers have also been concluded in, for example, Hungary and Poland.

It has been pointed out that tripartite consultations and negotiations in transition economies suffer from serious weaknesses. These stem from the limited room for manoeuvre in the difficult economic situation of the countries concerned, the absence of strong representative and effective social partners and the still insufficiently developed spirit of cooperation needed for effective tripartite consultations and negotiations.[31] It has also been pointed out that tripartite consultations and negotiations in transition economies have essentially dealt with the short-term social consequences of economic reform and they have not led to full-fledged "economic and social pacts" reflecting a genuine association of all parties in the elaboration of long-term economic and social strategies.[32] There is certainly much truth in these statements. However, even in Western Europe tripartite consultations and negotiations are far from free of such problems, even though they are less serious. More importantly, in spite of their limitations, tripartite consultations and negotiations have undoubtedly made an important – and perhaps indispensable – contribution to the transformation process in Central and Eastern Europe by giving it a minimal social dimension and thereby ensuring a minimum of social peace. They will most probably have to play a similar role in the future and every effort should therefore be made to improve their effectiveness.

Notes

[1] R. Portes: "Transformation traps", in *The Economic Journal*, Vol. 104, No. 426, Sep. 1993, p. 1183.

[2] M.I. Blejer et al. (eds.): *Eastern Europe in transition: From recession to growth?*, World Bank Discussion Papers, No. 196 (Washington, World Bank, 1993).

[3] D. Rodrick: "Making sense of the Soviet trade shock in Eastern Europe: A framework and some estimates", in Blejer et al. (eds.), op. cit.

[4] R. Jackman: "Economic policy and employment in the transition economies of Central and Eastern Europe: What have we learned?", in *International Labour Review*, 1994/3.

[5] Portes, op. cit.

[6] Jackman, op. cit., p. 33.

[7] T. Boeri: "Labour market flows and the persistence of unemployment in Central and Eastern Europe", presented at the OECD/ILO Technical Workshop, "The persistence of unemployment in Central and Eastern Europe", Sep. 1993.

[8] M. Burda: "Structural change and unemployment in Central and Eastern Europe: Some key issues", CEPR discussion paper No. 977 (1994).

[9] Among those who have brought attention to the issue of growing long-term unemployment in countries of the region, see M.E. Greenberg and S.B. Heintz: *Removing the barriers: Strategies to assist the long-term unemployed* (New York, Institute for East-West Studies, The Report of an Expert Working Group in Central and Eastern Europe, 1994).

[10] ILO and Commission of the European Communities: *The Bulgarian challenge: Reforming labour market and social policy* (Budapest, 1994), Ch. 2.

[11] ILO, *The Bulgarian challenge...*, op. cit., p. 158.

[12] *Trud* (Moscow), 21 Nov. 1991.

[13] One response has been to redefine the poverty line, but the fact that a very high and growing proportion of average family expenditure is spent on food supports a belief that the old measure was reasonable.

[14] In mid-1992 the new official definition of poverty set the minimum amount of meat per capita per year at 27 kilos, whereas the poor were expected to need 64 kilos per year in 1991. Similarly, in late 1992, to be counted as poor one had to have an annual consumption of less than 70 litres of milk, whereas the minimum set in the previous year's consumption basket was 120 litres. The poor also apparently need much less sugar than in the past. *Trud*, 16 Oct. 1992.

[15] T. Chetvernina: "The minimum wage in Russia: Fantasy chasing fact" (Budapest, ILO Paper No. 4, Mar. 1994).

[16] Unfortunately, the data were not calculated on a per equivalent adult basis, which is being rectified in subsequent surveys. K. Kordos: "Poverty measurement in Poland", paper presented at a Conference on Priorities of Social Policy in Poland in the Context of Foreign Assistance, Warsaw, 11-13 Mar. 1992.

[17] European Bank for Reconstruction and Development: *Transition Report* (London, EBRD, 1994).

[18] United Nations Economic Commission for Europe: *Economic survey of Europe in 1993-1994* (New York and Geneva, 1994), p. 5.

[19] M. Bruno: "Stabilization and reform in Eastern Europe: Preliminary evaluation", in Blejer et al. (eds.), op. cit.

[20] A. Szurmaki: "Infrastructure of the labour market", paper presented at a Conference on Priorities of Social Policy in Poland in the Context of Foreign Assistance, Warsaw, 11-13 Mar. 1992.

[21] For Hungary, for instance, see A. Nesporova: "The Hungarian labour market in 1993" (Budapest, ILO-CEET, 1994).

[22] In 1980, there were 219 students in universities per 10,000 student-age population; in 1991, the figure was 186 per 10,000. In 1980, there were 190 students in special technical schools per 10,000 population. See G. Standing: *Mysteries of unemployment in Central and Eastern Europe* (Geneva, ILO, 1994, mimeographed).

[23] G. Standing: "Recruitment, training and human resource developments in Russian industry", paper 5, presented to Conferences on Employment Restructuring in Russian Industry, Moscow and St. Petersburg, 21-28 Oct. 1992.

[24] M. Lado: "Women in the transition to a market economy: The case of Hungary", paper presented to Regional Seminar, Vienna, Apr. 1991.

[25] I. Tomes: "Social reform: A cornerstone in Czechoslovakia's new economic structure", in *International Labour Review*, Vol. 130, No. 2, 1991, pp. 191-198.

[26] M. Kabaj: "Elements of the programmes for counteracting unemployment", in *Rynek Pracy* [Monthly Bulletin of the Ministry of Labour and Social Policy], Jan. 1992, p. 30.

[27] Under the previous scheme, an unemployed person received 70 per cent of previous earnings for up to three months, 50 per cent for the next six months and 40 per cent thereafter. See Standing, 1994, op. cit.

[28] M. Ksiezopolki: "Social policy in Poland in the period of political and economic transition: Challenges and dilemmas" (draft, Oct. 1992), p. 17. Before the election in late 1993, the then Minister of State confirmed these predictions and was considering remedial measures, such as waiving the 12-month rule in high-unemployment areas.

[29] Central Office of Planning: *Poland 1992: The social and economic situation* (Warsaw, 1993, mimeographed), p. 7.

[30] K. Foti: "Rising unemployment in Hungary: Causes and remedies" (Budapest, Institute for World Economics, Working Paper No. 24, Aug. 1993), p. 19.

[31] L. Héthy: "Tripartism–its chances and limits in Central and Eastern Europe", in *Transformation of the industrial relations in Central and Eastern Europe*, IIRA 4th Regional Congress, Helsinki, 24-26 Aug. 1994.

[32] ibid.

4

PART FOUR

Industrialized countries

Unemployment in the industrialized countries:
A descriptive analysis

Unemployment began to rise in the industrialized countries following the first oil shock, when the rate of growth of economic activity dropped by half. Only Japan and the EFTA countries[1] (Austria, Finland, Norway, Sweden and Switzerland) escaped this trend (see figure 10). During the successive two decades unemployment has risen regularly in the European Community, apart from the period 1986-90, but has fluctuated in the United States and has risen sharply in the EFTA countries since the end of the 1980s.

A country-by-country comparison of trends in the various factors accounting for unemployment is instructive in several respects. First, economic growth has been on the whole similar throughout the industrialized countries between 1974 and 1994. In the United States and EFTA the maintenance or restoration of employment has been obtained by means differing widely from one country to another. Within EFTA, the relatively low increase in the active population has been largely absorbed by an increase in public employment. In the United States new jobs have been created at a fairly lively rate, admittedly at the cost of labour productivity gains.[2] The substantial and lasting increase in unemployment in the countries of the European Community also masks very different realities. The reversal of migratory flows, which were considerable in the 1960s between southern (Italy, Spain, Portugal, Greece and, at least according to a "migration ranking", Ireland) and northern Europe has played a major role in the context of a persistent slow-down of economic growth. Given the sustained increase in the active population, the creation of jobs in the countries of southern Europe, despite the fact that it was more rapid than in the 1960s, has not sufficed to maintain full employment. On the other hand, in the countries of northern Europe the increase in the active population has been more moderate, but since productivity gains have remained substantial, few jobs – or none at all – have been created during the last 20 years.

Finally, while unemployment has fluctuated at around 6 per cent in the United States since the early 1960s and has remained virtually unchanged in Japan, the picture is very different in Europe. Three periods may be distinguished:

– between 1974 and 1985 unemployment grew markedly in the countries of the European Community following each of the recessions caused by the oil

Figure 10.
Unemployment rate, industrialized countries, 1960-94 (percentage)

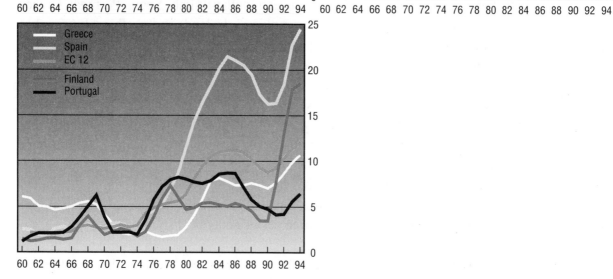

Source: Organization of Economic Cooperation and Development, *Economic Outlook* (June 1994), and reference supplement.

shocks, although it did not drop during the intervening upturns; it remained remarkably stable in the EFTA countries;

– from 1986 to 1990 the marked drop in unemployment in the Community may be attributed to the economic recovery which followed the oil counter-shock, creating many jobs as the rate of growth of the active population slowed down;

– finally, during the period 1990-94, the general recession affecting the whole of Europe nullified all the improvements on the labour market front during the preceding period: in 1994 unemployment returned to its 1985 levels, and even exceeded them, in most European countries; under the simultaneous effect of the slump in the former USSR, which essentially affected Finland, the deep and lasting economic recession in Sweden (where the situation has been described as a crisis comparable to that of the 1930s) and the Norwegian and Swiss recessions, unemployment rose sharply in EFTA.

Demographic growth and trends in rates of activity

Despite the slow-down in demographic growth, the rate of growth of the active population generally remained high in the 1970s and until the middle of the 1980s (see figure 11), under the simultaneous effect of:

Figure 11.
Economically active population, industrialized countries (average annual growth rate, percentage)

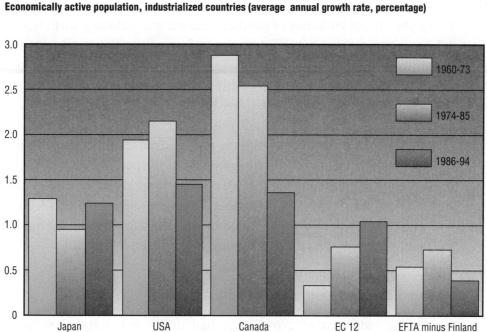

Source: Organization of Economic Cooperation and Development: *Economic Outlook* (June 1994), and reference supplement.

–   the increase in the population of working age, as the postwar "baby boom" generation reached working age and the age pyramid become distorted owing to a drop in fertility;

–   the shifts in migratory flows in Ireland and the countries of southern Europe;

–   the rise in rates of activity in North America and to a lesser extent in Scandinavia.

Since the middle of the 1980s the growth of the active population has considerably slowed down owing to the repercussions of the drop in the birth rate at the end of the 1970s on young people who are of working age today. Only in Germany, because of reunification and the massive immigration from countries of Eastern Europe, and in certain countries where there has been a sharp rise in activity rates (Austria, Netherlands, Spain, Switzerland) has there been an acceleration of the rate of growth of labour supply in the last decade. For the whole of the European Union the growth in the active population has speeded up because of the numerical effect of the incorporation of the eastern part of Germany; if no account is taken of this, however, labour supply is diminishing in the European Union. The phenomenon is even more marked in Scandinavia, where the active population is growing smaller. The 1990s will see a generally marked slow-down in the number of entrants to the labour market and an ageing of the active population throughout the industrialized countries.

For the whole of the period 1974-94, it is in the United States and Canada that the growth of the active population has been the most marked, reaching two per cent a year. In the countries of southern Europe and Ireland growth has reached 0.8 to 1.3 per cent a year, owing to the reversal of migratory flows, whereas in the northern countries of the European Union, where a rise in female rates of activity has been offset by more extended periods of education and the reduction of the rate of activity through early retirement, the rise has been only 0.4 to 0.6 per cent a year. In some countries, such as France, the trends in activity rates have had a clearly negative impact on the growth of the active population, partly because of the series of measures taken to directly affect labour supply (lengthening of the period of education, development of early retirement schemes, etc.) in a context of persistent unemployment. The most favourable trend in the active population has been noted in the EFTA countries, where a low rate of growth of the population of working age explains the moderate increase in labour supply despite a slight upward trend in activity rates.

Economic growth and employment

The reduction of growth has had different repercussions on employment depending on the degree to which it has been offset by a slow-down in productivity gains. Certain countries have succeeded in maintaining or sometimes speeding up the rate of job-creation at the cost of productivity gains. Generally speaking, the European countries, including EFTA, benefited considerably from the cycle of expansion which followed the oil counter-shock, but the jobs created at that time were entirely offset by the job losses caused by the recession of the early 1990s, so that employment has generally risen only a little in Europe since the first oil shock.

The slow-down in growth that followed the first oil shock had different effects on the industrialized countries (see figure 12): it was slight in the United States (−1.7 percentage points) but more pronounced in the European countries (−2.6 percentage points) and particularly in Japan and the southern countries of the European Community (−5 percentage points). Only in Finland and Norway did the overall rate of growth remain unchanged. The slow-down was also slight in Ireland.

Figure 12.
Gross domestic product, industrialized countries (average annual growth rate, percentage)

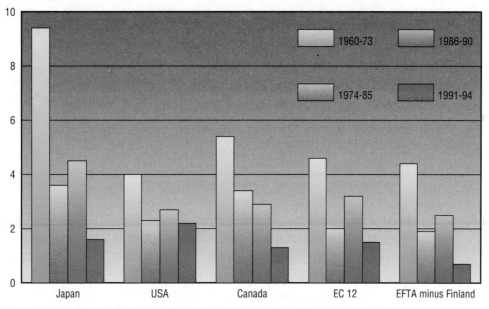

Source: Organization of Economic Cooperation and Development, *Economic Outlook* (June 1994) and reference supplement.

The employment impact of this slow-down of growth has differed widely from one country to another to the extent to which it has been largely, and sometimes entirely, offset by a slow-down in productivity gains. In the United States, the EFTA countries, the Netherlands, Ireland and, to a lesser extent, Japan, the slackening in productivity has completely offset the slow-down in growth so that jobs have continued to be created at the same rate as in the 1960s (see figure 13). In the northern countries of the European Community and Switzerland, on the other hand, despite the slackening in productivity, there was a marked drop in employment growth. In the southern countries of the European Community and Sweden employment creation was speeded up while growth declined. The fall in productivity was marked. A clear distinction thus appears between the different economic zones: while employment creation remained steady in both the United States and the EFTA countries, it was slight in the countries of the European Union throughout the period.

Figure 13.
Employment, industrialized countries (average annual growth rate, percentage)

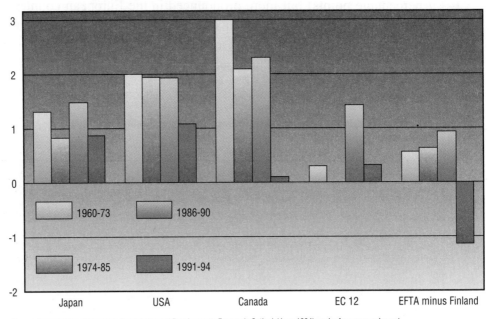

Source: Organization of Economic Cooperation and Development: *Economic Outlook* (June 1994), and reference supplement.

In most of the OECD countries the rate of employment creation between 1985 and 1990 returned to that of the 1960s, although growth remained lower by about two percentage points. Employment creation was particularly vigorous in the European Community owing to the economic upturn that followed the oil counter-shock and above all because productivity grew only slightly.

The United States, which entered the recession earlier than its European partners, has continued to enjoy a steady resumption of activity – the liveliest for ten years – since 1992; this was accompanied by a high level of employment creation. On the other hand, the recession which affected European economies at the beginning of the 1990s, and which in some cases has reached an extent unequalled since the Second World War, has affected employment all the more seriously in that productivity increases have been simultaneously maintained at high levels. Moreover, the EFTA countries have been affected by job losses, contrary to their previous experience: the recession has been deep and lasting in Norway, and above all in Sweden, where the growth of GDP has been negative for three consecutive years.

Given the widespread economic slump and its unfavourable repercussions on public finances, it has no longer been possible, as before, to make up for the loss of jobs in the private sector by creating jobs in the public sector, the more so as Sweden is at present formally engaged in bringing its macroeconomic performance (in terms of inflation, balance of public accounts and public debt) into line with those of the countries of the European Community, with a view to its participation in the Union.

The foregoing analyses make it possible to draw up a clear classification of unemployment trends for four zones.

In the United States the return to low unemployment after the second oil shock was made possible by maintaining a high level of employment creation despite a persistent slow-down in growth. On the other hand, productivity gains in the American economy declined markedly; the impact of demography on labour supply was substantial and was reinforced by the highest rise in the activity rate among the industrialized countries (over ten percentage points between 1974 and 1994). A study of working time shows that this has become considerably longer; thus the United States has not only had more persons at work, but these persons have also worked longer hours, which may seem like a dual feat of performance in the context of a persistently weak rate of growth.

Within the countries of the European Community, a distinction should be made between those of the north and those of the south. Because of the reversal of migratory flows in the early 1970s the countries of southern Europe have experienced a far higher rate of growth of the active population than those of northern Europe. Nevertheless, unemployment rose in both groups of countries. Whereas employment creation speeded up in southern Europe – but insufficiently given the growth of labour supply – very few jobs were created in northern Europe, which recorded the highest productivity gains in the industrialized countries with the exception of Japan.

The EFTA countries have long been admired for their excellent performance as regards unemployment, which rose only very slightly throughout the turbulent years of the oil shocks. Apart from favourable demographic trends due to a drop in fertility, Sweden and Austria have almost entirely absorbed the major reduction in growth by an equivalent fall of productivity. But unlike the United States, where employment creation appeared spontaneously in the private sector, employment has been maintained in Sweden by active employment support policies, essentially by creating public employment and almost systematically integrating the unemployed into training or "special works" programmes financed by the State. In the case of Switzerland the regulation of labour supply by immigration has been a major instrument for maintaining full employment.

Finally, in Japan, the reduction in growth has been considerable but has been completely offset by a reduction in productivity, especially in the tertiary sector.

As stressed in the previous paragraphs, the greater or lesser degree of success in combating unemployment in the industrialized countries is largely dependent on the different ways in which slower growth has been absorbed by reduced productivity. The countries which returned to low unemployment or maintained it after the oil shocks did so at the cost of productivity gains and hence incomes. Growth which produces more employment is less effective in improving individual incomes: to maintain a stable rate of inflation the sharing of growth between wage bills and profits must remain constant, which means that real wages must increase along with labour productivity.

Thus the United States has created more employment in proportion to growth than the countries of the European Community, but this has implied a smaller increase in real wages compatible with productivity gains (see figure 14). Many low-paid and often precarious jobs have made their appearance, mainly in the services sector. In the European Community, on the other hand, higher productivity gains have been associated with higher wage increases: the price of this has been the lasting exclusion from the labour market of a large and growing segment of the population. Seen from this angle the persistence of unemployment in Europe compared with fluctuations in the American unemployment rate seems due merely to ways of sharing rates of growth that are too weak to ensure both full employment and an increase in real

Figure 14.
Real wages and labour productivity, industrialized countries, 1974-94 (average annual growth rate,1974-94, percentage)

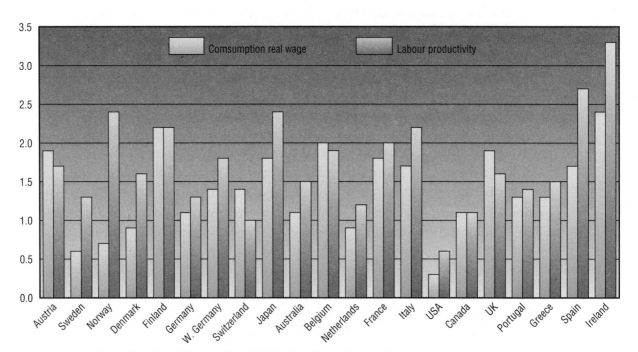

Source: Organization of Economic Cooperation and Development, *Economic Outlook* (June 1994), and reference supplement.

incomes: there is some justification for setting the concept of persistent unemployment in Europe against persistently stagnating incomes in the United States (or even decreasing incomes at certain times and among certain groups of workers). In the long run, the dilemma would appear to be to choose between two "forms of poverty".[3]

Sweden has also created more jobs at the cost of productivity but seems to have escaped this dilemma, at least for the time being. Although a slight increase in productivity has indeed been accompanied by a reduction in gains in the purchasing power of wages, it has also been accompanied by persistent inflationary pressures which were corrected in the early 1980s by major devaluations. The main difference from the American case is undoubtedly the fact that, thanks to a strong egalitarian tradition, wage austerity has not been accompanied by an increase in the wage spread and has thus not affected the lowest wages.

In rather simplified terms, we may define three different ways of responding to inadequate growth:

–   the American model: sharing low incomes by giving jobs to a large part of the labour force at the risk of creating a whole class of working poor;

–   the Scandinavian model: guaranteeing employment for all under satisfactory conditions by creating employment in the public sector, at the risk of building up inflationary pressures and depleting public finances;

–   the European model: protecting the incomes and working conditions of those who are in employment by reserving for them all the benefits of growth and ensuring decent incomes, through the costly unemployment benefit system, for a large and still increasing pool of unemployed.

Causes of rising unemployment

Economic policies and growth

The most obvious sign of the failure of the three models, American, European and Scandinavian, is their management of economic growth since 1973. Growth no longer offers a simultaneous assurance of full employment and a satisfactory improvement of incomes, conditions of work and standards of living for all.

A different sharing in economic growth

But why has growth been shared so differently in Europe and in the United States? There are two schools of thought. The first argues that the higher share of growth attributed to incomes in Europe is the result of strong rigidities in the

European labour market, which have prevented wages from decreasing, even in the presence of a high and/or rising unemployment rate. This kept real wages above their "market clearing level", that is, the level which would have allowed the creation of employment until full employment was reached; this, in turn, was responsible for the persistence of unemployment. The arguments related to the presence and the effects of rigidities in the labour market on employment will be discussed in the second section of this part of the report. An alternative view, presented in the following paragraphs, is that since employment has proved to be relatively inelastic to changes in real wages, the persistence of unemployment cannot be related to any kind of wage rigidity in the labour market. Instead, the different sharing of growth in the two continents is mainly explained by different trends in *exogenous* labour productivity. In the mid-1970s, levels of productivity and standards of living in the United States were markedly higher than those noted in Europe. The maintenance of higher productivity gains in Europe since that time is linked to the need to continue to catch up with American standards. The difference in technological progress between the United States and European countries, with the latter lagging behind, was important, and the constant introduction of more productive and capital-intensive technologies was continuing to generate labour productivity gains in Europe while these gains had to a large extent been exhausted in the United States. European labour productivity gains were, however, largely exogenous. Therefore, with higher labour productivity growth, *European countries would have needed a higher economic growth than the United States to maintain the same employment growth, the latter being required to preserve full employment.*

It would seem that the facts do not support the thesis that the persistence of unemployment in Europe is due mainly to the existence of rigidities in the European labour market. The rise of unemployment in Europe was essentially concentrated in periods of stagnating activity (particularly 1980-84). Whenever growth again became vigorous, unemployment dropped sharply (1986-90). The medium-term persistence of unemployment in Europe does not therefore appear to be a phenomenon linked primarily to labour market rigidities, but is the outcome of a persistent inadequacy of economic activity over the previous twenty years.

Why has growth been persistently inadequate? Does the blame lie with the restrictive orientation of economic policies?

Economic policies since the first oil shock

The appearance of unemployment is essentially linked with a break in the rhythm of growth in industrialized countries in the early 1970s. As emphasized by Muet,[4] the conditions that had permitted 30 years of balanced growth underwent an upheaval: the inflationary trends linked with the cycle of expansion at the end of the 1960s caused major disruptions in foreign exchange markets and the fall of the

Bretton Woods system; in this context, the first oil shock was of a dual nature, affecting demand by the massive transfer of income from industrialized countries to oil-producing countries, and supply by the rise in production costs induced by the change in the price of energy. Governments had never faced such a shock, which entailed a sharp decline in GDP growth simultaneously with a sudden increase in inflation, while external and government balances deteriorated. They reacted with expansionary budgetary policies and easy money policies. The result was a rapid return to sustained growth (although the rate was less than half that of the previous decade) but with persistent inflation.

In this context of growing disequilibria, economic policy reactions were very different following the second oil shock: the struggle against inflation and the re-establishment of the profit margins of enterprises became of prime importance. American monetary policy became restrictive and the rise in interest rates rapidly spread to the European countries. A wide divergence between budgetary policies in the United States and Europe then emerged: whereas increased public expenditure and reduced taxes combined to support activity in the United States, budgetary policies remained neutral or became highly restrictive in Europe (see box 1). The result was a return to high growth in the United States whereas growth remained slow in Europe.

It was not until the latter half of the 1980s, as a result of the oil counter-shock and the relaxation of monetary policies following the stock exchange crash of 1987, that growth picked up again in Europe, enabling it to catch up with the United States and make up for the delay accumulated at the beginning of the decade. In the early 1990s the end of the cycle of expansion in the United States, the drop in investment in Europe, the rise in household savings and the German recession which followed the boom of reunification, combined with highly restrictive monetary policies, gradually pushed Europe into recession. The American economy, under the impetus of the broad relaxation of monetary policy, in 1992-93 made its strongest recovery in ten years.

A high and lasting cost of disinflation?

The strong and persistent inflationary pressures which followed the first oil shock were at the origin of the tight budgetary and monetary policies of the early 1980s. Disinflation was, however, achieved by different means in the United States and Europe. High interest rates and appropriate exchange rate policies have played an important role, but as far as achieving disinflation through wages was concerned, the channels have been very different. It was "paid for" directly by the wage-earners in the United States, who saw a sharp drop in their real wages in the first half of the 1980s. In Europe, disinflation was rendered possible, indirectly, by the maintenance of a high level of unemployment.

Theoretically, the unemployment cost of disinflation should have been only transitory.[5] The economic system should have spontaneously returned to the equilibrium rate of unemployment, which is the rate compatible with stable inflation, called the NAIRU (non-accelerating inflation rate of unemployment).[6] But the reality shows that even once the disinflation process was achieved, unemployment remained high, and that the unemployment cost of disinflation was felt for a long time. This fact has been ascribed to both the increase in – and the slowness of the adjustment process to – the NAIRU: once disinflation strategies have moved unemployment above the NAIRU, it takes a long time for it to decline. The traditional labour market analysis explains both phenomena by various rigidities specific to the labour market, which should be removed in order to restore the equilibrating mechanisms. However, an alternative explanation, which seems more pertinent and appears to fit better with the empirical evidence, argues that the factors external to the labour market have played the major role.

The view developed in this report assumes that *the increase in the NAIRU is only temporary*. The influence of institutions is not rejected but their role is considered to be secondary and to have sometimes had ambiguous effects on wage moderation.[7] According to this view, the increase in the NAIRU is linked more to the terms of trade shocks induced by the oil shocks, and to the reduction in productivity caused by slower economic growth. It is thus largely endogenous to low growth and due to transitory supply shocks, but not structural and not due to specific labour market rigidities. Therefore, the NAIRU can be reduced through economic policies: an adequate macro-policy can reduce the terms of trade effect generated by an oil shock; sustaining growth or achieving increased wage moderation would also lower the NAIRU.

As far as *the return of unemployment toward the NAIRU* is concerned, the flexibility of prices and wages should allow the economy to return spontaneously to the NAIRU in the absence of any shock external to the labour market. If unemployment is higher than the NAIRU, real wages decline. At this point, however, views begin to differ on the channels through which the economy should return to the NAIRU. In a partial equilibrium analysis of the labour market, a decrease in real wages directly boosts employment until the unemployment rate returns to the NAIRU. This analysis does not allow the impact of shocks in, or feedbacks from, the rest of the economy to be taken into account.[8] In the macroeconomic framework used in this part of the Report, a decrease in real wages allows for increases in competitiveness and profits, which generate additional exports and investment and thus growth and employment until the NAIRU is reached. The direct influence of labour costs on employment remains weak and has to be complemented by general macroeconomic interactions. This explanation of the slowness of the return to the NAIRU is thus quite different from that in the partial equilibrium analysis of labour markets.

According to the macroeconomic explanation, the return to the NAIRU in an open economy operates through the deflationary process which improves competitiveness. But the decrease in real wages will not bring about these gains in competitiveness if it is implemented simultaneously in all countries. In addition, losses in the purchasing power of household incomes can counter the positive effect on growth of the increase in profits and competitiveness. So *the equilibrating mechanism of the Phillips curve is not sufficient in an open economy to permit a return to the NAIRU.* Macroeconomic policy is thus required. The need for such an intervention is reinforced by the fact that the macro environment has been largely unfavourable to growth, and thus to employment, because of inadequate macroeconomic policies and/or an inadequate functioning of the institutions determining the formation of interest rates and exchange rates. From this perspective, therefore, *labour market problems are only a consequence of a malfunctioning in the economy.* As such, the partial equilibrium analysis of labour markets appears too limiting: the decrease in real wages may not be sufficient to bring about a return to the NAIRU if mechanisms external to the labour market are taken into account. This comes from the fact that the demand for labour strongly depends on the expectations of production but remains quite inelastic to changes in real wages.

The lack of coordination and the deflationary bias of economic policies in Europe

The organization of economic policy in Europe since the end of the 1970s has largely been determined by the existence of the European Monetary System (EMS). Initially perceived as a mechanism to stabilize fluctuations in the exchange rates between European countries, and thus as a factor of integration of their economies, since 1980 the EMS has become a major instrument of anti-inflationary policy through the external constraints it imposes on the internal partners, both wage-earners and enterprises, with a view to keeping inflation under control and given the doubtful efficacy of devaluations. Thus, the relinquishment of monetary autonomy has been justified by the advantages of anchoring currencies to the mark and the convergence towards the German model of low inflation.

Monetary policy has thus been dictated by the German objectives of low inflation and in this sense has been tight. But budgetary policy has also suffered heavy constraints. No single country, when its economy is as open as those of Europe, can allow itself to practise an expansionist budgetary policy on its own. When interest rates are high, the cost to the budget is too heavy, the more so as the reflationary effect of budgetary stimulation is largely reduced by the high degree of interdependence of the European economies. The coordination of budgetary policies is thus essential. However, not only has no institutional mechanism been established to ensure this coordination, but it has been rendered still more complicated by the independence of the Bundesbank and the high level of interest rates. Now, in open economies, lack of coordination has a strong deflationary bias: no country has an interest in stimulating recovery, since the multiplier effect is largely attenuated by the effect of displacement

Box 1. The impact of budgetary policies in Europe and the United States since 1970

The impact of budgetary policy is traditionally measured by the variation in the balance of public accounts corrected for the effects of the economic situation, which is also known as the structural balance. It is necessary to compare the variation in the overall balance of the effects of automatic stabilizers, a rise in tax receipts and a reduction in benefits, particularly unemployment benefits, during a period of recovery, in order to isolate the purely discretionary – i.e. deliberate – orientation of economic policy. The OECD calculates the following structural deficits, which we shall adopt here: an improvement of 1 percentage point of GDP in the structural balance means that the *ex ante* restrictive effect of the whole series of discretionary measures of budgetary policy on economic activity has been of the order of 1 per cent of GDP.

The calculation of such budgetary indicators poses many problems, both theoretical and empirical. As emphasized by Sterdyniak,[9] among other things, should one consider, with OECD, that a rise in the interest paid on the public debt covers a deliberately expansionary orientation of economic policy? Is this expansionary effect not rather a result, albeit a paradoxical one, of a tightening of monetary policy, or is it merely the consequence of high deficits accumulated in the past? For these reasons we shall examine two types of indicators of orientation of budgetary policy: the structural deficit calculated by the OECD and the primary structural deficit (excluding the debt-servicing burden).

Whatever indicator is adopted, *budgetary policies were expansionary in the 1970s.* Their orientation in succeeding periods is more difficult to determine owing to the increase of the debt-servicing burden, which shows the impact of budgetary policy through the structural balance in a more favourable light.

If we take the structural balance as an indicator, *budgetary policies were relatively neutral in Europe between 1980 and 1993*, the cumulative impact over this period being somewhat restrictive, of the order of 1 point of GDP. Nevertheless, this neutrality over a period of 14 years covers shorter periods where the impact has been more marked: budgetary policy would thus have been restrictive between 1980 and 1987, the total impact at that time reaching 2.2 percentage points of GDP. Finally, owing essentially to the strong budgetary stimulus given by the reunification of Germany, the cumulative effect between 1988 and 1993 is somewhat positive, of the order of 1.2 percentage points of GDP.

On the other hand, if we look at the primary structural deficit, *budgetary policies were far more restrictive in Europe during the period 1980-93*:

by imports. On the other hand, every country benefits from the recovery of its neighbour. It is even in its interest to practise a restrictive policy and thus to "export" its unemployment. Implemented simultaneously, such policies of austerity, competitive disinflation, redressing current balances or public accounts, and pressures on wages, have cost Europe dear as far as employment is concerned.

Economic measures have been all the more difficult to coordinate in that growth requirements differed from one country to another in the 1980s. Growth was, it is said, "pulled back" in countries approaching full employment: it appears that in the only country with low inflation and whose favourable trade balance would easily have allowed it to play the role of leader in a coordinated recovery, namely Germany, unemployment was low and the ageing population appeared rather to favour a reduction in working time with slower growth than a high rate of growth permitting a large increase in incomes. German reunification nevertheless put an end to this state of affairs.

Box 1. *(cont.)*

the cumulative impact was 4.1 percentage points of GDP and was concentrated essentially over the years 1980-87. The employment cost of such a restrictive effect is obviously high.

In the three EFTA countries mentioned in the table, fiscal policies from 1980-93 were generally expansionary regardless of the indicator referred to, but this was essentially due to the large fiscal stimulus in 1992-93 (which had an accumulated impact of 3.6 percentage points over these two years). In fact, budgetary policies were particularly restrictive from 1980-87 (–2.4 percentage points) and afterwards generally neutral until 1991.

In the United States, whatever the indicator used, budgetary policy was on the whole expan-

sionary in the period 1980-93, the *ex ante* cumulative effect reaching 2.5 percentage points of GDP. But there were major changes of orientation in budgetary policy during this period, particularly if we look at the variations in the primary structural balance: under the first Reagan presidency the cumulative expansionary effect reached 3.9 percentage points of GDP, whereas the restrictive effect between 1984 and 1989, a period during which an attempt was made to rebalance public accounts, reached 2.9 percentage points of GDP. Finally, between 1990 and 1993, that is during the period of a marked slow-down in the economy, budgetary policy on the whole supported activity, the global impact attaining 2.1 percentage points of GDP.

Absolute cumulative variation in the structural balance as a percentage of GDP, 1979-93

	1980-93	1979-87	1988-93	1979-83	1984-89	1990-93
Structural balance as a percentage of GDP						
United States	–2.5	..	..	–1.9	0.4	–1.0
Europe 8	1.0	2.2	–1.2	..	..	..
EFTA 3	–3.5	3.4	–7.0	..	..	..
Primary structural balance as a percentage of GDP						
United States	–2.5	..	..	–3.9	2.9	–2.1
Europe 8	4.1	4.0	0.1	..	..	..
EFTA 3	–2.4	4.6	–7.0	..	..	..

Note: a negative sign shows an expansionary orientation, a positive sign a restrictive orientation. Europe 8 excludes Portugal (whose weight of GDP in the EC is 0.6), Luxembourg (0.05), Ireland (0.3) and Greece (0.5). EFTA 3 comprises Austria, Norway and Sweden.

Source: H. Sterdyniak and J. Creel: *Les déficits publics en Europe: causes, conséquences ou remèdes à la crise?* (forthcoming).

Today, although inflation has returned to historically low levels in most European countries, apart from Germany, economic policies continue to be restrictive in Europe. The struggle against inflation in Germany obliges interest rates to be kept high. In return, the constraints of indebtedness are severe, so that budgetary policy has little freedom of manoeuvre. Admittedly, during the 1993 recession, most countries allowed the automatic stabilizers to come into play, so that budgetary policy has played an expansionary role, at least cyclically. But the commitment of European countries to observe in the medium term the Maastricht criteria for the adoption of a single currency – inflation within the limit of 2 per cent above the average of the three countries with the lowest inflation, public deficit less than 3 per cent of GDP, and public debt not exceeding 60 per cent of GDP – obliges them to pursue policies to restore equilibrium, even when they have already regained a degree of macroeconomic stability (low inflation, healthy balance of foreign trade), but when their public finances are still in deficit. In such countries a restrictive budgetary policy is obviously inadequate, since the level of private savings spontaneously corresponds to the level of public indebtedness without creating pressures on foreign trade balances or excess internal demand, and unemployment remains persistently high owing to insufficient growth.

Labour market regulation

As discussed in the previous section, employment performance varied significantly in OECD countries in spite of similar growth rates. In the face of economic changes broadly shared by most OECD countries over the past two decades, it has become widely accepted that differences in labour market regulation must play a central – if not the central – role in explaining differences in labour market outcomes. The efficiency of the less regulated United States labour market has been compared with what has been termed as "Eurosclerosis",[10] the *overall* barriers to adjustment that the full range of European labour protection – e.g. strong unions, stringent employment protection, the generous provisions of the Welfare State – was argued to produce on employment growth. In the "perilous economic environment of the past two decades", it has been argued, "a trade-off was positioned between social protection and economic flexibility".[11] This section assesses the validity of this view that labour market rigidity was the main cause of poor employment performance in Europe. It begins with a review of the evidence with respect to major elements of labour market regulation that have often been identified as being responsible for poor employment performance.

Wage flexibility

Most fundamental to the debate on labour market regulation is the "disequilibrium real wage hypothesis". This asserts that the growth of real wages has exceeded that which is warranted, whether with respect to the growth of productivity or some fundamental disturbance resulting in a decline of output and demand. The existence of such a "wage gap" is said to lower firms' profits, and thus investment. Excessive wages, it is claimed, first trigger a round of "labour shedding"; the persistent failure of wages to adjust then results in labour displacement, since, as Krugman argues,[12] the reduced amount of capital available to firms would be invested in labour-saving "capital deepening" rather than in expanding output. Capacity thus shrinks, and higher levels of unemployment then become consistent with full capacity utilization.

Are wages in Europe "too high"?

Most empirical studies of the growth of real wages since the 1970s yield a relatively consistent story. In a climate of expanding output and productivity increase in the 1960s, real wages grew at high but "warranted" rates. They began to accelerate in Europe towards the end of that decade and continued to grow throughout the 1970s in spite of the lower productivity growth and supply shocks of that decade. "Labour's resistance" to accept the terms of trade reversals brought about by higher energy costs and, in several countries, the protection of real wages through automatic indexation mechanisms, have been offered as one explanation.[13] When unemployment rose in the late 1970s, it could thus be thought of as "classical" in origin;[14] excessive real wage growth outstripped the economy's ability to provide jobs for all who wanted them at current levels of demand.

Into the 1980s, at lower levels of growth of aggregate output throughout the OECD area, both real wages and productivity in European industry continued to rise. Since wage pressures in Europe may have induced firms to invest in labour-saving productivity improvements, the magnitude of the wage growth problem in many European countries in the first half of the 1980s may have been understated.[15] In the United States, on the other hand, the economy accommodated significant employment growth during the decade. But this was achieved against a backdrop of stagnant productivity growth, only moderate real wage growth and, in fact, real-wage decline for large segments of the workforce. The United States economy appeared to have added jobs at the expense of productivity and real-wage growth, whereas the trade-off in Europe showed up in higher real wages and productivity, but rising unemployment in a climate of low aggregate demand growth.

In the early years of the employment crisis, a significant factor behind rising unemployment might in part have been the sluggish adjustment of wages. By the mid-1980s, however, this no longer held true. As Bean records:[16] "Real wage gaps had disappeared in most countries by the mid-1980s, suggesting Keynesian unemployment," or unemployment caused by inadequate demand, rather than wages that were too high. With the objective of disinflation, regimes of macroeconomic policy austerity prevailed in Europe. Countries abandoned automatic wage indexation mechanisms, and real-wage moderation was such that wages trailed the continued growth of productivity in Europe. By the end of the decade, labour's share of value added in the economy had declined to its early 1970s level, and firms' profit levels had been restored. By the mid-1980s the labour market in much of Europe had still failed to "clear", but "excessive real-wage growth" no longer appeared a convincing explanation. This fall in the wage share probably helps explain, at least in part, why employment expanded so strongly in Europe during the period of recovery from the mid- to late 1980s. Significantly, however, even by the end of the decade, European unemployment remained high even before being exacerbated by renewed recession in the 1990s. This suggests that, despite the apparent absence of classical unemployment, other factors were causing the persistence of high unemployment.

Have industrial relations systems made wages rigid?

The wage-setting institutions of industrial relations have often been identified as a source of labour market rigidity. Two main claims have been made: first, that trade unions through collective bargaining raise the wages of their members above those of unorganized workers and, more generally, above those that would prevail in a purely competitive marketplace for labour; and, second, that trade unions tend to narrow the wage spread, primarily by raising the wages of their lowest-paid members. It is often argued that both effects may raise wages above their market-clearing levels, make them resistant to downward adjustment, thus lowering overall employment, and, by narrowing wage relativities, concentrate unemployment among workers with the lowest productivity. Since the speed of labour market adjustment may depend on how flexibly aggregate and relative wages adjust to change, the OECD has recently argued that greater labour market competition is desirable.[17] Since it acknowledges that *some* restraints on labour market competition are still desirable, very decentralized industrial relations systems are advocated as the best solution: "Enterprise bargaining structures are most likely to combine the benefits associated with competition-restraining practices without unduly limiting flexible wage formation. As long as companies are selling their products in competitive markets, there will be little scope for 'insiders' to raise wages beyond competitive levels." But the evidence for this view is at best unclear.

A literature comparing "corporatist" and centralized versus "pluralist" and decentralized forms of interest organization sought to link wage determination with macroeconomic performance. The observation that some economies had been better able to adjust wages consistent with the objectives of full employment and low inflation aroused interest in the institutional conditions under which the macroeconomic impact of wage bargaining could be internalized by bargaining agents. Attention dwelt on the extent to which wage bargaining was either centralized or co-ordinated by broad-based and authoritative interest representation groups with direct or indirect coordination by the State. With data from before the mid-1980s, a relatively consistent outcome of this literature is that optimal macroeconomic performance was found to be true of the most corporatist and centralized industrial relations systems, where the macroeconomic effects of wages on inflation and employment were internalized by powerful, centralized bargaining agents, or, conversely, the least corporatist or most decentralized systems where the discipline of market forces adjusted wages to employment. Countries in the "middle", where powerful bargaining cartels struck wage bargains at the industry level and where their wage deals could be legally extended industry-wide, were argued to perform worst of all. There was little incentive for employers to resist wage increases since their direct competitors shared the same fate and cost increases could be diffused throughout the economy in prices. Nor, it was argued, were there any incentives for unions to be concerned about the employment consequences of any but the industry "insiders", their members.

However, several doubts have been expressed over the validity of these conclusions: methodological concerns over how the performance of countries should be ranked with reference to their institutional structures would seem inevitable given the inherently qualitative nature of the variables concerned,[18] and correlations have thus rarely been robust or even statistically significant; nor, given the inherent complexity of industrial relations systems, the variety of paths of systemic adjustment, and the likelihood that other factors than labour market institutions have a more direct bearing on macroeconomic outcomes, can one comfortably distinguish the discrete role of industrial relations structures on prices and employment. Finally, the results no longer seem to hold good in the 1990s, or at least are far more ambiguous.[19] Symptomatic of this, of course, are the problems now faced by the "Swedish model", once emblematic of corporatist success, and now saddled with high public-sector deficits and a sharp rise in unemployment since 1990. There remain serious doubts, however, as to whether the structure of wage-setting institutions is to blame for this breakdown.[20]

These doubts over corporatist systems of industrial relations do not, however, prove the opposite case that decentralized systems are better. Union membership has fallen in many OECD countries over the 1980s and 1990s – and "precipitously"[21] in the United Kingdom and the United States, countries where decentralization of bargaining is predominant. In the United Kingdom and New Zealand, labour market reform has specifically targeted the structures of collective bargaining and trade unionism with the aim of intensifying labour market competition, lowering labour costs and increasing employment. A chief characteristic of decentralized industrial relations settings is that union density rates correspond closely to the coverage rate of collective bargaining; that is, the outcome of collective bargaining directly affects only those included in the agreement. (France, on the other hand, has the lowest union density rate in the OECD, but a very high coverage rate, since collective agreements are frequently legally extended throughout the economy.) In both the United States and the United Kingdom wage inequality has widened as union density has declined. For the United Kingdom, Schmitt[22] finds that 25 per cent of the rise in wage inequality can be attributed to the decline in union density, and others note that the greatest dispersion occurs in non-unionized firms. The decline of union density explains a similar share of the rise in wage inequality in the United States.[23] But rising wage inequality may also feed back negatively on union density rates by exposing unionized firms to greater wage competition and by giving greater incentives to employers to resist union organization. In short, unless governments would mandate employee representation at the enterprise level in countries where labour relations are decentralized (which is unlikely), the advocacy of enterprise bargaining, mentioned earlier, seems academic; in no such countries are union members a majority of the workforce. The benefits of their "competition-restraining" effect on the labour market are thus fragile and subject to erosion by greater labour market competition.

If unions in decentralized industrial relations settings allow relative wages to adjust more rapidly than in more centralized ones, then the positive trade-off should be in employment. In a general sense, the OECD presents evidence that this is the case,[24] although, for the United States, rising wage inequality and strong employment growth also appear to be associated with rising poverty. The picture for the United Kingdom should be more revealing, as the deregulation of industrial relations was explicitly intended to improve the jobs/pay trade-off. The results, however, have not been uniformly encouraging.[25] First, despite the decline in union density and decentralization of bargaining, real wages have increased at a higher rate than productivity growth. While the union/non-union wage differential has decreased, it has not increased aggregate employment as predicted. Nor has decentralized bargaining produced a superior inflation/jobs trade-off to more coordinated bargaining. Unemployment remains stubbornly over 2 million, whereas in the 1950-79 period it never rose to that figure. Finally, deregulation does not appear to have addressed the mounting problem of the severe deterioration in the employment prospects for the less skilled. The record for decentralization and deregulation of industrial relations would thus seem to be at best a trade-off between employment and inequality. It will also be interesting to follow closely future developments in New Zealand where industrial relations have undergone more dramatic reforms than in any other OECD country through the 1991 Employment Contract Act. It is, however, still too early to attempt any comprehensive assessment of the impact of these reforms.

The theoretical advantages of open, decentralized competition in labour markets must ultimately contend with the observation that the world's three most successful economies, the United States, Japan and Germany, all have vastly different institutional systems of wage determination, union density, levels of bargaining, coverage rates of bargaining and patterns of economy-wide coordination. On the one hand, the minimal conclusion to draw is that such differences simply do not matter in terms of aggregate employment and other macroeconomic variables. On the other hand, such differences may indeed matter, and may help to explain the relative success of such countries as Switzerland and Austria as well. Although the evidence as such cannot be anything more than indicative, some similar institutional features among otherwise different economies may have given them relative competitive advantage in recent years.

First, the United States aside, all of these economies share a relatively high degree of coordination in their wage bargaining intended to internalize trade-offs among wages, employment and prices. Significantly, the nature of coordination in Japan and Switzerland is horizontal across firms and can arguably be called "employer-driven". If defined solely from the perspective of the predominant locus of bargaining, then both countries are "decentralized" systems. Arguably such systems may further the objective of greater sensitivity to local labour market conditions, while nevertheless taking an economy-wide perspective on wage developments.

Second, flexible adjustments in relative wages can occur under widely differing industrial relations systems. In this context, it is striking that Austria, which is often at the top of corporatism rankings, is also the country in Western Europe with the highest inter-industry wage spread. Japan, too, is noted for its economy-wide earnings inequality (although narrow wage spread at the firm level). As Freeman and Katz observe: "Japan has sizable variation in wages across industries, which one normally associates with decentralized wage setting, but the percentage change in wages across sectors and firms in Japan is remarkably similar, which suggests a more centralized wage-setting mechanism."[26] Incomes policies are notoriously difficult to implement and sustain in the most decentralized countries, yet "in the 1970s Japan rapidly reduced its rate of wage inflation throughout the economy in a way that would do the most centralized wage-setting system proud". At the microeconomic level, the greater degree of real wage flexibility in Japan was associated with the widespread practice in major firms of profit-related bonuses, a variable component of pay that, depending on conditions, could amount to 30 per cent of workers' annual salary.[27]

As for Austria, wage bargaining is highly centralized at the industrial branch level, but, according to one author:[28] "the aim of the wage policy is not redistribution, either at the macro- or microeconomic level." Rather, while centralized wage bargaining produces roughly uniform nominal wage increases and is based on a consensus on a "constant ratio of wages to national income", considerable latitude is left for wage drift at the company level. In consequence, "industries with high productivity growth and strong unions have the highest effective wage increases". The maintenance of wage relativities and the speed of relative wage adjustment would therefore not seem antithetical either to the presence of strong unions or to high degrees of economy-wide coordination. Germany shares at least some of these wage-setting features, and its record on relatively low youth unemployment has been associated with both the quality and the design of its vocational training and with its low apprenticeship wages. But it is alone among OECD countries in seeing its wage spread actually narrow in the 1980s. Despite its relatively good economic performance and low level of aggregate unemployment, however, Germany also has a fairly high share of long-term unemployed. Both Japan and Germany, finally, have well-deserved reputations for integrating the lower-skilled into jobs through education and vocational training systems that increase their productivity.

Overall, the conclusion appears to be that a variety of institutional arrangements on national labour markets can cope with the challenges of labour market adjustment through wage flexibility and allowing relative wages to adjust, while at the same time incorporating employment objectives. Thorough decentralization, whether as the passive outcome of allowing market forces free rein or through conscious policies of deregulation, may have benefits not considered here, but also hidden economic costs. If anything, moreover, the evidence above suggests that the co-ordination of wage policy with macroeconomic objectives remains in some settings still possible, efficient and superior to atomistic competition.

Minimum wages

It is often claimed that the existence of minimum wages is associated in theory and in fact with negative employment effects. However, the bulk of empirical evidence, which is focused on young workers, largely finds these effects to be minimal. Indeed, recent evidence for the United States finds either that minimum wages have no effect, can increase labour supply and employment, or were *negatively* correlated to youth unemployment in the latter half of the 1980s.[29] Minimum wages established through wage councils were eliminated in the United Kingdom in 1993 on the theory that they negatively affected job creation. Dickens, Machin and Manning,[30] however, find that the effect of wage council minima on employment was neutral or positive between 1978 and 1990. The effects of regulating the minimum wage may be more substantial as its level approaches average earnings. The Netherlands and France have relatively high minimum wages. For the Netherlands, van Soest[31] finds that the minimum wage negatively affects both youth and adult employment. Only in France, however, did the minimum wage rise relative to the average wage during the 1980s. This rise,[32] in conjunction with greater efforts to enforce the minimum wage, has been argued to have contributed to the rise in youth unemployment in France. Others have estimated the impact of the minimum wage in France on youth unemployment to be statistically significant but relatively small and, indeed, far less severe than earlier assumed, to the point where the desirability of a sub-minimum wage for young workers can be questioned.[33] No effect of the French minimum wage has been found on adult employment.[34] In theory, minimum wages can push all wages up and negat-ively affect employment, but in the majority of industrialized countries statutory minimum wages declined relative to average wages in the 1980s.[35] In general, "most empirical evidence points to rather modest effects [of the minimum wage] on total equilibrium unemployment".[36]

Many European countries have separate, "sub-minimum" wages for young workers, which may be appropriate given the special vulnerability that the in-experienced face in the labour market. While the employment creation effect of such programmes can be substantial, they must also be evaluated with a view to determining whether a lower minimum wage for this group – or the absence of a minimum wage altogether – would produce substantial substitution effects to the disadvantage of employed adult workers.[37]

In practice, wage floors can be established not only by statutory minima for adult workers but through industry-wide bargaining and the practice in some countries for resulting minima to be administratively extended to all workers in the industry. The OECD argues on theoretical grounds that administrative extension may reduce competition in the product market and lessen job creation in labour-intensive industries by barring potential new entrants from competing on the basis of lower wages.[38] Workers of relatively low marginal productivity would be disproportionately affected. But the practice of legal extension does not occur in a vacuum, isolated from market forces – and, indeed, legal extension is preceded by bargaining, which itself can resist competitive pressures for only so long. Moreover, abolishing extension could in some settings undermine the benefits of coordinating wage movements. This is because extension gives employers incentives to participate in their respective federations, since bargaining outcomes may unfavourably affect the unrepresented employer. Extension may thus further the objective of wage coordination.

Non-wage labour costs

Another concern over the price of labour relates to the high component of non-wage labour costs (NWLCs) in total costs in some countries. This arises from the funding of social security programmes and other benefit entitlements out of firms' payroll taxes. It is argued that the high non-wage component of labour costs drives a "wedge" between the cost of labour to the firm and the wage at which employees would be willing to work. This constitutes a disincentive to hire and, through its negative impact on relative factor costs, sets in motion the process of the substitution of capital for labour referred to earlier.

NWLCs vary in proportion to total labour costs across countries. Increases in NWLCs can have negative short-term effects on employment, much the same as unwarranted wage increases can have. In the long run, "backward-shifting" of NWLCs onto workers' real earnings for the most part occurs, i.e. workers ultimately "pay" for longer vacations through their pay packets, etc. Evidence of this lies in the fact that countries with similar levels of productivity and similar labour costs nevertheless show great differences in the share of NWLCs in total labour costs.[39] The European Commission[40] finds that "the respective shares of labour costs and profits in value-added are also similar [across countries] and appear not to be affected to any great extent by the relative importance of employers' contributions in total labour costs". Rather, while the total package of remuneration is fixed by the level of productivity, differences in the composition of that package suggest that workers, employers and societies have considerable freedom to choose.

Since NWLCs are nevertheless an important component of total labour costs, European employers do perceive them to be a possible disincentive to hire.[41]

Would, then, a reduction in NWLCs boost employment? On the one hand, if reducing them results in a decline in social protection, then it is likely that workers will endeavour to offset the loss of income through higher wages. On the other hand, since wages may not immediately catch up, or could be managed through temporary incomes policies, the European Commission[42] argues that the reduction of NWLCs could be used as a medium-term employment strategy. Moreover, this strategy would be arguably more effective than reductions in wages, as a positive employment effect of the latter might be offset by a decline in consumption.

The NWLCs of workers of low marginal productivity deserve separate discussion. In nine EU countries the structure of NWLCs is "regressive", which means that, relative to wage levels, NWLCs represent a disproportionately higher share of the costs of employing a low-wage worker, since wage floors prevent the backward-shifting of NWLCs onto these workers. With the absence of such wage floors, however, the employment/unemployment trade-off would risk increasing the number of working poor. Since regressive NWLCs may be an additional factor in "pricing out" the low marginal productivity worker from employment, the scaling down or elimination of non-wage costs could have a beneficial impact on employment. This would preserve the institutional impact of wage compression, but simulate the differentials in total labour costs that would emerge in a competitive market. It would therefore appear that the reform of existing systems of financing unemployment and other social security benefits through payroll taxes should be given serious consideration. Discussion returns to the problem of payroll taxes below, and specific ideas for reform are evaluated.

Systems of unemployment benefits

Apart from the problems arising from the fact that they are financed through payroll taxes, systems of unemployment benefits are often blamed for aggravating the underlying employment problem through discouraging job search. Unemployment benefits comprise two components: an insurance component (UI) to which workers typically contribute and for which eligibility to claim benefits relates to previous work history; and an assistance component (UA), often means-related and of indefinite duration, to which those without work may have access once UI benefits expire or independently of prior work history. Approximately one-half of OECD countries have some form of guaranteed income support on these grounds. As for the structure of UI, the level (replacement rates) and duration of, and eligibility for, benefits vary widely among OECD countries. Consequently, in some countries, such as the United States, only a minority of unemployed persons as defined by the ILO may actually receive unemployment benefits, whereas in some European countries all such persons, as well as other categories of those without work, may receive benefits.

It is widely agreed that the level of unemployment benefits (i.e. the generosity of replacement rates) affects the duration of unemployment spells. Nickell's summary of the evidence is representative: "Studies indicate that the duration effects are significant but small, the general order of magnitude being that a 10 per cent increase in benefits leads to a 3 per cent rise in the average duration of unemployment spells."[43] Since the effects, while statistically significant, appear to be small, the level of benefit payments cannot by itself account for high levels of European unemployment: observed levels of unemployment are far higher than such estimates would predict.[44] By implication, reducing replacement rates or raising the "desperation" level at which the unemployed must search for jobs would require major rather than small reductions in generosity of payments.[45]

The duration of benefits is also believed to affect the duration of unemployment. Outflows from unemployment into jobs tend to be "spiked" about the period when benefit entitlements expire.[46] Nickell observes that "those countries where benefits are available for only a limited period (e.g. Canada, Norway, Sweden and United States) have much lower unemployment durations than those countries, such as Belgium, Germany, the Netherlands and the United Kingdom, where benefits are effectively payable for an indefinite period."[47] Layard also notes "a striking positive correlation"[48] between duration of benefits and duration of unemployment, as does the OECD[49] in finding a relationship between benefit duration and the magnitude of long-term unemployment.

For Layard, the real impact of benefit duration on unemployment "is how unemployment responds after a shock rather than its steady state level".[50] The existence of unemployment benefits keeps wages from adjusting downwards, and a variety of "insider/outsider" dynamics on both sides of the labour market may make unemployment persist. Disincentive effects may be greatest for the less educated and less skilled, whose reservation wages remain higher than market alternatives.[51] Long-lasting and generous unemployment benefits would then affect the composition of unemployment,[52] a view consistent with the observation that the long-term unemployed are disproportionately represented by those with the least education or skills or the least experience. All this suggests that, in addition to reviewing methods by which they are financed, other aspects of unemployment benefit systems offer fruitful scope for reform. These issues are taken up in a subsequent section.

Rules on employment protection

Employment security rules or high "firing costs" have often been cited as a deterrent to job creation. Such rules are varied and complex,[53] but may be thought of as embodying three considerations. First are rules on prior notification of dismissals; second are rules on the procedures governing dismissals, i.e. whom to select and how, criteria establishing unfair grounds for dismissal; finally, rules govern the amount of severance pay to which the dismissed employee is entitled. Regulation on each often varies with the seniority, age, employment and social status of the individual concerned. The case against employment protection is fairly straightforward in theoretical terms: by making labour a more fixed factor of production, allocative efficiency is argued to be distorted and labour market adjustment slowed; by adding to the cost of labour, employment protection would constitute a disincentive to hire.

Surveys of European employers record the perception that stringent employment protection laws impede job creation.[54] High firing costs may induce firms to use their existing workforce more intensively, and may lower the future demand for labour as firms substitute capital for it.[55] Drawing from data over a 29-year period for 22 countries, for example, Lazear[56] finds that employment protection reduces the employment/population ratio, but acknowledges that this finding is very sensitive to his model's specifications. Wells and Grubb and Wells[57] have argued that the extent to which societies protect full-time jobs of indefinite duration limits the number of such jobs that an economy can produce.

Do theory and perception match actual outcomes on the labour market? A number of European economies in the 1980s allowed firms to circumvent stringent employment protection rules with the objective of job creation. The results have been mixed. Changes in laws permitting the use of fixed-term contracts in France increased the number of these contracts, but the removal of administrative approval for dismissals did not appear to give a substantial boost to hiring; in Germany, the eased availability of fixed-term contracts appeared to alter hiring behaviour hardly at all.[58] When Spain relaxed the terms under which firms could hire workers on a temporary basis, job creation rebounded. In fact, the majority of jobs created in Spain since 1987 have been temporary jobs; but a disproportionate share of those entering unemployment has also been accounted for by temporary workers whose contracts have expired. There, the greater ease with which firms can circumvent stringent employment protection laws by hiring on a fixed-term basis has not appeared to have substantially lowered unemployment. The Spanish unemployment rate, for example, continues to be at the top of the European league.

Why does employment protection not appear substantially to alter labour market adjustment? One reason is that adjustment can occur through several different paths. A review of patterns of labour adjustment in Belgium, France, Germany and the United States,[59] finds for the three European countries that employment has indeed adjusted more slowly to changes in output than in the United States. But adjustment in hours worked is similar across the countries: employment protection has not significantly altered whether adjustment has occurred to changes in output; rather it is the adjustment path that has varied – specifically, whether adjustment has been achieved through changes in working time or in the numbers employed. It may be for this reason – i.e. the availability of systemic offsets – that employment protection in some settings is not a major disincentive to hiring.

The creation of stable, long-term jobs may in any case have little to do with firing costs. As Drèze argues,[60] the determinants of long-term, "regular" jobs have mostly to do with the existence of openings and firms' expectations on the stability of future demand: "If the prospect for continued employment is there, severance pay (though relevant) is not a major issue. But if the prospect for continued employment is lacking, then no regular job is at hand, irrespective of the severance pay issue." Reducing firing costs would "not have a major influence on the supply of regular jobs". This view is consistent with the observation of a high rate of employment creation in Europe following the economic upturn of 1986.

However, while employment protection may not be a significant deterrent to labour hiring and may not foreclose adjustment, it could still cause slower adjustments. If firing costs make firms slow to hire in an upturn, they may also make them slow to shed labour in a downturn. Thus, the impact of employment protection may be to reduce the volatility of employment fluctuations over the cycle, while leaving overall employment relatively unchanged. Labour is hoarded in a downturn, and job creation may be slower to rebound as business conditions improve,[61] a view that seems to fit the dynamics of European unemployment.

In fact, the dual effect of labour hoarding and slower hiring may actually be to *raise* total employment over the cycle more than would occur in environments where employment protection is weak.[62] As Bean observes, this employment effect would be even more substantial if it were plausible to assume that employees trade off greater employment protection for lower wages, as they may do over the long run or at a specific moment in time, as during "concession bargaining" in the United States, or in conjunction with considerable wage flexibility, as in Japan, or by adjusting both wages and working time to the objective of employment stability.[63]

In sum, theory and perception may exaggerate the inflexibility of employment protection. As the McKinsey Global Institute recently concluded: "While many employers complained about inflexibility in interviews, the evidence showed when companies were forced to react to dramatic changes in the market place, they were able to overcome these barriers. The transaction costs of hiring and firing play a relatively minor role."[64]

If labour is still shed in Europe when necessary, is the process of labour market reallocation any different than in settings with minimal firing costs? How quickly employment adjusts out of declining sectors and into expanding ones is argued to be important, since slow adjustment may lower the economy's growth of output and productivity.[65] Burgess considered the effect of employment protection on employment reallocation in ten OECD countries and for 20 two-digit industries (International Standard Classification of Occupations) within each. Differences in employment protection did seem to influence the speed of reallocating labour in the predicted way, but he finds the evidence to be neither "particularly strong" nor "compelling". The McKinsey Global Institute[66] found the evidence even less compelling: More "trial and error" and weaker employment security in the United States do not seem to determine greater hiring there, relative to Europe. "Overall flexibility of the European economy does not seem to lag behind the US in terms of total gross job creation and destruction." Similarities in patterns of labour reallocation have also been found by the OECD, and, for the United States and Canada, by Baldwin, Dunne and Haltiwanger, irrespective of differences in firing costs.[67]

Summing up

The foregoing review of evidence on the impact of key aspects of labour market regulation on employment suggests that it is far from clear that labour market rigidities are the major cause of high unemployment. It follows from this that it is by no means obvious that labour market deregulation is the solution for high unemployment.

The prominence that the reform of labour market regulation retains in high-level policy circles makes it important to know whether labour market regulations are merely "downstream" *mechanisms* that produce different labour market outcomes, or whether they are part of the *underlying "upstream" causes* of those outcomes. Depending upon which view is correct, reform can be expected to have a long-term and salutary impact on labour market performance or merely exchange one set of problems for another.

Our reading of the evidence suggests that labour market regulations have not been part of the underlying causes of labour market performance problems. Whatever their regulatory patterns, signs of fragility appear in all OECD labour markets in the mid-1990s. In settings such as the United States, where rules do not impede a variety of adjustment paths, fragility takes the form of widening income distribution and rising poverty, or concerns over employment security or a "core" of stable jobs set against a periphery of precarious employment. In the more regulated settings of many European countries employment may be stable or secure for those who have jobs – inflows into unemployment are lower – but a significant share of the labour force may be excluded from employment altogether, or channelled into the secondary labour market of temporary, fixed-term or even concealed work. Over two decades of turbulence and change, no OECD labour market has remained unaffected: *labour market performance has deteriorated when compared with the stable environment of growth that prevailed until 1970. And this deterioration has occurred irrespective of differences in labour market regulation.* If employment creation but rising inequality on one side of the Atlantic and high unemployment on the other are two sides of the same coin, this would suggest something more fundamental behind poor labour market performance, whereas differences in labour market rules might account for *different patterns of inadequacy*. In this sense, and as has been argued in previous ILO work on labour market flexibility, the "unemployment rate" alone is an inadequate measure of labour market performance as it fails to capture the full range and variety of labour market slack.[68]

The foregoing discussion has also shown that some evidence supports the view that labour market rules may plausibly contribute to the persistence of unemployment and displace employment at the lower end of the earnings scale. But, even without consideration of their benefits, that the costs of labour market rules are in any major way a barrier to labour market performance is far from convincing. From the foregoing evidence it cannot be said that the level of wages continues to be a significant problem and, indeed, their reduction would only have a meagre impact on unemployment. Nor do statutory minimum wages appear in any general sense to affect aggregate unemployment. Some relatively institutionalized countries where wages are coordinated beyond the level of the firm do not appear to have performed poorly. Modern labour market theories of "efficiency wages", "implied contracts", or "norm-guided" labour market behaviour[69] furthermore suggest that there are good reasons why wages do not clear the labour market in the first place, quite independently of explicit or formal mechanisms of rigidity. Recent empirical evidence for many countries suggests that, irrespective of the presence of trade unions or other formal regulation, wages across countries only marginally adjust to changes in unemployment, and not in a way that would clear the market.[70]

Employment protection rules do not convincingly seem a barrier to hiring or firing. If rigidity in European labour markets is a problem of the magnitude that many have suggested, how could the European Union countries have added 17 million jobs during the upturn of the late 1980s – more than were added by the United States over the equivalent period? Nor can the level of unemployment benefits account for high unemployment, and there are, moreover, problems of timing: why was European unemployment lower and United States unemployment higher in the 1960s when differences in labour market regulation between both sides of the Atlantic were prevalent then as now? Why has high unemployment persisted despite the declining power of trade unions and changes since the 1980s in many European countries which *weakened* labour market regulation? It could of course be argued that deregulatory changes have not proceeded fast or far enough, but there are also clearly other factors behind poor labour market performance.

"If the cause of persistent unemployment among European countries was similar to the cause of rising inequality in the United States, then the key policy issue is not labour market flexibility. Rather, the issue is international shifts in trade, employment and technology, which were manifested in different ways in different economies".[71] But, in addition to the labour market, there may be other regulatory spheres situated between these broad trends and their downstream consequences on employment.

A recent study targets the product rather than the labour market, and makes two central observations on the relationship between regulation and job creation.[72] First, it finds that a number of anti-competitive regulations in European product markets – ranging from restrictions on opening or operating hours, to zoning laws, and to a variety of other regulatory barriers to entry – are found to impede employment creation. Second, it is primarily anti-competitive product market regulation which works against job creation – not labour market regulation. Relative to job creation, labour market "rigidities" are found by and large to play a "relatively minor" role, confined in most instances to the lower end of the earnings distribution, and rarely constitute "binding constraints". While, in the logic of some observers, the message of deregulation would extend to *all* markets, with product-market and labour-market deregulation proceeding hand-in-hand, the main implication of the McKinsey study is that the matter of labour market regulation may be wrongly conflated with problems in another regulatory sphere: "Deregulation in the labour market will… lead to a higher number of low skill, low wage jobs. Deregulation in the product market, however, will lead to job creation across the board".[73]

This debate over labour market regulation is, however, not simply an academic one but has implications for the reform of existing labour market regulation. Some concrete proposals for reform are in fact on the current policy agenda in several countries. It is important that the social partners be involved not only in the general debate on these proposals but also in the actual formulation of new regulations. Social concertation in this area will be essential for arriving at a harmonious balance between the competing demands of economic efficiency and social protection.

Reducing unemployment

Macroeconomic policies

Mass unemployment has affected essentially the countries of the European Community for two decades. In the United States the nature of the problem is different: the economy fluctuates cyclically around a NAIRU of about 6 per cent. The problem is not so much to create more jobs as to return to a productivity growth rate enabling the historical rises in American incomes to be restored.

In Europe the opposite situation prevails: the growth of incomes has remained satisfactory, and productivity has continued to grow, although at a markedly slower rate since the first oil shock, but larger and larger numbers of workers are finding themselves excluded from the labour market. This section will examine possible remedies to this endemic plague of European economies.

The case of the former EFTA countries is different. Although its member States have recently experienced a rise in unemployment, which still nevertheless remains lower than 6 per cent throughout EFTA, excluding Finland, they do not for the time being have to face unemployment of the same kind as the countries of the European Community. They have experienced neither long-term unemployment nor massive unemployment of youth and less qualified persons. Nevertheless, there exists the risk that this cyclical unemployment will gradually become transformed into structural unemployment. Sweden, for example, has always managed to maintain a low rate of unemployment by taking the unemployed into public employment, training programmes, youth measures, subsidized employment and relief work. If this policy were to be discontinued under a strategy of reducing the public deficit in the medium term, for example, unemployment might become persistent and even increase rapidly if future recovery were not sufficiently vigorous. The debate on the solutions to the problem of persistent unemployment might thus become a topical one in Northern Europe.

The growth necessary to return to full employment

In the absence of any major external shock, and assuming that present economic policies will be maintained, the prospects as regards unemployment as projected in the long-term scenarios constructed by various organizations, such as the OECD and the *Observatoire français des conjonctures économiques* (OFCE) are gloomy: growth is far from adequate to bring Europe back to full employment. The MIMOSA long-term scenario came to the conclusion that most countries are hampered by severe macroeconomic constraints: inflationary pressures due to low productivity gains in the United States, absence of margins in the budgets of most countries due to a large backlog of public debt and high rates of real interest compared with the growth rate. Long-term interest rates remain high even where easy money policies have been adopted, because of their formation on financial markets independently of the level of short-term rates and the low level of inflation. Moreover, these constraints are mutually reinforcing in a highly interdependent world. The growth of consumption is held back by that of wages and by persistent unemployment. Since demand is weak, investment by enterprises is low. In the absence of suitable economic policies "the secret of growth seems to have been lost."[74]

Table 21 shows that unemployment is above all a problem for European countries. Only Austria, Iceland, Japan, Norway, Portugal, Switzerland and the United States should have, according to OECD forecasts, unemployment rates lower than 7 per cent in 1995. Countries such as Austria, Belgium, Canada, Finland and Ireland would need a growth rate of more than 4 per cent in order to return to an unemployment rate of 5 per cent by the year 2000. Certain European countries, such as Denmark, Greece, the Netherlands and Portugal, would need a growth rate of the order of 3 to 3.5 per cent.

Table 21. **Forecasts of unemployment rates in the year 2000 (assuming that economic policies remain unchanged) and of growth required to reach a 5 per cent unemployment rate in the year 2000**

Country	GDP[1]	Productivity[1]	Employment[1]	Active population[1,2]	Unemployment rate in 2000	Required growth[1]	Unemployment rate in 1995[3]
USA	2.2	1.1	1.1	1.1	**5.8**	**2.6**	5.8
Japan	3.3	2.7	0.6	0.6	**2.8**	**2.4**	2.8
Germany	3.0	2.5	0.5	0.1	**8.2**	**4.4**	10.0
France	2.2	2.1	0.1	0.5	**14.0**	**6.2**	12.2
Italy	1.9	2.0	–0.1	0.2	**13.2**	**5.6**	11.9
United Kingdom	2.2	1.9	0.3	0.4	**9.4**	**4.1**	8.2
Spain	3.0	2.0	1.0	0.8	**23.7**	**12.2**	24.4
Portugal	3.0	2.1	0.9	0.6	**5.5**	**3.2**	6.9
Greece	2.5	1.4	1.1	0.2	**6.9**	**3.4**	11.0
Netherlands	2.0	1.2	0.8	0.2	**6.8**	**2.8**	9.5
Denmark	2.0	1.7	0.3	–0.2	**8.2**	**3.4**	10.5
Ireland	2.0	1.8	0.2	0.8	**17.9**	**8.0**	15.4
Belgium	2.0	1.8	0.2	0.0	**11.8**	**5.1**	12.7
Sweden	2.0	1.9	0.1	0.2	**8.3**	**3.4**	7.8
Norway	2.0	1.8	0.2	0.4	**6.1**	**2.5**	5.2
Switzerland	2.0	1.3	0.7	0.2	**1.3**	**0.5**	3.8
Finland	1.0	1.0	0.0	0.0	**17.7**	**6.9**	17.7
Austria	2.0	1.3	0.7	0.0	**1.2**	**0.5**	4.6
Iceland	2.0	1.0	1.0	0.8	**5.3**	**2.1**	6.2
Canada	2.0	1.0	1.0	1.3	**11.5**	**4.9**	10.2
Australia	2.0	0.9	1.1	1.6	**11.7**	**5.0**	9.5
New Zealand	2.0	1.5	0.5	0.8	**9.5**	**4.0**	8.1

[1] The average rate of growth forecast between 1995 and 2000 (source: OFCE 1993). [2] Source: Eurostat projections. [3] Source: OECD forecasts (Paris, 1994).

A key element in solving the problem of high unemployment is thus policies to raise rates of economic growth. The possible contribution of expansionary macro-economic policies to achieving this will first be discussed. This will be followed by a discussion of longer-term growth strategies.

The scope for expansionary macroeconomic policies

Traditionally, three instruments are available for macroeconomic regulation: the national budget, interest rates and exchange rates. When capital circulates freely, interest rates and exchange rates are linked: monetary policy becomes an exchange rate policy, variations in the interest rate serving as much for macroeconomic regulation as for fixing the level of exchange rates.

The effects of budgetary and/or monetary stimulation on growth and employment (see box 2) are well known, even if highly controversial. Policies aimed at reflating the economy, whether by lowering interest rates or by budgetary stimulation, are today weakened by two phenomena: the greater openness of economies on the one hand, and the deregulation and growing integration of international financial markets on the other.

The principal mechanisms hindering an expansionary policy are the effect of displacement by imports and loss of competitiveness consequent on the development of inflationary pressures. Today these effects tend to be reinforced by the growing openness of economies. If the multiplier for public expenditure is still fairly high in relatively closed economies such as that of the United States, it becomes very low, and even less, for small, open economies. Reflation of the economy, if practised in a single country, risks engendering an external deficit which may soon become unsustainable and give rise to heavy financial market speculations on a devaluation of the exchange rate. France had this unfortunate experience in 1982-83.

On the other hand, coordinated recovery is a way of breaking these constraints. It offers many advantages:

–   it limits the effects of displacement by foreign trade (since imports and exports are stimulated to the same degree and loss of competitiveness is reduced since all the commercial partners are subject to more or less the same inflationary pressures) and national external deficits, particularly when coordination takes place between a group of countries trading intensively with each other and less with the exterior. Such a group comes close to being a relatively closed economy; one naturally thinks of Europe and particularly of the European Union;

–   it reinforces the initial expansionary effect, since each country stimulates the growth of its trading partners.

Owing to the free circulation of capital, the flexibility of exchange rates and the integration of international financial markets, long-term interest rates – and, to a lesser extent, exchange rates – have run out of control. It is difficult to determine the factors accounting for trends in long-term interest rates. The latter may depend on the world supply and demand of capital. They may also depend on anticipated growth, inflation and public deficits on international markets. Thus, an expansionary budgetary policy practised without opposition from the Central Bank – i.e. using fixed short-term real interest rates – may have unfavourable effects on long-term interest rates: if financial markets anticipate, rightly or wrongly, that the medium-term consequences of budgetary stimulation of the economy will take the form of inflationary pressures causing the Central Bank to react by raising the short-term interest rates, or that there will be an increase in the budget deficit that will be difficult for the markets to finance without pressures on the supply of capital, any reflation of the economy by budgetary means will risk being thwarted by a rise in interest rates.

The fear that an increase in the budget deficit may result in an increase in long-term interest rates is linked with a particular interpretation of the operation of financial markets and macroeconomic equilibrium. If an increase in public savings is to draw off available capital at the world level to such an extent that it results in a rise in its price, firstly, this phenomenon must be sufficiently broad in scope (which is not necessarily the case given the size of international financial markets integrated at world level); secondly, the economy must be in a position where there is a deficit in savings accompanied by dynamic investment. If this were the case, there would be excess demand on the market for goods, which would appear unlikely in a situation of underemployment and in the absence of inflationary pressures and pressures on production capacity. On the contrary, the present period of low inflation and large excess of production capacity would appear to indicate that industrialized countries are suffering rather from insufficiency of demand. There is therefore no reason why an increase in public savings should result in pressures on capital markets, except in the absence of irrational and self-validating behaviour of financial markets. It would thus be necessary, in any recovery resulting from an increase in the budget deficit, to explain to financial markets the temporary and marginal nature of this increase in public savings and to convince them that the drop in short-term interest rates will be lasting.

The introduction of an expansionary monetary and budgetary policy faces a number of obstacles which would appear to set major limitations on the latitude for manoeuvre in most industrialized countries today: large public debts and fiscal deficits, accentuated by the 1992-93 recession, which lead to fears that public finances will get out of control and that there will be long-term problems of servicing public debts; the particular set of problems linked with the fixed exchange rate system in Europe, which has lost its status as an instrument of economic policy and is complicating the coordination of economic policies owing to the independence of the Bundesbank; and, more generally, the Maastricht objectives of convergence for Europe with a view to adopting a single currency, seem to leave budgetary policy little freedom, either in the States of the European Union or in the States which are candidates for entry in the near future. On the other hand, monetary policies would appear to enjoy considerable freedom of manoeuvre, given the high level of real interest rates, at least in continental Europe, while inflation remains generally under control.

Is the coordination of economic policies possible, at least in Europe?

Having noted these shared constraints, we must now examine some country-specific factors that stand in the way of a coordinated expansionary policy. Certain countries may consider that they have already done much in the way of budgetary stimulation: the United Kingdom, whose deficit today amounts to 8 per cent of GDP, whereas public accounts were still balanced before the recession; certain smaller European countries like Denmark, which have introduced a certain form of budgetary stimulation; even Germany, for which the high budgetary cost of re-unification since 1989 can be likened to stimulation by means of public expenditure.

Figure 15.
Rate of production capacity utilization, 1994 (percentage)

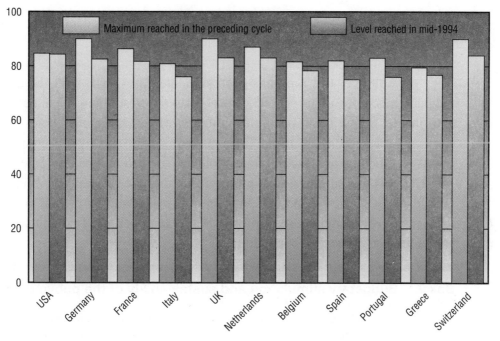

Source: Organization of Economic Cooperation and Development, main economic indicators, October 1994.

In other countries the macroeconomic situation is still unbalanced: this is the case particularly in Italy, which has only recently succeeded in reducing inflation and balancing its external accounts within the context of a still galloping public debt. Prices are still rising sharply in certain countries of the south such as Greece, Portugal and Spain. The United Kingdom also shows a trend towards accelerated wage rises as soon as sustained growth is achieved, the present virtual stability of prices being in this respect exceptional. In other countries, however, inflation is no longer a constraint.

It is, moreover, somewhat unlikely that recovery in Europe or the United States will be checked by supply constraints in the short run: the level of utilization of production capacity is low (see figure 15). Moreover, most countries have unemployment rates markedly above the NAIRU.

A coordinated expansionary strategy might, for example, adopt the following means of action:

—   a coordinated reduction of short-term interest rates, which would immediately bring about a lasting devaluation of European currencies;

—   a reduction of the social contributions of employers, which would, by reducing labour costs, make it possible to avoid the inflationary pressures caused by devaluation and the resumption of growth and would also have a favourable impact on the demand for labour;

– a direct budgetary stimulation, for example by reducing the taxes paid by households or increasing public investment.

A policy of this kind has been simulated by OFCE with the aid of a multinational macroeconomic model. Short-term interest rates have been reduced to zero in real terms; the resulting devaluation of European currencies is 15 per cent for the first year. Employers' social contributions have been reduced by 2 percentage points of GDP; taxes affecting households have been reduced by 1 percentage point of GDP (this measure has been preferred to an increase in public investment, since high levels of public expenditure and compulsory deductions prevail in most countries today; the present trend is thus more towards a reduction of compulsory deductions than a further increase in expenditure).

Box 2. Budgetary stimulation and sustainability of the public debt

The public debt is today very high in industrialized countries, with the notable exception of Japan, and the primary balance required in order to stabilize the process of indebtedness has markedly increased. This being so, many observers conclude that public budgets have no freedom of manoeuvre at all.

Account should be taken of two factors which modify this pessimistic view. The problem of sustainability of the public debt is to a large extent linked with the excessively high level of real interest rates in a context of slow growth.[75] This indicates first of all that recovery should begin with a drop in the rates of interest; in addition, temporary public deficits in periods of low activity do not lead to the point where the public debt is unsustainable: an increase in the fiscal deficit results in a rise in household incomes, and hence consumption, which is in the long run theoretically likely to bring about a sufficient increase in activity to wipe out the rise in

the indebtedness ratio. Thus, lower rates of interest and reflation of activity combine to slacken the momentum of public indebtedness. Only when demand reaches a satisfactory level should the stabilization of the public debt be sought by means of a budgetary policy of rebalancing public accounts.

In addition, in certain countries, the level of the public debt does not appear to be a problem in itself: when macroeconomic equilibrium is satisfactory, i.e. when external accounts are balanced, external indebtedness is low and there are no major inflationary pressures, a high level of public debt merely corresponds to a keen desire for private savings, to the extent to which the debt is financed essentially by internal agents. In an unemployment situation, diminishing the public debt is unjustified, since, given an excessively high level of private savings, it would be necessary to support demand in order to improve the employment situation, as indeed macroeconomic conditions permit.

The result is a reflation of activity of about 5 percentage points over a three-year horizon, without major inflationary tendencies and without impairing the fiscal balance or the foreign trade balance. Nevertheless, given the improvement in productivity and the effects of a higher activity rate noted earlier, the reduction in unemployment amounts to only 2.5 percentage points throughout the European Union. Although the effect is pronounced, it is still inadequate for a return to full employment.

Adapting to the global economy

While all avenues for raising growth rates through changes in macroeconomic policy should be explored, attention also needs to be paid to the growth-augmenting benefits of successful adjustment to changes in the global economy.

In a free trade framework, dynamic adjustment should lead each region to specialize in activities where it has a comparative advantage. The industrialized countries should therefore concentrate their production in high-technology, high value-added and capital-intensive industries. International markets for such products are already expanding, and should expand further with the rapid development of the NICs and the transitional economies. In its definition of a competitive strategy for Europe, the European Commission White Paper (1993) on growth, competitiveness and employment underlines the importance of "office automation, computing, electronics, optical instruments and surgical material". More generally, markets linked to environmental products and services – the demand for which is likely to increase rapidly in developed as well as in rapidly developing economies – to health care and to culture appear very promising for the industrial world. According to the White Paper, the development of such activities should have a net positive effect on employment, even when the losses due to the abandonment of low-skilled and labour-intensive activities are taken into account.

The "high-road" adjustment in industrial countries should focus on different, although closely linked, strategies. Developing comparative advantages is one fundamental direction. Another focus should be on improving non-price competitiveness. Comparative advantages, represented by initial production-factor endowments, should more and more come to be replaced by competitive advantages linked to qualitative factors capable of improving the global efficiency of the production system (White Paper): quality of education, investment in human capital, investment in research and development, high quality of infrastructure and services, all of which enhance initial production-factor endowments. More generally, the emerging theory of endogenous growth underlines the importance of qualitative factors as main determinants of long-term productivity and growth. Beyond all fundamental issues raised in earlier parts of this Report, long-term solutions to persistent unemployment also rely on increasing the potential rate of growth of industrial economies. Supply-side improvements associated with the accumulation of physical and human capital and/or knowledge, or with technology, education and infrastructure, are very likely to be the essential driving force behind long-term sustainable growth.

Delaying the "positive" adjustment measures outlined above by adopting the "low road" of protectionism would only impede the process of globalization, postpone the development of the less industrialized world and in the end deprive

OECD countries of one of the most promising solutions to persistent unemployment and/or insufficient growth: the huge markets in the South and East.

Instead of complaining of "social or monetary dumping" from low-wage countries, the industrialized world could decide to take the "high road" of high technology and high value-added industries. But in order to avoid the temptation of resolving employment problems through protectionism, industrial countries would need to implement a whole set of policies aimed at re-establishing satisfactory growth and employment in the North. Active and coordinated economic policies to sustain growth, reforms of systems of financing social benefits, transfers aimed at re-distributing the gains from free trade to directly affected activities or workers, public investment in physical and human capital, are the indispensable tools that should be used on the way towards successful globalization.

The industrialized world could benefit significantly from a generalized increase in international trade and demand. Simulations with macroeconomic models carried out by the *Observatoire français des conjonctures économiques* (OFCE) estimate the overall positive effect on world growth of a strategy of broad and successful integration of developing and transition economies into the global economy. It is too often forgotten that, if Northern countries have a major role to play in the development process of the South and East, huge positive feedbacks are also likely to occur from this adjustment and to have very positive impacts on the North. These are what sometimes have been known as "trade reverse linkages". In the simulation quoted below, the integration policy is twofold:

–   substantial financing is accorded to the South and the East: loans and direct investments, increasing to a magnitude of 1 per cent of OECD GDP after eight years (the equivalent of the American Marshall Plan for Europe after the Second World War), would be received by the South and East;

–   Northern markets would be widely opened to developing and transitional countries' exports.

Although this scenario remains quite utopian in some of its assumptions (the transition process is assumed to succeed rapidly in Eastern Europe and attract large direct investment, developing countries are assumed to be able to absorb additional capital transfers efficiently, a real political and social consensus is assumed to allow for a rapid opening of Western markets), it shows to what extent this strategy could solve some of the actual problems of the industrial world. In OECD countries GDP could be 5 per cent higher after eight years, and the unemployment rate could fall by 1 to 3 percentage points depending on the country.

This kind of simulation nevertheless only projects the induced effects on employment of higher trade between the industrialized countries and the developing and transitional economies. It does not take account of the problem of increasing unemployment of low-skilled workers or of growing social inequalities between different categories of workers. These issues will be taken up in a following section.

In determining their trade policies the industrialized countries should recognize that they have a major role to play in the evolution of the global economy. The future of world trade and development depends largely upon their behaviour, e.g. whether they follow a pattern of integration or move towards more protectionist policies. Imports from low-wage countries are likely to destroy a large number of unskilled jobs in the North, thus increasing unemployment and social inequalities. This could lead industrialized countries to adopt protectionist attitudes which would definitely hamper the whole process of globalization. But it needs to be remembered that free trade is likely to increase global productivity and the welfare of all countries participating in international trade. Under certain conditions, industrialized countries could profit massively from an increase in world trade. Although developing countries and the former centrally planned economies may indeed endanger some sectoral activities in the industrialized world, they are also a huge potential market for Northern exports. In addition, if poor growth records in industrialized countries during the last two decades are connected with the saturation of demand in rich countries, the expansion of new markets could even be *the* solution. This follows from the argument of some economists[76] who view the fundamental force behind the shift from full employment to unemployment in industrialized countries as residing in the saturation of demand for many consumer durables – industries that traditionally accounted for large shares of employment. Historically, there had been a positive correlation between productivity growth and employment in these basic industries because productivity increases resulted in declining consumer prices and thus expanded demand. High rates of growth in demand in turn allowed for rapid growth in output and net employment growth in spite of rising labour productivity. It is argued that the demand for these goods is now saturated with the result that although continued productivity increases (required by stiffer competition) may still result in lower consumer prices, this no longer leads to expanding output and employment. In short, countries that have not been successful in shifting employment from higher productivity growth goods-producing industries to lower productivity growth service activities have generally experienced little employment growth. Appropriate policies – short-term subsidies to damaged sectors, adequate measures to allow for balanced growth in the North, development of high-technology activities – could lower, if not totally offset, the costs of free trade and competition. In purely economic terms, the gains could overcome the losses. Industrialized countries may not at present be willing to implement the necessary effort of redistribution and reform. But in ethical terms, as stressed by Sterdyniak and Mathieu, "do they have the right to force developing and transitional countries to pay for the richest countries' incapacity to adapt to the new world economy?"[77]

Labour market regulation

As foreshadowed in the discussion of the causes of unemployment in the previous section, this report is of the view that the underlying causes of poor employment performance such as slow growth and product market distortions may be more important than differences in labour market regulation. This subsection will begin with a discussion of the limitations of labour market deregulation as a proposed solution to the employment problem. It will then present some alternative proposals which appear to provide ways of reducing unemployment without aggravating inequality and poverty.

Deregulation: Trade-offs or net gain?

The pure neo-liberal position is that the competitive market is the most efficient and effective form of economic organization; that any form of government regulation and control is an artificial constraint upon the market and distorts its operation; and that if such artificial restraints are removed, a more efficient market organization will emerge naturally of its own accord. In this framework the economy is composed solely of self-interested individuals, sometimes acting as workers and consumers, sometimes as business firms, relating to each other through the market-place. The framework does not naturally recognize the social actors and has no organic place for labour market regulation. Of course, in all countries, real-world policy environments are more complicated than in theoretical models and no-one has really advocated totally deregulated labour markets. But it is also true that neo-liberal theory on unemployment and its solution, and on how labour markets work, have influenced policy. In such cases, the policy that is advocated is a very thorough, albeit still less than complete, deregulation of labour markets. It is important, therefore, to consider the implications of very extensive labour market deregulation as one polar extreme of a continuum of proposals for the reform of labour market regulation.

When theory is matched with the evidence reviewed earlier, the relationship of labour market regulation to labour market performance does not emerge as one of a simple negative correlation; in other words, the absence of rules does not automatically and unambiguously improve performance, nor does the presence of regulation unambiguously impede adjustment and worsen performance. The relationship between rules and performance would appear far more to be in the nature of trade-offs. Thus, as Krugman observes:[78] "There is a well-understood way to reduce OECD unemployment, but it involves creating more jobs at the expense of more extensive and more severe poverty." In a world of slow growth, hesitant demand, macroeconomic policy austerity, and pervasive technological change, policy choices may for the most part be in the nature of dilemmas or trade-offs, rather than unambiguously "plus-sum" options.

There are, of course, no "natural experiments" upon which to base conclusions on the impact of deregulation. Of course, if modern theories of the labour market are correct, i.e. that the labour market functions in ways that are qualitatively different from other markets, then there can be no purely deregulated setting anyway. The closest one can come to natural experiments in labour market deregulation may be the United Kingdom, and, perhaps even more dramatically and more recently, New Zealand. In both countries a variety of institutional rigidities in the labour market did indeed hamper employment adjustment once economic conditions deteriorated. In neither country, however, has deregulation resulted unambiguously in improved labour market performance.[79] Experience in New Zealand is still too recent to evaluate; while one can point to a number of different outcomes on the labour market, it would be difficult to assign the causes of those outcomes, whether positive or negative, to the impact of deregulation *per se* or to the economic cycle.[80] But neither is the longer term effect of deregulation as seen in the United Kingdom anything but mixed: Recent research results "conclude that the Thatcher reforms succeeded in reducing union power and increasing the incentive to work – and may have increased the responsiveness of wages and employment at the micro level. But they did not improve the responsiveness of real wages to unemployment nor the transition for men out of unemployment, and were accompanied by rising wage inequalities that do not seem to reflect the working of an ideal market system. While there are glimmers of improved market adjustments and responsiveness that may do the British economy well in a prolonged boom, there is no strong evidence that the British labour market experienced a deep microeconomic change".[81] In short, to date, deregulation has solved some problems while creating others – the very definition of a trade-off. This suggests that the most meaningful debate is not that between deregulation versus regulation, but on the sort of regulatory reforms in the labour market that changes in the economic landscape will require. Discussion of such reforms may find fault with some existing laws and practices but must also acknowledge the benefits of labour market regulation.

Flexibility and the organization of working time

The doubts raised in the foregoing discussion do not imply that one should favour a myopic defence of the regulatory status quo. To do so would ignore the very real demands for labour market flexibility that both the problems of employment creation and the evolution of production systems would seem to require – and some existing regulations on the labour market may impede. There is no better example of such impediments and how they can be overcome through legislated or negotiated change than those relating to the length and organization of working time. While the present report has dwelt on other critical areas of labour market regulation, the main elements of change in working time organization deserve a brief highlight.

If workers were freely able to choose their own hours of work, and firms were able to adjust the organization of their work to accommodate these choices, it is likely that employment would benefit. There are, of course, many reasons behind the standardization of working time schedules, but regulatory constraints are among these. Three examples may be given. First, constraints or ceilings on maximum working time as measured over discrete time periods often apply. Work beyond a certain time threshold may be proscribed, whereas hours worked in excess of lower thresholds may be considered overtime hours and compensated either through premium pay, paid time off, or both. The 1980s witnessed a trend in many countries toward the averaging of maximum hours over a longer period: indeed, in the United Kingdom, by 1990, one in 16 employees had "annualized" working time schedules.[82] For the firm, such scheduling allows a better matching of production needs with working time, while minimizing overtime pay costs. For the worker, greater latitude in scheduling work and leisure is a major benefit, particularly when greater flexibility in working time organization is coupled with overall reductions in individual working time.

Second, law and agreement have often limited the scheduling of work performed outside normal time periods, e.g. shiftwork, nightwork, Saturday or Sunday work. A major trend has been the linking of reductions in individual working time with the greater use of capital equipment through the expansion of shift work. For the firm, responding to the peaks and troughs of demand is one advantage, and the more rapid amortization of capital equipment another. Additional jobs are often created, and, provided that workers are able to select their schedules voluntarily, they may benefit from a better division of their time between work, additional training, and leisure.

Third, the pronounced growth of "non-standard" forms of employment (e.g. part-time and temporary employment) suggests that there are powerful reasons for opting for other than regular full-time employment on both the supply and demand sides of the labour market. Where regulation stringently applies only to regular full-time jobs, some evidence suggests both that employment opportunities arising from non-standard work are forgone, and, that where non-standard work exists, it is more likely to be involuntary.[83] Moreover, constraints on the uptake of part-time opportunities may also be embedded in benefit systems. The Confederation of British Industry, for example, finds that many of the long-term unemployed are dissuaded from part-time opportunities because their earnings do not offset the abrupt decline in the benefits to which they were entitled while unemployed. It notes that benefit reform policies in the United Kingdom have begun to address this "poverty trap" by recognizing part-time work as "a legitimate longer term option".[84] There would seem, in short, to be scope for job creation through the continued reform of regulatory – and purely organizational – constraints on the organization of working time. The balance to be struck in expanding such opportunities is to provide the protection required to ensure that the choice of new distributions between market work and non-market activities is voluntary.

The benefits of labour market regulation

The bulk of empirical research on labour market regulation has explored only the cost side of the equation. The main risk in such an approach is that costs, if not balanced by benefits, may be magnified. Costs of individual labour market rules are exaggerated if no allowance is made for the fact that they may also be offset by benefits arising from them. As Blank and Freeman observe: "The standard 1980s economists' study of unemployment insurance or income support is an exercise in estimating distortionary labour supply or related costs".[85] There is an extraordinary absence of empirical findings on the link between on the one hand unemployment benefits and, on the other, efficient job search or on its relation to consumption stabilization, or whether the existence of unemployment insurance encourages industrial restructuring by mitigating the risks involved. The absence of empirical evidence on the benefit side of labour market regulation seems pervasive. Admittedly, the benefits of regulation are often intractable or unwieldy to quantify. Measurable costs incurred by the firm may register benefits elsewhere in the economy or with various time lags; that is, costs imposed at the micro level may reap longer-term benefits for the economy as a whole. What, for example, is the *net cost*, i.e. outlays and savings, of occupational safety and health regulations?

A major economic benefit from regulation derives from the fact that it often responds to market failures. This implies that the presence of regulation improves market functioning in economic terms, i.e. that intervention can produce better economic outcomes than free markets: "many social insurance programmes provide 'goods' that competitive markets intrinsically cannot provide because of the presence of moral hazards, externalities, or other forms of market failure, which means these programmes cannot be criticized for crowding out market alternatives".[86] For example, individual firms that voluntarily offered sickness benefits might suffer the risk of adverse selection in attracting illness-prone workers. In the absence of regulation, they would not rationally offer such benefits. They would, instead, face a strong incentive to hire only young, healthy workers.

Table 22 reconstructs the economics of labour market regulation from the standpoint of the benefit side of the equation. Again the empirics of the argument are largely (although not entirely) undeveloped in the literature, but this is merely a methodological matter. If many labour market rules are designed to remedy market failure, their removal will, of course, imply a resurgence of efficiency losses. For example, employment security has been associated with both the propensity of firms to train and the willingness of workers to invest in human capital;[87] the dismantling of employment security may result in an economy-wide underinvestment in training. Since labour market regulation conveys economic benefits, *economic flexibility may crucially rely on the presence rather than the absence of labour market regulation. In this sense, the economic advantages of competitive freedom in product markets ought not to be con-*

Table 22.　**Benefits of labour market regulation**

Regulation	Benefit	Theory
Employment protection	(1) Ensures employment stability	(1) Employment stability is valued, not only by the worker but by the firm, as the transaction costs of hiring, training and turnover may be lower than if employment is volatile.
	(2) Results in increased internal labour market flexibility	(2) Labour market adjustment is channelled through the internal labour market, through a higher degree of "functional flexibility", and a greater degree of internal mobility, through broader job design, job rotation, access to training, or a greater reliance on merit rather than security in job assignment.
		The greater need for functional flexibility also implies the need for initial and continuous training. The volatility of product markets and the rapid rate of technological change place a greater premium on training. In the absence of stable and longer-term employment relationships, there may be an under-investment in training, a market failure that results from the reluctance of firms to invest in employees who may leave and take their newly acquired training with them to other firms.
	(3) Improves labour market mediation	(3) Systems that bias adjustment toward internal mechanisms, i.e. those with relatively strong employment security constraints, may in fact cope with situations of permanent decline in demand in more efficient and equitable ways. Short-time working as opposed to mass layoffs may be an efficient way of internalizing the costs of external adjustment, as both alternatives are equally cost-effective to the firm, a reduction in hours worked is far more preferable to the worker than unemployment, and this would allow labour force adjustment to occur through attrition.
	(4) Increases in the speed of transition	(4) By allowing displaced workers to look for alternative employment while still employed, prior notification lowers the incidence of non-employment and thus speeds the adjustment of employment. This forces firms to internalize the externalities of their decisions, i.e. to internalize some of the costs of employment displacement, so that what is a cost for the firm may be an efficiency advantage for the economy by way of a speedier transition.
	(5) Leads to productive efficiencies	(5) Employment security may lead to firms adopting long-term planning horizons and competing through the product market rather than through the labour market. Adjustment would occur through production strategies, through higher rates of product innovation and the exploitation of high-margin product niches.
Wage: minimum wage, wage floors, compressed wages	(1) Associates income distribution with market incentives	(1) The minimum wage is a mechanism for income redistribution with major advantages, as it makes the social objective of income redistribution consistent with market incentives, i.e. the incentive to work, as well as having a budget-neutral impact, as distinct from a redistribution through transfer payments.
	(2) Stimulates labour supply	(2) In this sense, the minimum wage can add to a country's potential growth through an expanded employment/population ratio.
	(3) Has a positive effect on school enrolment	(3) A positive correlation may exist between increases in the minimum wage and school enrolment suggesting that the withdrawal of youths from the labour force as minimum wages increase may be the result of further schooling.
	(4) Leads to productive efficiencies	(4) The endogenous relationship between pay and productivity, for example channelling firms' competitive strategies towards improving management and productivity through a "shock effect", reducing opportunism and short-term thinking, and refocusing competition through the product market by the cultivation of high-margin niches and faster rates of new product innovation.
	(5) Reduces the number of working poor	(5) The absence of a shock effect through wages runs the risk of perpetuating competition through a low-pay, low-productivity trap. It may also degenerate into downward competitive spirals as "bad" conditions drive out the "good". If the market-led decline in the wages of the low-skilled goes unchecked, this could lead to a rise in the "working poor".
	(6) Leads to a culture of cooperation and commitment in the workplace	(6) Modern productive efficiency relies on significantly higher degrees of labour-management cooperation. In a world where competition is increasingly based on "quality at the source" and a rapid response to changing markets, cooperation, trust and commitment to organizational objectives are essential in the workplace. Compressed earnings or a narrower dispersion can foster these necessary conditions.

Regulation	Benefit	Theory
Unemployment benefits	(1) Allow efficient job search	(1) An unemployed worker who receives unemployment benefits will be better able to concentrate on finding a job, rather than having to worry about things such as changing consumption patterns and other changes that are entailed by a loss of income.
	(2) Produce economic benefits by fostering a better match between labour supply and demand and by reducing future spells of unemployment	(2) Unemployment benefits raise the reservation wage with which the unemployed evaluate job offers, and allow the unemployed to search for a job that is better suited to their skills and their requirements. Therefore, in the future, they would be less likely to leave such a job either voluntarily or by force, thus reducing future spells of unemployment, lowering costs of unemployment benefits programmes and improving productivity.
	(3) Foster macroeconomic stabilization	(3) Unemployment benefits allow the unemployed to maintain their consumption habits during unemployment which provides an automatic fiscal stimulus to the economy by increasing purchasing power at times of slack consumer demand, particularly if the pay out of benefits and the taxes that finance them are countercyclical.
	(4) Redistribute income to low-income households	(4) If low-income households and low-skilled workers are more prone to spells of unemployment, unemployment benefits serve as an income redistribution mechanism, especially if taxes financing unemployment benefits are progressive.
	(5) Encourage structural adjustment	(5) Structural change in an industry or a region may require the redeployment or mobility of labour across sectors. Income protection may reduce resistance to such structural change and encourage adjustment to occur, thus the economy shares in the private adjustment costs of individuals, industries and regions. Existence of unemployment insurance encourages structural adjustment to take place.

flated with the deregulation of labour markets. Marsden,[88] for example, argues that the exigencies of modern productive efficiency rely on trust relations in the firm and the construction of "cooperative exchange". The latter, he argues, is facilitated by greater equality of treatment, e.g. firm-wide employment security, and greater wage compression. On the macro side, Persson and Tabellini[89] present evidence for 56 countries finding a strong negative correlation between income inequality and growth in per capita GDP. Finally, rules that protect the income and employment security of workers may create incentives for competition to occur more through product market innovation and product market strategy. Labour market "rigidities" may therefore promote "productive efficiency". In the case of Germany, for example, it has been found that, as labour is a relatively greater fixed factor of production in industry, systemic stability depends upon the long-term focus of firms relative to their product markets and shareholders, and on a broad regulatory pattern that supports that stability.[90]

Why wage cuts are not a solution

The persistence of unemployment has frequently been ascribed to the prevalence of excessively high wage costs caused by labour market rigidity. Proponents of labour market deregulation therefore argue that the struggle against unemployment should take the form of a reduction of wage costs. Four reservations should be made as regards a strategy of this kind. First, the share of wages in value added, which had sharply increased following the first oil shock, has been reduced to a level comparable to that prevailing before 1974 (see figure 16); indeed, the policies of

Figure 16
Share of the wages in the value added, 1973-93

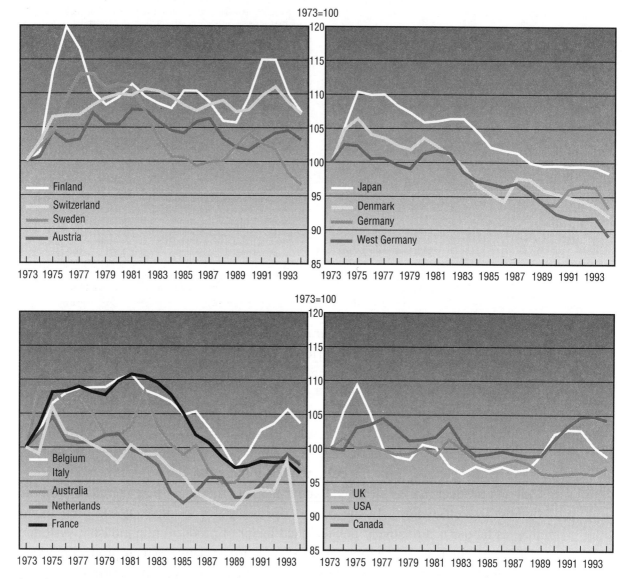

Source: Organization of Economic Cooperation and Development, *Economic Outlook* (June 1994), and reference supplement.

wage moderation or even austerity of the 1980s brought down wage rises to below the rate of growth of productivity. To the extent to which this situation persists in the face of a high level of unemployment, it would hardly appear necessary to encourage this trend beyond the level it has reached today.

Second, the effects of substitution between capital and labour virtually vanished during the 1980s: although the enormous rise in interest rates, combined with moderate advances in real wages, has made the cost of capital relatively stable compared with that of labour, growth has still remained fairly capital-intensive. The substitution mechanism is slow, since it operates only through the renewal of capital: for every period substitution operates only for the fraction of capital newly acquired. A change in the relative costs of capital and labour through a wage cut would thus have only a very slight impact on employment since factor substitution is limited.

Third, a strategy to reduce wage costs will increase competitiveness only if it is applied in a single country. If all European countries resort to it with the aim of reducing unemployment (in other words, exporting it to their trading partners), gains in productivity will no longer be achieved, or will be achieved only at the level of trade outside the Union. This will markedly reduce the positive effect on growth given the relatively closed nature of the economy of the European Union. Since the effects of competition from low-wage countries appear on the whole moderate in European countries, increasing competitiveness by comparison with low-wage areas will have only a marginal effect on employment.

Box 3.   The empirical findings on the influence of labour costs on employment

Estimates of the labour cost elasticity of employment have given rise to copious literature, and particularly – problematically – to findings differing widely depending on the methods used.

The main studies made on the long-term ratios in the manufacturing sector arrive at three conclusions:[91]

– estimated elasticities vary between 0 and –0.8 for most countries, a range which gives no satisfactory answer; elasticities are usually of the order of –0.3 to –0.5;

– the case of France is characterized by elasticities which are always below 0.3 and often nil;

– a major result stressed by Hamermesh[92] is that the employment-wage elasticity is less important for skilled workers than for unskilled workers, which pleads in favour of a reduction of the cost of unskilled work.

This being so, if we, say, adopt an elasticity of –0.3, which is a high value compared with available estimates, this means that labour costs must be reduced by 3.33 per cent in order to obtain a 1 per cent increase in employment. If the initial unemployment rate is 10 per cent, and the effect of the higher activity rate is 0.5, employment must be increased by 11.8 per cent in order to reduce unemployment by 5 points. Labour costs must therefore be reduced by 39.3 per cent, even if one only takes into account the partial equilibrium of the labour market and ignores the induced effects on wages (hence on incomes and consumption), on profits of enterprises (hence on investment and growth), and on public finances if contributions affecting labour costs are to be reduced. Moreover, given the fact that employers' social contributions represent between 0 and 50 per cent of gross wages in Europe, if the share is 50 per cent, contributions must be reduced by at least 80 per cent; this would be difficult for social security systems and public finances in general to support.

Finally, and more basically, a policy of reducing wage costs can be effective only to the extent to which the demand of enterprises for labour is sensitive to its cost, which remains a moot point (see box 3). It seems that, empirically speaking, labour costs are only very marginal in determining hiring decisions, which depend mainly on anticipated production, i.e. demand.

A priori, lowering direct wages has an uncertain macroeconomic effect on employment. The drop in wage costs will bring about a fall in the unit costs of production and hence an improvement of competitiveness and/or profit for undertakings, which will enable them to increase their investments; these two factors support growth and hence employment. If, moreover, the choice of production technology depends on the relative cost of the factors of production, a drop in wages can have a beneficial effect on employment by substituting labour for capital. Nevertheless, the drop in incomes of households has a strongly negative effect on their consumption, which, depending on the degree of openness of the economy, may more or less offset the positive effects of investment and foreign trade.

It should be noted that the effects of a reduction in wages depend essentially on the characteristics of unemployment: if it is genuinely due to inability to hire because labour costs are too high, then a reduction in wages may well result in the hiring of large numbers of workers. If, on the other hand, unemployment is due essentially to a deficiency in demand, then enterprises will not hire if they have no sales prospects, even if costs are drastically reduced. In this case reduced wages will have the opposite effect to that intended since, if the economy is not open enough, the reduction of consumption will more than offset the reflation by exports and growth will slow down.

Simulations made with the aid of the MIMOSA macroeconomic model,[93] in which enterprises do not, *a priori*, suffer from the constraints of excessively high labour costs since their level of self-financing was entirely satisfactory in 1994, show that the employment effect of lowering wages throughout the European Community is virtually nil. The positive effects of a strategy of this kind are a slow-down in inflation and an improvement in the foreign trade balance, two objectives which today have become secondary in a community which already enjoys a favourable external balance and whose level of inflation is under control.

Adjusting labour market regulation

In addition to the doubts expressed earlier over the employment creation effects of wage cuts, the strong negative distributional impact of such a strategy needs to be recognized. This is particularly serious in a context where there is growing concern over the related problems of growing wage inequality between unskilled and skilled workers and reduced job opportunities for the unskilled. As discussed in Part 1 of this report, opinion remains divided over the main underlying cause of this phenomenon, the main differences revolving around the relative magnitudes of the roles of technical change and import competition from low-wage economies. Be this as it may, a serious economic and social problem exists, and solutions need to be found. Indeed, the importance of finding viable solutions extends beyond the national boundaries of individual industrialized countries. It should be recalled from the discussion in Part 1 that the sustainability of global trade expansion under the Uruguay Round depends to a large extent on the effectiveness of positive adjustment measures in the industrialized countries. A major part of the adjustment problem resides precisely in the need to manage the redeployment of low-skilled workers to higher-skilled jobs, or at least to generate adequate employment opportunities in non-tradeable sectors of the economy.

The best solution would, of course, be the expansion of tradeable production in the context of expanding world trade and higher rates of investment and growth in the global economy. In such a context the problem of low-skilled workers needs to be tackled through education and training policies designed as part of overall efforts to shift employment towards higher-productivity activities. But this will require a supportive institutional framework and not a deregulation of the labour market. This is a particularly important issue in view of the rise of new production systems which require both a more skilled and a more versatile workforce as well as extensive cooperation between managers and workers. These developments pose important challenges in terms of the reform of existing labour market institutions. These issues will be discussed below, mainly in connection with the question of education and training.

It is unlikely, however, that positive adjustment measures in the context of expanding trade and higher growth will provide a complete solution. Other institutional reforms are necessary to remove disincentives to the hiring of low-skilled workers and to job search by such workers. Some interesting recent proposals for such reforms will therefore also be reviewed below. A basic attraction of these proposals is that they seek to prevent the rise in inequality and poverty that the deregulation path would create while reducing some of the disincentive problems arising from existing labour market institutions. They all involve some measure of redistribution but not necessarily higher than current levels. They promise strong gains in equity and other social benefits as well as some improvements in economic efficiency. We begin with a discussion of the challenges posed to labour market institutions by the rise of new production systems before considering proposals for dealing with the problem of low-skilled workers.

New challenges for labour market regulation

Labour market regulation does affect overall labour market adjustment, but the most important issue is to know the *kind of adjustment* most appropriate to future demands. If jobs and workers' skill bases will obsolesce more rapidly in the future, either institutional support for the firm as both the agent and the locus of long-term adjustment is required, or firms may be left free in their employment security decisions and institutional support would then focus on the sort of extra-firm training infrastructure that would improve the functioning of the external labour market.

The heterogeneity of national institutions and experience faced by otherwise common directions of changes in production suggests that there is no one path to regulatory reform. But all environments, particularly those where coordination is most lacking, will have to adjust to new prerogatives that appear to ratify a profound tendency toward decentralization – in production, in decision-making, in quality and control. The new systems of production narrow the distinction between labour and management, placing a premium on close cooperative relations and blurring the older division of labour and lines of authority.

Among the principal aims of labour market regulation will be to promote cooperation and "employability security",[94] where worker preparedness is at the very least dissociated from "job security" traditionally understood, if not necessarily employment tenure within a given firm. It stands to reason that regulatory solutions cannot be defined by technicians and imposed by government. Solutions will require the active participation of lower-level workers and managers, and hence a commitment and allegiance that will be obtained only if those who are to participate in the new institutions and structures are active in the process through which they are created. The role of government at national level is, it can be argued, just as likely to be strengthened as it is to be diminished – but it will be changed, in the sense of not imposing new regulations, but rather of fostering discussion and debate and establishing a procedural framework in which the new institutional structures can be worked out.

These general propositions can be illustrated with reference to two key issues: training and workplace industrial relations.

Training

It is now almost accepted wisdom that training should develop flexibility in workers, who are likely to change jobs several times in their working lives. The ability to learn to do new jobs well in a short amount of time is a key factor in a worker's long-term employability. Flexibility means having been brought to a relatively high level of cognitive knowledge so that learning new tasks does not seem at all formidable. Germany and Japan may direct the objective of training-supported, rapid job change more toward intra-firm labour markets. Of course, this does not necessarily preclude more frequent *job* changes by individuals in the future; such a scenario could occur internally within the firm (or network of firms) and, in fact, would probably do so.

The institutional requirements for this brand of flexibility are apparently great. At the level of the firm, they are associated with radically different internal labour market structures which, in the Japanese case, emphasize job rotation, "employment" – rather than "job" – security, narrow wage spreads and a flexible wage component with low entry wages improved by experience and tenure with the firm, and the willingness of employees to be widely deployed both within the firm and within an interfirm network. Such a system can only be maintained by an initial education system that has as its objective to raise the attainment of the average performer. Significantly, in both Germany and Japan, this bias towards long-term flexibility also requires a close relationship *at the macro level* between the public and private sector and financial institutions, and between workers and employers, a broader system of "incentive structures"[95] argued to convey "comparative institutional advantage".[96]

The challenge is therefore to develop the required institutional framework. Deregulation is not the answer, since more and better training cannot be ensured in the context of deregulated labour markets. Deregulation is likely to increase levels of labour turnover, reduce the core workforce and increase numbers of temporary and part-time workers; these developments will all erode the incentive to train. For example, assuming the decline of firm-based employment security, "there will be a greater need for 'market-makers', including independent career advisers, employment agencies and so on. This is a social cost to set against the efficiency gains which may result from the flexibility of employment from which firms will benefit",[97] according to the Director of the United Kingdom's National Institute of Economic and Social Research. Moreover, such market-making would only seem feasible in the presence of a strong, extra-firm training component. Firms facing relatively few constraints on employment security would be less willing to provide on-the-job training claiming that governments should make workers "job-ready". Exceptionally, firms might provide for highly firm-specific skills, that is for training which is the least useful to workers should they be displaced or wish to move to other firms. In labour markets characterized by this sort of flexibility, firms are also less likely to provide training that would increase long-run productivity based on worker innovation, since such training is generally tied to employment security and worker participation. "Flexibility" and "deregulation", in this view, are in fact separate concepts, more opposite in meaning than synonymous.

Given the possibility of profound changes in production systems, and assuming that the implications of those changes are as outlined above for education and training and employment security, one is confronted by yet another set of trade-offs. The advantage of some highly institutionalized settings would appear to be the "head start" that they have in adjusting education and training systems to the future or longer-term demands of rapidly changing production systems. The advantage of deregulated environments resides in relatively more rapid external labour market adjustment, although, as noted, this may be increasingly at the risk of training bottlenecks in the absence of regulatory reform that would shift the burden of adjustment costs borne disproportionately by individual firms and individual workers. Another trade-off relates to labour-management cooperation. Deregulated settings such as the United States appear rich in new, innovative forms of firm-level cooperation; but the benefits of some more regulated and coordinated environments, such as Germany and Japan, lie in the widespread diffusion of a national model of labour-management cooperation.

Industrial relations and workplace performance

New production systems require extensive cooperation between labour and management and the participation of workers in business decisions from which they were previously excluded. Despite a parallel trend toward the "decollectivization" or "individualization" of labour-management relations, new production trends also converge with benefits usually associated with workplace employee representation:

–   there will be an increasing premium on labour-management cooperation and bottom-up participation, both vertically and laterally in the firm's organization. The "voice mechanism" associated with workplace employee participation has been associated with lowering firms' transaction costs by instilling greater commitment and long-term continuity in relationships;[98]

–   "high-performance" workplaces[99] require an infrastructure of education and training, and willingness to retrain, which calls upon the traditional training function of trade unions. Moreover, the value of trade union participation in training programmes may be to ensure a component of general training in addition to firm-specific training. This would enhance the external labour market mobility of the workforce and suggests a positive externality that unions provide in decentralized systems;

–   the intensity of competition and rapid adjustment to technological change requires continuous improvements in productivity. Such improvements cannot be delivered in top-down fashion but require the "empowerment", problem-solving and participation of workers involved at the planning rather than just the implementation phase of organizational change. Evidence suggests that workplace employee participation is associated with the more rapid and efficient diffusion of new technologies;[100]

–   while there are powerful trends towards the decentralization of operational decision-making, modern production organization is also pushing towards new forms of network organization, to the extent where overall "productivity" of the firm may be less and less a single-firm matter.[101] The question will be which institutional solutions can ensure (1) the availability of qualified labour in the external labour market, and (2) best prevent bottlenecks in production from occurring as a result of the slow diffusion of "best-practice" techniques. Trade unions have traditionally played a role in such challenges of labour market intermediation between the firm and its external environment.

Alleviating unemployment and problems of low pay

As indicated earlier, a major social and labour market problem in industrialized countries is the declining job prospects for low-skilled workers. This is reflected either in a concentration of unemployment (particularly long-term unemployment) among this category of workers or in low pay (in both a relative and an absolute sense) for those in work. While the long-term solution clearly lies in positive adjustment to the changing world economy and in education and training policies, there is a serious immediate problem to be tackled. Finding adequate solutions is of strategic importance for maintaining freer trade and investment flows in the global economy, since the persistence or aggravation of unemployment and problems of low pay will fuel protectionist pressures. It is of course also a serious problem of inequality in its own right in the industrialized countries. We discuss below some proposals for dealing with the problem. These are of two varieties: subsidies directed towards employers, which are especially relevant where existing institutions prop up the wages of the low-skilled; and subsidies directed towards workers themselves, of particular relevance where wage floors are weak.

Tax-financed employment creation

Two broad policy routes encouraging the creation of low-productivity jobs, especially in the non-tradable sector, can be envisaged. The OECD[102] seems to favour labour market deregulation and warns against the alternative route of "tax concessions or employment subsidies". It is true that subsidies for low-paid jobs would not be a viable policy against unemployment unless they had substantial effects. But the same applies to labour market deregulation, whose effectiveness is still much debated. In terms of efficiency, there may well be little to choose between the two strategies.

The fundamental difference between allowing market forces to press down wages and conditions of employment in private services on the one hand and subsidizing employment there on the other is distributional. The question is whether private service workers as a whole should pay for increased employment by cuts in relative pay, or whether the costs should be borne generally out of higher taxation. There is no *prima facie* case in favour of deregulation (with its adverse distributional effects) and against subsidies (without such effects). It may be that the taxpayers would not accept the direct burden of reducing unemployment (irrespective of indirect benefits) and that, therefore, the costs would have to be borne by a section of society (low-paid workers) without the market power to refuse them. This, however, would be a political judgement and could not be seriously justified on the grounds of the allocative inefficiencies of subsidies.

The idea that jobs could be created by an expansion of tax-financed government expenditure can be extended beyond the realm of subsidies to low-skilled private service activities. It is important to note that such a policy has different effects from those resulting from traditional deficit spending.[103] The compensating rise in taxation chokes off the multiplier by redistributing spending power from existing taxpayers to those who find jobs as a result (e.g. in the public sector itself or within supplier sectors if the spending is on infrastructures). This limits the creation of jobs and, by the same token, leads only to a small rise in the demand for tradables; however, it prevents any substantial worsening of the balance of payments (the more so as the redistribution of consumption from higher-income groups to the erstwhile unemployed should typically reduce import demand).[104]

The pattern of government spending can also be targeted to provide work for groups especially affected by the lack of jobs. Thus, the concentration of unemployment (and non-employment) on the less educationally qualified, or on those living in particular areas, can be taken into account in devising an appropriate pattern of expenditure increases. Within the public sector (and public-sector contracts) preference could be given to the long-term unemployed, with confidence that this represented net additional jobs rather than the displacement of other workers. Obviously a balance has to be struck between the benefits of different spending patterns and their opportunity costs, but within public spending programmes the variation in social costs of employing different categories of people can be explicitly taken into account.

Subsidizing the working poor

In addition to transfers to businesses toward the objective of employment creation, there remains the problem of the working poor, particularly in those environments in which institutional forces do not prop up their wages. A proposal for low-wage employment subsidies has been put forward by Edmund Phelps[105] to deal with this problem. He argues that "since the earnings of the very disadvantaged are so very low it would seem entirely feasible for society to introduce institutional changes, involving the apparatus of government, to improve the earnings of the very disadvantaged". He advocates a "system of subsidies (possibly in the form of tax credits) to qualifying business enterprises for their employment of low-wage workers". This would increase the incentive to enterprises to hire such workers and thereby increase both job opportunities and earnings for the low-paid. It has several advantages over other possible mechanisms. For example, a scheme such as the Earned Income Tax Credit in the United States suffers from the drawback that firms respond by offering lower wages to those eligible for the credit. Similarly, schemes to "auction" employment subsidy funds to firms would be vulnerable to fraud. Moreover, as commented on later, benefit transfer programmes would "privilege a class of persons (the unemployed or welfare recipients) in the competition for jobs at the expense of others with no less a moral claim".

There are several grounds for such subsidies. Firstly, there are clear moral grounds for alleviating the hardship of the most disadvantaged. Secondly, there will be social benefits from the reduction of social pathologies arising from high unemployment and poverty. Indeed, the value of these social benefits constitutes a basic justification for paying the wage subsidy. Thirdly, there will be gains from increased mobilization of human resources and savings in welfare payments. Finally, there may be gains in terms of allocative efficiency through the strengthening of the motivation of the low-paid to retain a job and work diligently. This lowers the wage necessary to motivate employees and helps to lower unemployment more generally. The only drawback is the efficiency cost of higher taxes than may be necessary to fund the subsidies. But the benefits are likely to outweigh this.

Problems of financing

It is a very important, though often underappreciated, feature of the contemporary Welfare State that the net cost of the additional public spending to the taxpayer is far less than the gross cost if the workers concerned would otherwise have remained unemployed. If the gross "replacement ratio" is put at 50 per cent of the average wage, a realistic figure in the light of available estimates,[106] the government recoups, in additional taxation and in reduced payments for benefits, roughly half of its increased spending. In most OECD countries for which estimates are available, net "replacement ratios", which take taxation into account, are higher and can reach 80 per cent or more.[107] This would imply a net cost of job creation by the public sector of a mere 20 per cent (or even less) of the gross cost. Though in practice costs would be somewhat higher, since some of those newly employed would have been ineligible for benefits, these figures do suggest that in most countries the opportunity cost of additional infrastructures or public services is likely to be quite low.

Against these various advantages must be set two possible costs. The first is that such policies would lead to a rising share of government in the economy, something that countries have generally opposed in the last decade or so. This cost, however, is open to question. Ideology apart, there is no coherent economic reason for aiming at a particular "optimal" size of the public sector.[108] And in the light of the virtual stagnation in government investment recorded over the last 20 years in the industrialized countries of Western Europe, very strong arguments could be made in favour of greater public intervention in the provision of badly needed infrastructure and social overhead capital.

The second cost is more serious. Whatever the offsets mentioned above, there must be *some* additional element of taxation reflecting the fact that the unemployed will have higher incomes and consumption when they find jobs. If total consumption and the absorption of tradables are to be held constant, then this will have to be paid for with lower consumption elsewhere in the economy. A crucial issue, therefore, is the acceptability of such higher taxation for the purposes of financing spending increases which will cut unemployment.

The NAIRU model provides a framework for analysing this issue.[109] If one were to assume that the economy was already at the NAIRU (even though in a number of Western European countries it is likely that unemployment is at present above the NAIRU), then a rise in employment, together with a decline in the post-tax incomes of the employed, would seem to be a recipe for rising inflation. Measures to deregulate the labour market and force down wages in private services appear much more promising. They would raise the living standards of higher-paid workers through a lowering of the price of the private services which these workers typically use, and so motivate the better-off to show wage restraint. Though labour market deregulation would tend to have the greatest impact on weaker sections of the labour force, it could still help to secure bargaining moderation overall by its redistributive effects in favour of the better-off. The deregulatory route, in other words, would seem to hold out the possibility of simultaneously increasing employment and reducing the NAIRU – precisely what is required.

Higher taxation, by contrast, tends to increase the NAIRU. The only way of preventing this would be by a determined effort to gain support for the (modest) additional taxation required. This may not be impossible if it is borne in mind that the benefits from improvements in public services and the infrastructure are widely distributed among the population. And further widespread benefits would accrue from reduced social tension and conflict consequent upon the reduction in unemployment.

However, such policies have not only to gain electoral support, but, just as important, to evoke the appropriate response in the wage bargaining process. If people vote for higher spending and taxation, but then pass on the extra tax by securing compensatory wage increases, the whole process will be frustrated by rising inflation. Sooner or later the government will have to cut back on demand, and the initial expansion of employment will be reversed. Thus, to make the higher employment sustainable, powerful bargaining groups must not take advantage of tighter labour markets. Some wage restraint is needed; there would seem to be few or no alternatives if full employment is to be pursued in a relatively egalitarian fashion.

Cuts in working time are seen by some as such an alternative. For a given impact on employment, a problematic question in the case of work-sharing,[110] the two proposals have similar implications for consumption since the employed have to accept some reduction in living standards as their hours of work fall (though not in proportion since the cost of supporting the unemployed declines). The main difference is that in the case of work-sharing the benefits accrue in the form of increased leisure time, while public spending yields improvements in public services. In distributional terms the latter are probably more progressive since the benefits are likely to accrue disproportionately to the poorer sections of the population most dependent on public facilities (and the increased leisure may be perceived as of less value to low-paid workers). More fundamentally, however, work-sharing carries the connotation that there is an excess supply of labour in relation to social needs and that the available work should, therefore, be shared more equally. This is surely implausible in the context of the benefits that improvements in public services could deliver. While reducing working time holds out great advantages, it would be wrong to think that it must have the central role in any policy for reducing unemployment.

Reform of unemployment benefit systems

There is widespread agreement among economic policy makers that most unemployment benefit systems operating in advanced industrialized countries are in need of reform. As discussed earlier, the longer people are unemployed, the more their skills erode, the more discouraged they become in searching for jobs, and the more wary employers become of hiring them. For these reasons, the long-term unemployed are disadvantaged in the labour market. The appropriate policy response to this problem may be to make it more profitable for firms to hire the long-term unemployed and for these unemployed to find jobs; that is, to restore market incentives while retaining protection, and to move from mere *protection* of the unemployed to *promotion* of their re-employment.

A variety of benefit reform proposals have received serious attention in various quarters. Some of the shortfalls of existing systems seem widespread. For example, benefit administrations themselves could be improved through tightening. It is not just the long-term unemployed who need to be enabled and motivated to seek work; the civil servants distributing the unemployment benefits also need incentives, but the latter are often absent in many European countries since it is common for unemployment benefits to be financed at the national level, but administered and distributed at the local level. Thus the national government reaps all the financial reward when benefits are withdrawn from those ineligible to receive them, but the local authorities bear all the costs of doing so. If, instead, the national government gave the local authorities fixed grants, and then left these authorities to incur both the costs and benefits from their administration of unemployment benefits, civil servants would gain a greater incentive to target these unemployment benefits to those actually entitled to receive them.

Methods of financing unemployment also deserve attention. It is common to finance unemployment benefits out of payroll taxes levied on employers. When that happens, the unemployment benefit systems may discourage employment simultaneously in two separate ways: they not only lengthen job search and raise jobseekers' expectations of wages, whose levels are high by comparison with unemployment benefit, but also raise employers' labour costs by increasing their tax bill, since it is unlikely that payroll taxes will be fully borne by employees through their wages, at least in the short term. Financing unemployment benefits through expenditure taxes (such as VAT) may generally be expected to have a smaller contractionary effect on labour demand: expenditure taxes lead to lower labour costs and higher take-home pay than do payroll taxes. This raises firms' incentives to employ and workers' incentives to seek work.

A related proposal is to lower the cost of unskilled labour through introducing progressivity in the financing of unemployment benefits. Unemployment massively affects the lowest-skilled categories, namely those whose level of education is the lowest. Given the extent of the problem, certain writers have proposed to reduce contributions in respect of low wages. This has already partially been implemented in France as a solution to the problem of regressiveness of social contributions.

Two means of action have so far been discussed:

– exempting from employers' social contributions the fraction of the wage which is below the minimum wage: this measure would have a strong impact on the wage costs of the least-skilled workers (the cost of labour would, for example, drop by 28 per cent in France, to the level of the minimum inter-occupational growth wage), but would be extremely costly (5.5 per cent of GDP in France);

– to exempt only the wages of workers earning incomes in the region of the minimum wage: this measure is less costly to the national budget but makes wage increases very expensive for the undertaking when a worker moves from an exempted level of remuneration to a non-exempted level.

Measures of this kind can be financed in two ways: either by increasing tax deductions from households, which would have a dampening impact on consumption and an uncertain impact on overall employment, or by increasing the cost of another factor of production: energy or the highest salaries, which would produce a substitution effect in favour of the least skilled categories. This would either reduce emissions of gases resulting in a greenhouse effect or relax the labour market for the most skilled workers, while ensuring neutrality at the macroeconomic level. Nevertheless, the extent of the substitution effects involved remains highly uncertain.

Quite understandably, reform proposals have in particular targeted the phenomenon of long-term unemployment in its relation to the duration of benefits. Brief details of the major proposals, their rationales, and also their drawbacks, are presented in table 23. Another proposal would replace unemployment benefits by employment vouchers.[111] If the money governments spend on unemployment benefit

Table 23.   **Reforming unemployment benefits systems**

Proposal	Rationale	Downside risks
(1) Retain generous payouts but reduce duration of unemployment benefits	Generous benefits are required to give people the opportunity to make judicious and productive job matches, but long-term unemployment which generous benefit *duration* may encourage is a waste of human resources. Short-term unemployment helps to restrain wages and inflation, whereas long-term unemployment has no significant influence in this respect.	Since benefit entitlement programmes may influence behaviour with considerable lag effect, it is possible that putting a cap on the upper duration of unemployment benefits would still find many long-term unemployed without jobs at the expiration of the benefits. If those remaining unemployed at the expiration of benefits are given training, intensified job counselling, or public-sector jobs, the effect may be merely to shift the underlying problem into the slightly more remote future. If shorter benefit duration merely means earlier eligibility for continued unemployment assistance, the smaller is the incentive of the short-term unemployed to find jobs, regardless of how short the duration of unemployment benefits is.
(2) Legislated severance pay as a substitute for unemployment benefits	Severance pay which rises with job tenure gives a fixed and limited amount to the unemployed persons providing an incentive to find work promptly. Unlike unemployment insurance, the unemployed receive a lump sum severance payment and thus the flexibility of how the funds are used is increased; since unemployment insurance increases the length of unemployment, this is a disincentive to find work. Unemployment benefits give firms incentives for higher turnover, whereas severance pay has the opposite incentive effect of inducing longer-term employment relationships and, with this, the incentive to provide and acquire training.	Severance pay and long-term employment relationships work in Japan because employees are, in return, occupationally mobile with a broad range of skills. Without broad skills, the long-tenured employee who loses a job may face re-employment difficulties. Severance pay may be positively related to length of unemployment spell since firms are reluctant to hire labour if uncertain of the strength and stability of a business upturn. Severance pay may therefore not improve unemployment especially in economies prone to long recessions.
(3) Making unemployment benefits less conditional on unemployment	Unemployment benefits continue after the unemployed have found work. The marginal return to finding employment is lower the more that benefits are "clawed back" with market work. If benefits are not withdrawn or only partially withdrawn for a limited period, the return to finding employment would rise and the unemployed would try harder to become self-sufficient.	There may be "deadweight costs" arising from the fact that some of those permitted to retain their unemployment benefits would have sought and found work anyway. "Displacement" may occur since this proposal would allow the unemployed to accept lower wage offers and who might then displace incumbent employees who may then be turned into unemployed and be entitled to retain some of their unemployment benefits when re-employed.
(4) The conditional negative income tax	Everyone of working age files a tax return. All those with incomes above a threshold level would be required to pay income taxes. For those below this level, people who are demonstrably willing to work and retrain to find work, would receive "negative income taxes, that is payments from the government." This proposal would reduce tax fraud, provide less disincentive to work than existing unemployment benefits systems, be less demeaning than means-tested benefits and be simple to administer. It could better fulfil equity objectives of unemployment benefits systems since it uses income rather than employment as the criterion for redistribution.	In order to provide a socially acceptable level of support to those with the lowest earned incomes, the tax rate on those at the upper end of the income distribution would have to be increased. The gains from the increased incentives to work among the unemployed must be set against the losses from the decreased incentive to work among those in the middle and upper income ranges.

could be redirected so as to provide an incentive, rather than a disincentive, to create employment, many countries – and particularly those where unemployment benefits are comparatively generous – might reap a large benefit. Such a benefit transfer programme would seek to give the unemployed – particularly the long-term unemployed – a new option: to use a portion of their unemployment benefits, if they so wish, as vouchers for employers that hire them. In this way unemployment benefit systems, which currently impose an implicit tax on work, could be the source of employment subsidies for the people who need these subsidies most, namely, the long-term unemployed.

A policy that eliminates the inefficiencies created by current unemployment benefit systems clearly gives positive returns to the public. To the unemployed, the amount the government spends on unemployment benefits may not appear very substantial; but if these funds along with forgone tax revenues were offered to employers as wage subsidies, they might have a very substantial effect on employment. The voluntary nature of the programme would appeal to both the supply and demand sides of the labour market. Employees could end up receiving substantially more than their unemployment benefits, and many employers could end up paying substantially less than the prevailing wages.

Since the least educated and lowest-skilled are disproportionately represented among the long-term unemployed, lowering the cost of employing such persons along the lines discussed above would seem a promising remedy. A variety of institutionally reinforced wage floors may be pricing low-productivity workers out of jobs, but reductions in the direct wages that such workers receive could be dysfunctional, since reducing the earnings that the low-skilled can command on the labour market would provide little incentive for them to seek market work while increasing the incentive to engage in alternative, anti-social behaviour. This is one reason why the reduction of the labour costs of the low-skilled could be achieved through subsidizing their employment in the way discussed in the previous paragraph. There would, however, be risks of incurring deadweight costs, of encouraging fraud, or privileging only those currently in receipt of unemployment benefits. Simpler in the view of some economists would be to exempt employers of those most disenfranchised from the labour market of the whole or part of NWLCs associated with their employment. This would increase the demand for these workers, while augmenting their earnings. Shortfalls on the budget revenue side would in part be made up by the fiscal gains of lower unemployment (in both higher tax revenue and lower benefit expenditure). Other methods of recuperating budget revenue income would also seem plausible, as highlighted in the previous section.

Of course, the ideas presented in the foregoing paragraphs do not in themselves constitute firm policy recommendations. However, they do offer a sample of innovative thinking on how labour market policies may adjust to the changing economic environment.

Notes

[1] Throughout this part of the report the term "EFTA" will be used to designate the countries that were members for most of the period under review here.

[2] The concept of labour productivity used in this section arises from the identity:

$$\text{Labour productivity} = \frac{\text{GDP}}{\text{Employment}}$$

Therefore GDP growth = employment growth + labour productivity growth.

For a given rate of economic growth, employment creation can be high and labour productivity low, or the opposite.

[3] A.B. Atkinson et al.: *Pour l'emploi et la cohésion sociale* (Paris, Presses de la Fondation nationale des sciences politiques, 1994).

[4] P.A. Muet: "La persistance du chômage en Europe", in P.A. Muet (ed.): *Le chômage persistant en Europe* (Paris, Presses de la Fondation nationale des sciences politiques, 1994).

[5] This result holds as long as there is no monetary illusion or hysteresis effect. Empirical results show that those conditions are usually respected except for the case of the United Kingdom. See Muet, op. cit.

[6] It would be noted that the NAIRU is not necessarily the unemployment rate which would prevail in a situation of full employment.

[7] The theoretical debate concerning the effects of the wage bargaining structure on the evolution of wages is far from clear-cut. While it has generally been agreed that a centralized wage bargaining system would enhance wage moderation, recent developments show that it may have had, on the contrary, inflationary effects. The empirical evidence of the impact of industrial relations on NAIRU levels is very controversial and conclusions differ widely from one study to another. For more details see L. Calmfors: *Wage formation and macroeconomic policy in the Nordic countries* (Oxford, Oxford University Press, 1990); and idem: "Lessons from the macroeconomic experience of Sweden", in *European Journal of Political Economy*, Vol. 9, No. 1, Mar. 1993.

[8] This has been identified as the main weakness of new labour market theories: the focus on labour market mechanisms which can explain "stylized facts" but remain far from the synthesis they would like to propose. See A. Perrot: *Les nouvelles théories du marché du travail* (Paris, La Découverte, 1992).

[9] H. Sterdyniak et al.: "Lutter contre le chômage de masse en Europe", in *Revue de l'OFCE* (Paris), No. 48, Jan. 1994.

[10] H. Giersch: "Eurosclerosis", Kiel Discussion Paper No. 112 (Kiel, Kiel Institute for World Economics, 1985).

[11] R. Blank and R. Freeman: "Evaluating the connection between economic flexibility and social protection", in Rebecca Blank (ed): *Social protection versus economic flexibility* (Chicago, University of Chicago Press, National Bureau of Economic Research Comparative Labor Market Series, 1994), p. 1.

[12] P. Krugman: "Slow growth in Europe: conceptual issues", in Robert Z. Lawrence and Charles L. Schultze (eds.): *Barriers to European growth: A transatlantic view* (Washington, D.C., Brookings Institution, 1987).

[13] J. Elmeskov: *High and persistent unemployment: Assessment of the problem and its causes* (Paris, OECD, 1993), p. 20.

[14] C. Bean: "European unemployment: A survey", in *Journal of Economic Literature*, Vol. XXXII, June 1994.

[15] Krugman, op. cit.

[16] Bean, op. cit., p. 577.

[17] OECD: *The OECD jobs study: Evidence and explanations: Part II: The adjustment potential of the labour market* (Paris, OECD, 1994), p. 52.

[18] See, for example, D. Soskice: "Wage determination: The changing role of institutions in advanced industrialized countries", in *Oxford Review of Economic Policy* (Oxford), Vol. 6. 1990, and R. Freeman and L. Katz: "Rising wage inequality: The United States vs. other advanced countries", in Richard Freeman (ed.): *Working under different rules*, A National Bureau of Economic Research Project Report (New York, Russel Sage Foundation, 1994).

[19] See A. Pankert: "Industrial relations, employment and economic performance in the OECD area" (Geneva, ILO, 1994, mimeographed).

[20] For an argument that assigns significant blame to Swedish labour market regulation for current unemployment, see A. Lindbeck et al.: *Turning Sweden around* (Cambridge, Massachusetts, MIT Press, 1994), pp. 90-94 in particular.

[21] Freeman and Katz, op. cit., p. 53.

[22] Research by John Schmitt, cited in Freeman and Katz, op. cit.

[23] Freeman and Katz, op. cit.

[24] OECD: *The OECD jobs study...* op. cit., table 5.15.

[25] See for example, G. Standing: *Unemployment and labour market flexibility: The United Kingdom* (Geneva ILO, 1986); and, more recently, D. Blanchflower and R. Freeman: "Did the Thatcher reforms change British labour market performance?", in R. Barrell (ed): *The UK labour market* (Cambridge, Cambridge University Press), 1994; and D. Metcalf: "Deregulation of the British labour market, 1979-94: Description and evaluation" (Geneva: ILO, 1994, mimeographed).

[26] Freeman and Katz, op. cit., p. 52.

[27] R. Dore: *Flexible rigidities* (Stanford, Stanford University Press, 1986).

[28] M. Marterbauer: "Eurowatch: Do institutions matter?" in *New Economy*, Vol. 1, No. 1, 1994, pp. 58-59.

[29] R. Freeman reviews recent literature in "Minimum Wages–Again!", in *International Journal of Manpower*, Vol. 15, Nos. 2/3, 1994. See also *Industrial and Labor Relations Review*, Vol. 46, No. 1, 1992, which is devoted to a discussion of recent research on the minimum wage.

[30] R. Dickens, S. Machin and A. Manning: "Minimum wages and employment: A theoretical framework with application to the UK wage councils", in *International Journal of Manpower*, op. cit.

[31] A. van Soest: "Youth minimum wage rates: The Dutch experience" in *International Journal of Manpower*, op. cit.

[32] A. Wood: *North-South trade, employment and inequality* (Oxford, Clarendon Press, 1994), p. 317.

[33] S. Bazen and J. Martin: "The impact of the minimum wage on the earnings and employment of young people and adults in France, 1963-1985", in *OECD Economic Studies* (Paris), Vol. 16, Spring 1991; and G. Benhayoun: "The impact of minimum wages on youth employment in France revisited: A note on the robustness of the relationship", in *International Journal of Manpower*, op. cit.

[34] Bazen and Martin, op. cit.

[35] OECD: *The OECD jobs study...* op. cit., Ch. 5.

[36] J. Elmeskov, op. cit., p. 27.

[37] van Soest, op. cit.

[38] OECD: *The OECD jobs study...* op. cit., Ch. 5.

[39] S. Nickell: "Implications for labour markets in Western Europe and the UK", paper presented at ILO Anniversary Seminar, United Kingdom Employment Department, 16 Sep. 1994, p. 25.

[40] European Commission: *Employment in Europe 1994* (Brussels: European Commission, Directorate-General for Employment, Industrial Relations, and Social Affairs, 1994), p. 130.

[41] ibid.

[42] ibid., p. 131.

[43] S. Nickell: "Unemployment and the benefit system", in *Employment Policy Institute Economic Report*, Vol. 7, No. 13, Oct. 1993, p. 2. For a thorough review of the literature, see A. Atkinson and J. Micklewright: "Unemployment compensation and labor market transitions: A critical review", in *Journal of Economic Literature*, Vol. 29, No. 4, Dec. 1991.

[44] G. Burtless: "Jobless pay and high European unemployment", in Lawrence and Schultze, op. cit., p. 154.

[45] Atkinson and Mickelwright, op. cit.

[46] R. Moffitt: "Unemployment insurance and the distribution of unemployment spells", in *Journal of Econometrics*, Vol. 28, No. 1, Apr. 1985.

[47] Nickell, 1994, p. 2.

[48] R. Layard: Discussion of Michael Burda: " 'Wait unemployment' in Europe", in *Economic Policy*, Vol. 3, No. 2, Oct. 1988, pp. 417-418.

[49] OECD: *The OECD jobs study...* op. cit., Ch. 8.

[50] Layard, op. cit., pp. 417-418.

[51] P. Krugman: "Past and prospective causes of high unemployment", paper presented at the economic symposium of the United States Federal Reserve Bank of Kansas City, Jackson Hole, Wyoming, 25-27 Aug. 1994 (mimeographed).

[52] Atkinson and Mickelwright, op. cit.

[53] For a thorough review of these intricacies see M. Emerson: "Regulation or deregulation of the labour market: policy regimes for the recruitment and dismissal of employees in the industrialized countries", in *European Economic Review*, Vol. 32, No. 4, Apr. 1988, pp. 775-817.

[54] Results of the European Community's 1989 survey of European employers in European Commission: *European Economy*, No. 47, Mar. 1991.

[55] R. Paredes: "Job security and labour market adjustment", in A. Adams, L. Riveros and E. King (eds.): *Managing the social cost of adjustment* (Washington, D.C., World Bank, 1993; mimeographed).

[56] E. Lazear: "Job security provisions and employment", in *Quarterly Journal of Economics*, Vol. 105, No. 3, 1990, p. 700.

[57] See, for example, B. Wells: "Does the structure of employment legislation affect the structure of employment and unemployment?"(undated, mimeographed): and D. Grubb and B. Wells: "Employment regulation and patterns of work in EC countries", in *OECD Economic Studies*, No. 21, Winter 1993.

[58] For a discussion of the impact in France and Germany see C. Buechtemann: "Does (de)-regulation matter?: Employment protection and temporary work in the Federal Republic of Germany", in G. Standing and V. Tokman (eds.): *Toward social adjustment: Labour market issues in structural adjustment* (Geneva, ILO, 1990).

[59] K. Abraham and S. Houseman: "Does employment protection inhibit labor market flexibility?: Lessons from Germany, France and Belgium", in Blank, op. cit.

[60] J. Drèze: *Work-sharing: Why? How? How not...*, Centre for European Policy Studies, Paper No. 27 (1986), pp. 14-15.

[61] G. Alogoskoufis and A. Manning: "On the persistence of unemployment", in *Economic Policy*, Vol. 3, No. 2, Oct. 1988, pp. 431-432.

[62] S. Bentolila and G. Bertola: "Firing costs and labour demand: How bad is Eurosclerosis?", in *Review of Economic Studies*, Vol. 57, No. 3, July 1990.

[63] Bean, op. cit.

[64] McKinsey Global Institute: *Employment performance* (Washington, D.C., McKinsey & Company, 1994), Section 2, p. 15.

[65] S. Burgess: *The reallocation of employment and the role of employment protection legislation*, Discussion Paper No 193 (London, London School of Economics, Centre for Economic Performance, 1994), p. 4.

[66] McKinsey Global Institute, *Employment performance*, op. cit., Section 2, pp. 5-6.

[67] OECD: *Employment Outlook* (Paris, OECD, 1994), Ch. 3. See also J. Baldwin, T. Dunne and J. Haltiwanger: "A comparison of job creation and job destruction in Canada and the United States", Working Paper No. 4726, (Cambridge, Massachusetts, National Bureau of Economic Research, 1994).

[68] Standing, op. cit., p. 8, pp. 17-18.

[69] See, for example, R. Solow: *The labour market as a social institution* (Oxford, Basil Blackwell, 1990).

[70] D. Blanchflower and A. Oswald: *International wage curves*, Working paper No. 4200 (Cambridge, Massachusetts, National Bureau of Economic Research, 1992).

[71] R. Blank: "Changes in inequality and unemployment over the 1980s: Comparative cross-national responses" (1994, mimeographed), p. 18.

[72] McKinsey Global Institute: *Employment performance*, op. cit.

[73] ibid, section 5, p. 5.

[74] H. Delessy et al.: "Croissance: Le secret perdu?", in *Revue de l'OFCE*, No. 46, July 1993.

[75] Sterdyniak et al., op. cit.

[76] This argument is developed by E. Appelbaum and R. Schettkat: "The employment problem in the industrialized economies" (Geneva, ILO, 1994, mimeographed).

[77] C. Mathieu and H. Sterdyniak: "L'émergence de l'Asie en développement menace-t-elle l'emploi en France?", in *Revue de l'OFCE* (Paris), No. 48, Jan. 1994.

[78] P. Krugman: *Past and prospective causes of high unemployment*, op. cit., p. 31.

[79] Recent analyses include Metcalf, op. cit. and R. Harbridge: *Labour market regulation and employment: Trends in New Zealand* (Geneva, ILO, 1994, mimeographed).

[80] Harbridge, op. cit.

[81] Blanchflower and Freeman (1994), pp. 74-75.

[82] ILO: "Towards full employment", document for discussion at the Informal Tripartite Meeting at the Ministerial Level on Employment, Geneva, 10 June 1994, p. 13.

[83] Grubb and Wells, op. cit.

[84] Confederation of British Industry: *Tackling long term unemployment: A business agenda* (London, 1994), pp. 34-35.

[85] Blank and Freeman, op. cit., p. 32.

[86] ibid.

[87] OECD: *Employment Outlook* (Paris, OECD, 1993), Ch. 4.

[88] D. Marsden: "Regulation v. deregulation: Which route for Europe's labour market?", in *Employment Policy Institute Economic Report*, Vol. 8, No. 8, Nov. 1994.

[89] T. Persson and G. Tabellini: "Is inequality harmful for growth?", in *American Economic Review*, June 1994.

[90] Among other titles, the rich and rather varied literature on how regulation channels incentive structures in microeconomic behaviour includes, for example, D. Soskice: *The institutional infrastructure for international competitiveness: A comparative analysis of the UK and Germany*, paper prepared for the International Economic Association Conference, Venice, Nov. 1990; R. Boyer: *Les capitalismes vers le XXIᵉ siècle: Des transformations majeures en quête de théories*, CEPREMAP Discussion Paper, 25 Mar. 1994; on the role of labour market regulation in promoting "productive efficiency", see W. Sengenberger: "Protection, participation, promotion: The systemic nature and effects of labour standards", in W. Sengenberger and D. Campbell (eds.): *Creating economic opportunities: The role of labour standards in industrial restructuring* (Geneva, International Institute for Labour Studies, 1994), Ch. 2; from a business strategy perspective, see M. Porter: *The competitive advantage of nations* (London, Macmillan Press, 1990), Ch. 12 in particular.

[91] For a résumé, see B. Dormont: "Quelle est l'influence du coût du travail sur l'emploi?" in *Revue économique*, Vol. 48, No. 3, May 1994.

[92] D.S. Hamermesh: "The demand for labour in the long run" in O. Ashenfelter and R. Layard: *Handbook of labour economics*, Vol. I (Amsterdam, North-Holland, 1986); and idem: "Labour demand: What do we know?", NBER working paper no. 3890 (1991).

[93] *Revue de l'OFCE*, op. cit.

[94] So described by United States Labour Secretary Robert Reich before the International Labour Conference, June 1994.

[95] Soskice: *The institutional infrastructure...*, op. cit.

[96] The concept of "comparative institutional advantage" has been recently advanced by D. Soskice in an unpublished manuscript, 1994.

[97] A. Britton: "A world of minimal job security", in *Financial Times*, 27 Sep. 1994, p. 15.

[98] This is documented for the United States in R. Freeman and J. Medoff: *What do unions do?* (New York, Basic Books, 1984).

[99] Former United States Labor Secretary Ray Marshall describes criteria for high-performance workplaces in "The importance of international labour standards in a more competitive global economy", in W. Sengenberger and D. Campbell (eds.): *International labour standards and economic interdependence* (Geneva, International Institute for Labour Studies, 1994).

[100] Cross-national comparisons on advanced manufacturing technology diffusion in relation to differences in labour market institutions are discussed in G. Vickery and D. Campbell: *Managing manpower for advanced manufacturing technology* (Paris, OECD, 1991).

[101] W. Sengenberger and D. Campbell (eds.): *Is the single firm vanishing?: Inter-enterprise networks, labour and labour institutions*, Forum Series on Labour in a Changing World Economy, No. 1 (Geneva, International Institute for Labour Studies, 1993).

[102] OECD: *The OECD jobs study...* op. cit., Vol. 2.

[103] See A. Glyn and R. Rowthorn: "European employment policies", in J. Grieve Smith and J. Michie (eds.): *European unemployment* (London, Academic Press, 1994).

[104] V. Borooah: "Income distribution, consumption patterns, and economic outcomes in the United Kingdom", in *Contributions to political economy*, Vol. 7, 1988.

[105] In Atkinson et al., op. cit., Ch. 6.

[106] See R. Layard, S. Nickell and R. Jackman: *Unemployment, macroeconomic performance and the labour market* (Oxford, Oxford University Press, 1991), and *Employment Outlook* (Paris, OECD, 1993), Ch. 3.

[107] See G. Schmid, B. Reissert and G. Bruche: *Unemployment insurance and active labor market policies* (Detroit, Wayne State University Press, 1992), table 11.

[108] W. Beckerman: "How large a public sector?", in *Oxford Review of Economic Policy*, Vol. 2, No. 2, Summer 1986.

[109] W. Carlin and D. Soskice: *Macroeconomics and the wage bargain* (Oxford, Oxford University Press, 1990).

[110] Drèze, op. cit.

[111] D. Snower: *Unemployment benefits: An assessment of proposals for reform* (Geneva, ILO, 1994, mimeographed).

5 PART FIVE

The challenge of global full employment

Introduction

The preceding parts of this report have shown how formidable is the challenge of restoring full employment in most parts of the world. Indeed, all recent reports or studies of the employment problem have noted that there is no simple and painless solution. National action is constrained both by internal obstacles to reform and external economic forces. At the same time, international cooperation has weakened in the face of overwhelming forces of global change and seems extremely difficult to restore. The present report has confirmed as much, but there are compelling reasons why the international community cannot afford to let matters rest there.

First, however difficult this may be, it is imperative to find viable solutions to the twin problems of mass unemployment in the industrialized countries and of widespread underemployment and poverty in developing countries. The current employment situation represents an enormous waste of resources and an unacceptable level of human suffering. It has led to growing social exclusion, rising inequality between and within nations, and a host of social ills. It is thus both morally unacceptable and economically irrational. In contrast, the benefits of achieving full employment are clear: other things being equal, it will make for better social integration, a higher level of output and a greater degree of equity.

The second, and related, reason is that if most countries accept the defeatist attitude that full employment is unattainable then this by itself is likely to contribute to a worsening of the current situation. This is not only because national policies will thereby fail to give the required priority to the employment objective; it is also because such attitudes will make it more difficult to develop the cooperative international action that is essential for improving the global employment situation. The reason for this is that it is difficult to mobilize international action around an objective many believe to be unattainable, so in this sense a defeatist attitude towards full employment becomes a self-fulfilling prophecy.

Both the unacceptability of the current world employment situation and the negative consequences of a defeatist attitude towards the possibility of improving it constitute powerful arguments for a renewed commitment to the objective of full employment at both the national and international levels. There is an international labour Convention (the Employment Policy Convention, 1964 (No. 122)) which calls for a commitment to full employment that has been ratified by over 80 member

States. The formal provisions thus exist; it only remains to increase the efforts to translate its objects into reality.

A third compelling reason is that there is scope for effective action at both the national and international levels. There will in fact be vast benefits from a common and serious commitment by all nations to achieving full employment. For example, this will greatly facilitate the process of developing a new cooperative framework for managing the global economy. Coordination of macroeconomic policies and ensuring an orderly system of international exchange rates would be easier if all countries attached high priority to full employment as an objective of domestic policy. "When one government worries more about inflation than unemployment and the other takes the opposite view, they can be expected to disagree about the costs of acting jointly."[1] Similarly, a common commitment to full employment will make it more likely that a higher level of demand will prevail in the global economy. This will in turn provide a more supportive international environment for countries undertaking economic reforms. For example, trade liberalization will impose lower short-run costs and higher benefits when there is sufficient effective demand in the world economy. More fundamentally, high levels of effective demand in the industrialized countries, which still account for 79 per cent of world production, will invariably improve the growth prospects of developing and transitional economies through improved demand for their exports and increased foreign investment. In contrast, if countries seek isolationist solutions to the employment problem and attempt to impede further progress towards integration of the global economy, then world welfare will be impaired. This could lead to a more divided, unequal and politically turbulent world. In particular, if the industrialized countries succumb to protectionist pressures, the prospects of material betterment for the vast majority of mankind will be blighted. It is apposite in this connection to recall one of the fundamental principles contained in the Declaration of Philadelphia, to the effect that "poverty anywhere constitutes a threat to prosperity everywhere".

Nevertheless, given the current widespread scepticism over the prospects of achieving full employment, it is instructive to review the experience of the period between 1950 and 1973, when full employment actually prevailed in the industrialized countries and the employment situation improved in the developing countries. An understanding of the factors which made this possible can provide useful lessons for the actions that are necessary to find an escape route from the current impasse of high unemployment. Current circumstances are admittedly very different, but an analysis of the past can nevertheless provide important pointers to key requirements for the restoration of full employment.

The era of full employment

The current mass unemployment stands in striking contrast to the situation that prevailed in the industrialized countries in the not too distant past. During the 1950s and the 1960s, leading industrial countries not only enjoyed full employment but had over-full employment. In addition to being able to employ all their own people, these countries provided jobs for labour from abroad. In countries such as France and the Federal Republic of Germany nearly 10 per cent of the labour force came from other nations. During the period from 1950 to 1973 the industrialized countries experienced a historically unprecedented expansion of production and consumption at a rate of nearly 5 per cent a year. This was accompanied by a huge increase in world trade, particularly in manufactured products.

Most developing countries also participated in and benefited from this world-wide prosperity. Many Asian and Latin American countries embarked on a veritable industrial revolution in these post-war decades.

This period of simultaneous prosperity for the North and the South evidently came to an end with the first oil shock of 1973. Since then, the rate of growth of the OECD and the world GDP has nearly halved. It is therefore not surprising to find the high rates of unemployment recently experienced by the OECD – rates which were unthinkable in the preceding period. It is for the same reason that for a large number of countries in the South, in contrast to the greater employment opportunities and the significant rises in the average standard of living that prevailed earlier, the last 15 years have been marked by deindustrialization, considerable falls in per capita incomes and much increased underemployment and open unemployment.

There were three key features of the system that ensured full employment. First, the post-Second World War international economic system gave high priority to the objective of full employment. It is a recurring theme in most official documents of the new post-war international economic order. Thus, for example, the contracting parties to GATT in the very first clause of the Preamble declared themselves as "Recognizing that their relations in the field of trade and economic endeavour should be conducted with a view to *raising standards of living, ensuring full employment and a large and steadily growing volume of real income and effective demand, developing the full uses of the resources of the world...*" (emphasis added). Thus, under GATT, free trade was not regarded as an end in itself, but explicitly as a vehicle for promoting effective demand and full employment. Similarly the ILO's Declaration of Philadelphia, adopted in 1944, calls for the attainment of full employment as a major objective of national policies. Second, there was a social consensus in the industrialized countries over institutional arrangements in respect of setting of wages and prices, the distribution between wages and profits, and the state fiscal, credit and welfare policies that guaranteed minimum living standards and maintained aggregate demand. In the sphere of wage setting, for example, productivity wage bargaining which flourished during this period played a key role both in keeping a rough balance between the share of wages and profits in the national product and also in helping to provide an adequate rate of growth of consumer demand. Third, at the international level, the global economic system functioned under stable monetary and trading arrangements.

Towards the end of the period serious difficulties arose at both the national and international levels; these began to interact with each other in a cumulatively adverse way to the detriment of the system as a whole. The Bretton Woods monetary system broke down in the late 1960s. By the early 1970s, the system was so fragile that it disintegrated under the impact of the two oil shocks, thus pushing the world economy into a period of prolonged slow growth which began in 1973. The social consensus of this period which was crucial to the functioning of the economic system as a whole broke down.

The breakdown of the Bretton Woods system and the international rules of coordination meant that the balance of payments disequilibria between nations arising from the first oil shock could not be resolved at a rate of growth of world demand compatible with full employment and low inflation. Most economists at the time believed that the introduction of floating exchange rates would make the system more flexible and remove an important restraint on economic growth. In practice this turned out to be an illusion, and the asymmetrical adjustment processes of the international economic system soon reasserted themselves. Countries which followed Keynesian expansionary policies in the wake of the oil price shock increasingly became balance-of-payment-constrained and were faced with the prospect of currency depreciations in inflationary conditions. The simultaneous breakdown of the internal rules of coordination with respect to wages and prices made it more difficult to use exchange rate movements as an equilibrating device in the international sphere.

In particular, it could be argued that two changes in the international financial system that originated in the late 1970s have exacerbated problems of increased global unemployment. The first is the increased international mobility of capital as a result of relaxation of previous controls. The second is the dramatic increase in trading in global markets for currencies, currency futures, and a wide variety of "derivative" instruments. There has been not only an explosion of activity in foreign exchange and capital markets but a change in the nature of the activity.

In 1971, just before the collapse of the Bretton Woods fixed exchange rate system, about 90 per cent of all foreign exchange transactions were for the finance of trade and long-term investment, and only about 10 per cent were speculative. Today those percentages are reversed, with well over 90 per cent of all transactions being speculative. Daily speculative flows now regularly exceed the combined foreign exchange reserves of all the G-7 governments.[2]

The most important of these flows are speculative investments in foreign exchange markets and purchases of a wide variety of derivatives – financial instruments whose prices are linked to the behaviour of some underlying asset. These changes in the global financial system have contributed to long-term interest rates that are high by post-Second World War standards. A significant fraction of investors now have a real alternative to investing their money either long-term or short-term. When both short-term and long-term rates seem unattractively low, flows of funds into these more speculative types of investment are likely to increase dramatically. As a consequence, long-term investors as a group are now able to extract an inflation premium that was not available before the explosive growth of these speculative markets, and this has created a permanent tendency towards high long-term interest rates across the entire world economy, rates which lead directly to higher rates of unemployment and slower rates of global growth.

But the new reality is not just that real interest rates are high but that the elimination of capital controls has deprived nearly all countries of the ability to insulate themselves from them.

In short, when large economies such as Germany and the United States raise interest rates, other countries must follow or suffer very large outflows of capital. In theory, countries have another choice: they can simply let their currency float downward relative to the currency of the high-interest-rate country. But devaluations are a problematic instrument for stemming capital outflows, since they fuel speculative pressures. High levels of capital mobility provide a strong bias towards restrictive monetary policies in the world economy. Countries that fail to align their interest rates with those of the large economy with the highest interest rate risk substantial capital outflows and intense speculative pressures on their currencies.

What policy lessons do we learn from this experience with respect to the requirements for obtaining sustainable full employment with low inflation? These may be summarized as follows:

–   an extremely important lesson is that, in the present interdependent global economy, it is necessary to have efficient and consistent rules for coordinating mechanisms in *both* the internal and the external spheres. As we saw in the preceding analysis, mechanisms of both types have lost their efficacy and are interacting with each other to generate ever more severe consequences for the economy;

–   as far as the internal mechanism is concerned, what is required is a means of restricting money wage demands in line with the country's changing macro-economic potential, so as to avoid leap-frogging inflation. The alternative would be the continued waste involved in keeping high unemployment (with increasing NAIRU as unemployment grows) in order to restrain inflation. It is certainly sensible to seek cooperative arrangements between workers and employers which can avoid this waste;

–   at the international level there is a need for symmetrical adjustment in the balance of payments in order to raise the rate of growth of the world economy. Under the present system this is not ensured, yet for full employment to be achieved it is important to have symmetrical adjustment between deficit and surplus countries. It is worth noting that, even in a world of conflicting national objectives and free capital movements, the task of international coordination will be much easier if the domestic mechanisms for securing non-inflationary growth are working adequately. This will enable countries to use the exchange rate much more freely to attain external balance. There is in fact a close interaction between the internal and external instruments of coordination. The internal mechanisms, for example, will work more effectively the smaller the fluctuations in the world economy and therefore the smaller the required changes in the exchange rate.

Restoring full employment: international action

It is clear from the foregoing that a fundamental requirement for restoring full employment is the creation of an institutional framework for cooperative international action in finding optimal solutions to the pressing problems of unemployment and related social ills. This involves overcoming threats to the sustainability of positive trends in the global economy as well as creating the basis for cooperative, positive-sum policies. The need for this grows more pressing by the day. With the extent of globalization that has occurred so far there has already been a reduction of national policy autonomy in a number of areas. This has already bred significant misgivings, uncertainty and insecurity. If globalization is to proceed benignly then it is clear that the loss of national policy autonomy has to be compensated by the development of an international policy. For example, the increased liberalization of capital flows has led to reduced national autonomy as regards macroeconomic policy, and the difficulties created by this need to be resolved by viable mechanisms for international coordination of macroeconomic policies as well as reforms to the international monetary system. In particular, problems arising from the large increase of speculative financial flows in the foreign exchange and financial derivative markets need to be adequately resolved. The objective should be to reduce destabilizing effects on exchange and interest rates, to channel a greater proportion of world savings to productive real investments, and to lower real long-term interest rates. The last-mentioned is a vital determinant of levels of investment and job creation. Proposals for the reform of the international monetary system such as a transaction tax on financial flows and target zones for exchange rates accordingly deserve serious consideration, not least from the standpoint of their potential contribution to attaining higher levels of employment.

Another important area for greater international cooperation is that of labour standards. As noted in an earlier section of the report, the growth of transnational production has undermined the effectiveness of traditional instruments of labour policy and of collective bargaining. Competition for foreign investment and the increasing footlooseness of production tend to lead to the debasement of labour standards. This clearly needs to be countered by giving a fresh impetus to international cooperation to enforce basic labour standards. There are clear mutual benefits for all groups of countries in the continued progress of trade liberalization and in increasing flows of foreign direct investment. There are also short-run transitional problems which need to be managed. These problems, whether in industrialized, transitional or developing countries, are mainly social in nature. They include job losses, the need to change jobs and acquire new skills more frequently, and the threat of growing inequality and social exclusion. At the heart of these concerns are jobs and the income, social recognition and participation that they provide. These problems understandably generate deep social and political anxieties and provide fertile breeding grounds for protectionist and even xenophobic responses. Since protectionist sentiment is in turn often aggravated by perceptions that some countries are obtaining an unfair competitive edge by violating basic labour standards, progress in the universal enforcement of these standards is important for preserving an open global economic system.

The common challenge of adjustment to a rapidly changing global economy that is faced by all countries should also be recognized as an important area for co-operative international action. The development of common principles with respect to how the process should be designed and implemented would help in promoting orderly adjustment. High social costs are likely to generate social tensions that can abort adjustment efforts in individual countries. This in turn will slow progress towards a more open and productive economy. It is therefore important for the international community to make adequate provisions for adjustment assistance to countries facing the largest problems in this respect, such as the least developed and most severely indebted countries. Such assistance could include the stronger implementation of debt-relief measures for severely indebted countries as well as enhanced trade preferences of the least-developed countries.

An important step towards achieving greater international cooperation would be to bring current social problems and anxieties to the fore of the global agenda. International attention has been focused for too long on political and economic issues to the unfortunate exclusion of vital social ones. It is imperative to correct this at a moment when social problems threaten to undermine progress towards exploiting opportunities for greater material and social well-being. The World Summit for Social Development which will be held in March 1995 is therefore a timely and welcome event. But it is important that this summit does not end up reinforcing the artificial separation of economic and social issues by dealing exclusively with the latter. If it deals only with the minutiae of social problems and palliatives for these, without confronting underlying economic causes, then a historic opportunity will be wasted.

The Summit has three issues on its agenda: social integration, the promotion of productive employment, and the alleviation of poverty. The fundamental solution to these three interrelated problems lies in the creation of the conditions for generating higher rates of growth of output and employment in the world economy. This is the only viable long-run basis for solving the social ills that plague the world today. Without growth and the creation of more productive jobs, no amount of tinkering with social measures will offer lasting solutions. Equally, however, without resolving social problems the required levels of economic growth and job creation cannot be sustained. This is why the summit should be the occasion for defining a programme of action that exploits the synergies that will result from simultaneously tackling the economic and social problems of the day.

Even more important than defining a plan of action, however, is the creation of an institutional framework for ensuring that global economic and social problems are continuously dealt with on a unified basis. For example, with universal commitment to achieving full employment as a primary objective of policy the foundation will have been laid for this to happen. The coordination of economic policies and the operation of global trade, financial and investment systems will then need to be viewed from the standpoint of their impact on employment outcomes. These outcomes would in turn be the primary determinant of social outcomes such as the distribution of income, the degree of social integration, and levels of poverty.

A specific step in this direction would be to include ministers responsible for employment and social affairs in deliberations on economic policy at both the national and international levels. This could be reinforced by improved coordination and closer collaboration between international agencies responsible for economic and financial policies and those responsible for employment and social policies.

These institutional changes to give greater weight to the social dimension of economic policies will, of course, need to be backed up by the formulation of feasible proposals for action on specific issues. Many of these issues are technically complex and political consensus around proposals for action will be difficult to achieve. But a start has to be made somewhere and more attention needs to be devoted to these issues in the research work and policy analyses of international agencies. The ILO, for its part, intends to promote this, both in its own work and in its collaboration with other agencies. The outcome of such work will provide the basis for substantive consideration of proposals for action by policy-makers at both the national and international levels.

Notes

[1] P.B. Kennen: *Managing exchange rates* (London, Routledge, 1988), p. 83.

[2] J. Eatwell: "The global money trap: Can Clinton master the markets?", in *The American Prospect*, 12 (Winter 1993), p. 120.